DATE			

❦ *The Children of the Dream*

The Children of the Dream

BRUNO BETTELHEIM

The Macmillan Company

Collier-Macmillan Ltd., London

Library of Congress Catalog Card Number: 69-10505

Sixth Printing 1970

The Macmillan Company
866 Third Avenue, New York, N.Y. 10022
Collier-Macmillan Canada Ltd., Toronto, Ontario

Printed in the United States of America

For permission to include previously published material by Stanley
Diamond, grateful acknowledgment is made to Mr. Diamond, to The
Society for the Study of Social Problems, *Social Problems*, Vol. 5, No. 2,
1957, and to *Dissent*, Vol. 4, 1957.

❧ *To Jeremiah Kaplan*

CONTENTS

ACKNOWLEDGMENTS

In the spring of 1964 a grant from the New World Foundation enabled me to spend seven weeks studying communal rearing in the Israeli kibbutz. I am most grateful to the foundation for this opportunity and must hope that the following report does not disappoint their trust.

None of it would have been possible, however, without the splendid help of many people in Israel to whom I remain immensely grateful. Many of them, through what they told me, wrote large parts of this book. First and foremost among them were the many kibbutzniks and their children who gave so much more of themselves to my venture than mere time and interest.

At Atid[1] in particular, everyone was generous beyond expectation. Only their wish for anonymity prevents me from thanking them by name, even the kibbutznik who for weeks let me have his own room, let me sleep in his bed, at consid-

---

[1] Hebrew, meaning *future*; the fictitious name used in this report for the kibbutz at which I was based.

erable inconvenience to himself. (While it is a misnomer
here to speak of his "own" bed, since it is merely the bed
assigned him by the kibbutz and not his private possession,
this does not alter his generosity a whit.) But his was only
one of the host of kindnesses too numerous to mention. Beyond the best I can do here with words is the lasting grati-
tude I feel for how readily they gave in all things, with both
hands.

There were many others in Israel without whom this book
would have been the poorer: psychologists and psychiatrists,
sociologists and newspaper men, members of labor unions
and the army, professors at the Hebrew University, and just
people I met casually, in transit. Unfailingly, in their own
ways, they helped me to understand them and the issues I
was trying to grasp.

Some time before my visit to Israel I had invited Charles
Sharp to produce a documentary movie at the University of
Chicago's Orthogenic School. The assignment was to illustrate the treatment, over time, of one of the severely emotionally disturbed patients who are treated at this mental
hospital for children. Impressed by how much the film he
made was able to show of what is impossible to describe for
the reader in words, I felt it would be worth trying to do the
same for kibbutz children. Sharp, in turn, became interested
in my study plans and in the challenging idea of the kibbutz.
So he joined me for several weeks at Atid and there produced his movie, *The Kibbutz*, on which it was a pleasure
and privilege to have worked with him. (As of this writing,
The Kibbutz had received the Gold Award [First Prize] at
the International Film and TV Festival of New York, 1966,
and the Golden Eagle award of CINE, 1967. In addition it
was chosen "for its excellence" by the American Film Festival, 1967, to represent the United States at international
motion picture events abroad, and by the Educational Film
Library Association, 1967, for festival showing.) Together

we produced a second documentary during our stay in Israel, on child rearing particularly. This one is presently being readied for public showing.

Several of my friends read early drafts of the manuscript, and I gained much from their criticism and suggestions—particularly those of my friends at the University of Chicago, Professors Ben Bloom, Jacob W. Getzels, and Morris Janowitz—but also Len Atkins, Dr. Al Flarsheim, and Dr. Peter Wolff. I wish to thank them here, and the several others who helped me to clarify some of the thoughts in this volume.

To Professor Bloom, to Hanoch Rinot, Israel's Director General of Education, and to Moshe Smilansky, director of the School of Education of the University of Tel Aviv, I owe my thanks for valuable information on Israeli education in general and on kibbutz education in particular. I am grateful to Professors S. N. Eisenstadt, Carl Frankenstein, and the late Yonina Talmon of the Hebrew University for the time they gave me, and for their help in understanding kibbutz youth and family life. I wish also to thank Professor Erik Erikson for permission to reproduce his model of personality growth and development.

Most of all I wish to thank my friend and collaborator Ruth Marquis. She encouraged me from the first to undertake this study, read the thousands of pages of tapes in transcription, helped me to select which of this mass of data to use, and in what way. Many of the thoughts expressed in the following pages took their final form thanks only to discussions with her. The readability of what follows is owed to the loving care with which she transmuted the often cumbersome way in which I expressed my thoughts into what—at least to me who knows their original form—seems an easier prose, without depriving it of its personal flavor.

BRUNO BETTELHEIM

❧ *The Children of the Dream*

I

An Experiment in Nature

How intimate is the link between the nature of a society and how its children are raised? Or as we have so often asked: Is man the father of society, or society the father of man? This question becomes no less burning with the passing of millennia. Today it is posed by the Israeli kibbutz but also by the communes of China and by the Soviet experiments with raising children in institutions.

Here in America it is posed by the slum child: Can such children, if they continue to live in the slums, still learn to become citizens who will forever do away with the very conditions that bred them? Or does a better life for them depend on their removal from the slums in their formative years?

Reflecting on this riddle of society and child, David Rapaport once remarked that "The upbringing of children in the agricultural collectives in Israel is for the social scientist what an 'experiment of nature' is for the natural scientist [1958]."

For many years, before he wrote this, we had talked together of the theoretical issues raised by such a method of rearing children, and of our serious dissatisfactions with those reports we had seen on how kibbutz children grow up. He was critical of them on the basis of his firsthand experience, having lived in an early kibbutz, and of his profound understanding of human psychology; I on the basis of my experience with the institutional rearing of children, which contradicted the claims that to rear children in groups must be damaging to mental health. Each of us felt that no one had yet explored kibbutz educational methods for "what they can teach us about the relationships between instinctual drives, ego, and environment, that is to say, about the relationship between the life of a society and the upbringing of children in it [Rapaport, 1958]." Such a study, we felt, was badly overdue.

Since that time other reports of kibbutz education have appeared, foremost among them in this country being Spiro's *Children of the Kibbutz* (1958). But although an important study, it seemed to raise as many questions as it answered. My own impatience came from what appeared to me an unexamined and unwarranted assumption that child rearing methods that are standard in our middle-class culture are therefore best in all cultures. This I could not accept, since my professional activities had made me all too aware of serious shortcomings at home. So in reaction to Spiro's book, and to parallel reports by some psychiatrists who could see nothing good in the communal rearing of children, I wrote a defense of kibbutz education (1959, 1962). Indeed, the more I studied Spiro's book, the less could I agree with some of the interpretations he gave his own data. Nor did some of his conclusions seem to me supported by what he wrote about kibbutz education.

Since his was *the* book on the subject, it seemed important to voice my objections. So I spent much time writing a long critical essay of his report. I am glad now that better sense won out, and I destroyed what had grown into a lengthy monograph. I realized that when all was said, he had been there, and I had not.

There could be no doubt either of Spiro's sincerity or intelligence. So if he had arrived at what to me seemed erroneous interpretations, they might still be the right ones, derived from a "feel" of things he had gotten on the spot. Though his findings did not always accord with his data, they might still be correct and represent a "higher" truth. After all he had lived with the problem, and with kibbutzniks; he had not just observed. The only way to be sure if my objections were way off or not was to go and find out for myself. But that prospect was still in the future.

In retrospect I am very glad I arrived at this conclusion. Because later, in Israel, my own observations taught me that he was more often correct than my untested judgments had allowed, even though, as the reader will see, the conclusions we arrived at differed in very important respects.

Nevertheless the fact remains that Spiro's book failed to deal with significant issues, some of them raised in the aforementioned article by Rapaport. As suggested there, every society, as it brings up the next generation, presents the child at each step of his growing up with the particular demands flowing from the way of life particular to that society. These demands reach the child through the attitudes he encounters in the persons who take care of him most—attitudes that both enable and compel him to solve the problems brought on by his development. And by problems are meant the repeated crises between personal endowment, aspiration, and what his society permits and requires. The very way he resolves these crises brings him closer and closer to becoming a viable and effective member of that society.

Much of the importance for us of kibbutz rearing lies

in the fact that all these factors shaping personality can be studied there directly. They do not have to be unearthed at a distance of centuries (as when we study past cultures), or across the gap that divides Western man from present-day preliterate society. We will gain little, though, from our study of the kibbutz, unless we free ourselves of the inclination to take our own system of rearing for granted. If unbiased, however, such a study might not only teach us how kibbutz education accommodates to changing social conditions but, by implication, it should deepen our understanding of Western education. It might even begin to suggest how we might reform our educational system to meet better our changing social conditions.

❧ Reasons for the Study

IT WAS PROBLEMS SUCH AS THESE, AND DISSATISFACTIONS WITH the available literature on kibbutz education, that moved me to look for some answers myself.

But there were also more specific and immediate reasons. Among the pressing problems still unsolved in American child rearing are those of the slum child, of the restless dissatisfaction of youth in general, and of particular disturbances among them, like drug addiction or juvenile delinquency. Since the Israeli kibbutzim seem to be free of such afflictions, that alone seemed potent reason to ask if their educational methods could be applied to our problems.

Moreover, the feeling is widespread that if we are to help the culturally deprived child—whether in city slums or impoverished rural areas—he had best be reared in an environment different from his home, since his home life often makes him unfit for the world he must later enter. But can children be reared successfully away from their mothers, as kibbutz children are? Prevalent feeling in the West seems to be that this is disastrous for the child.

At this moment the need in America seems to be twofold: We need, at the beginning of the educational venture, to have day care centers for the children of working mothers and for those children whose parents cannot offer them a suitable home. There we must ready such children for what might roughly be called a middle-class way of life, and for acquiring the knowledge they will need to live it successfully and happily—though our current efforts, even in preschool care, often focus on too narrow an academic goal. At the other end of the schooling sequence our task is to provide for the underachiever, the dropout, the delinquent, for all those who find life empty of meaning and purpose. Throughout their schooling (and not just their schooling) we must provide the kind of experience that will keep them from looking at school as something alien to their existence.

About the day care so needed in America, prevailing opinion is typified in a statement by the Children's Bureau, which says: "Young children need individual attention from their parents, and do not fare well in groups." Following Rene Spitz's studies (1945, etc.) of the disastrous effects on infants brought up in groups, and his description of "institutionalism," it was assumed to be most damaging for any young child to be reared without benefit of a single mothering person who took care of him more or less exclusively. And this, though Spitz's findings were based only on patently bad institutions and thus begged the question of what the child's fate might be if he were not raised in the kind of institutions made infamous by Dickens.

In recent years it is perhaps John Bowlby (1951, etc.) more than any other person, following Spitz, who has shaped public opinion on this matter. After extensive review of the relation between maternal care and mental health, he concluded it to be "essential for mental health that the infant and young child should experience a warm, intimate, and continuous relationship with his mother (or permanent mother substitute) in which both find satisfaction and enjoyment." If this were indeed true, it would bode ill for the mental health of children raised communally.[1]

Bowlby stresses three factors as being specially pernicious to the child's mental health: First, no chance to form a close relationship to a mother figure during the first three years of life; second, maternal deprivation (separation trauma) for limited periods; and third, inconstancy, or changes from one mother figure to another during the first three years of life.

Of these, the first (lack of closeness to the mother) is not entirely avoided. While the mother is important, the relation to her is severely diluted by relations to the child's caretakers and the peer group. More important, the third condition (intermittent mothering) certainly prevails in the kibbutz with the frequent changes of caretakers and the children's moves from one house to another as they reach a new age-grade. Since the particular functions of these child care workers, as distinguished from those of the teachers, are not to be found in our society we have no suitable name for them. Hence I shall call them by their Hebrew name which is *metapelet*. (The Hebrew *metapel* means "to take care," hence a metapelet is one who takes care. The plural of *metapelet* is *metaplot*, but to simplify matters I shall refer to them in the plural as *metapelets*.)

It is more difficult to talk about the second condition (separation trauma), since the mother's role is affected by the child's early relations to many persons besides his mother, and because the separation from his mother is a

---

[1] See Appendix E on the communal arrangements for child care in the Israeli kibbutz.

daily occurrence. Yet the effects of these conditions can hardly be as traumatic for the kibbutz child as postulated in the theoretical models of Bowlby and Spitz. Though raised in groups from infancy on and not by his parents, he seems nevertheless to fare very well—much better, in fact, than those American children in need of day care.

The more reason to study this radical and apparently successful experiment in the rearing and education of children! Particularly so when it proceeds within the framework of a democratic society, involving people very much like ourselves. At least they are people whose educational aspirations—though different in a shunning of competition and any desire for private property—are otherwise much like our own.

While data on the kibbutz itself are extensive, reports on its educational system are scant, not only in the English literature, but also in Israel, though less so. Most American students of the kibbutz have not been specialists in child rearing and education; also, their findings have been contradictory. Interestingly enough, even the anthropologists among them, committed as they are to the principle that a culture must be understood on its own premises, take an *a priori* critical view of the rearing of children away from their parents. Because of findings on United States children raised in this way, they seem convinced it must have shortcomings anywhere.

On the other hand, when objective tests were applied (as by Albert I. Rabin, for example, 1958) Israeli children so raised compared very favorably with corresponding American youth. No dropouts in the kibbutz; no youngsters who merely find life absurd. Their performance in later adult life sheds further doubt on views critical of kibbutz education, because they are described as hardworking, responsible citizens, devoted to their communities and nation. The problem of how these children manage so well, though in infancy and childhood they spend most of the day and all night away from their parents, remains unanswered. So does the question of what experience is provided—educational, social, and emotional—to enable them to grow up so well, though not reared by their parents.

Thus I determined to study the kibbutz again, not to find out how they organize the day for infants and children, but to learn what prepares the children so well for adult life without their running into those difficulties that beset so many of our children raised at home. It also seemed important to shed some light on the question: Why is it that United States children raised in institutions find it difficult, by and large, to adjust later in life, unlike the children raised in Israeli kibbutzim?

❧ The Sample

I WANT TO STRESS AT THE OUTSET THAT THIS REPORT IS not intended as a complete tracing of all or even most important aspects of kibbutz rearing or of personality formation from infancy to adulthood. Nor should it even be viewed as a definitive story of how the kibbutz child is socialized. First, things are still very much in flux—not only as regards the kibbutz itself and its educational methods, but also the place of the kibbutz in Israeli society, on which the first two depend. Second, there was only the one kibbutz at Atid where I gained some fuller understanding of how its children are raised, and even that not completely, while all the rest of kibbutz life I could only grasp in part. (*Atid* means *future* in Hebrew. As noted in the Acknowledgments, it is the name used in this report for the kibbutz at which I was based while in Israel.)

What follows is thus a very personal, impressionistic report, derived from my study of one kibbutz mainly, though based on observations at several other kibbutzim. It is as objective a review as was possible to this particular observer, who was often a participant-observer as well.[2]

On the other hand, my concentrating so largely on Atid turned out to be less a handicap than I expected and feared. During the several years in which I had planned and prepared for the study, I was told again and again how different the various kibbutz movements are, and how unique was each one of its settlements. It seemed natural for those kibbutzniks I met to insist that only their own embodied the true kibbutz spirit, and to study any other simply would not do. But even non-kibbutzniks, including social scientists who had studied these settlements, usually insisted that the particular kibbutz they knew best was the one to investigate. Also I had listened to long discussions about the great differences between settlements embracing different political viewpoints: those of the right, left, and middle of the road.

I soon found that my worries were unjustified as to whether the study, principally, of one single kibbutz would invalidate my findings. Except for the orthodox religious kibbutzim, which I did not include in this study—of which I am told there are only twelve, or less than 5 percent of all kibbutzim, and which in many ways are very different from the rest[3]—I found the more or less random sample of kibbutzim I visited, in all the other three movements, astonish-

---

[2] See Appendices A and B on the nature of data collected, the problem of a common language, and the choice of a field.

[3] According to the *Israeli Yearbook of Statistics* (1964), the kibbutz population totaled 80,024 in 1963, with the following distribution among the movements. There were seventy-four left-wing kibbutzim with 27,450 members; fifty-eight middle-of-the-road kibbutzim with 22,352 members; and seventy-six right-wing kibbutzim with 24,467 members. Orthodox kibbutzim numbered twelve and were split into two different groups (based on differences in the stringency of orthodoxy) with 3,169 in one group and 537 in the other. Finally, there were ten unaffiliated or independent kibbutzim, with 2,084 members.

ingly similar to the one I studied intensively. That is, I found them similar in all those respects that interested me—how the children fared in them—and only slightly dissimilar in most other respects.

Incidentally, the terms left wing, middle of the road, and right wing, must be understood through kibbutz eyes, and not in terms of American politics. To us, even the right-wing kibbutz movement would be viewed as communistic, with its absence of private property, its atheism, its radical socialist views. In Israel the difference between the movements is that the *left-wing* is the most doctrinaire, most centrally directed, and closest to Russian communism; though even in this movement there had been some disillusionment with the Soviets since the persecution of Jews under Stalin. The *right-wing* movement, though still communist in its abhorrence of private property and its broad control of the individual's life, comes closest to what in America would be the socialist position and is least centrally directed. It is also politically active within the Israeli government, while the left-wing movement at the time of my visit remained in opposition.

The recent six-day war, and all events leading up to it, had a considerable effect on the left-wing movement. Among the kibbutz-born especially, there was disgust with Russian communism because of its anti-Israeli stand. Under pressure from them, left-wingers of the founding generation were forced to reexamine and discard their old ideological and emotional attachment to both Russian and international communism, and move closer to the Israeli socialist position of the other two movements. As a result, the left-wing movement too, entered the government, and seems in the process of resolving many of its differences with the other two movements.

This development aside, political views among kibbutzim of the three movements were indeed different at the time of my visit, and so were their stated views on Russia, for example, or the Arab question. But in practice, even their political differences seemed insignificant when compared to how alike they were in protecting their own way of life against, for example, influences coming from the rest of Israel, or such pressing social issues as those presented by the influx of North African Jews. Nor was there any essential difference in how the various movements handled their relations to the children, though they believed that the differences were very great indeed.

Later, for example, I shall discuss how parents in the left-wing movement are not allowed to put their children to bed, while in another movement the parents' putting their children to bed is a near sacred routine. This is viewed as a difference of crucial importance and is widely discussed, but really makes little essential difference to the child in the end.

One gets the feeling that what happens here is like what often happens when minority groups struggle for their existence against a surrounding majority, but also strain to preserve their unique difference from very similar minorities with whom they share all essential attitudes, values, and ways of life. Among kibbutzim, small ideological differences are stressed out of all proportion, in the struggle to maintain an identity unlike any other, exactly because they are so essentially alike. In this process of polarization the fundamentals they share are so taken for granted as to be largely overlooked.

If I found significant differences in how life unfolds in the various kibbutzim, I found they depended not so much on the particular movement a kibbutz belonged to, but on such factors as how big or how old the kibbutz. A kibbutz of two thousand members is something entirely different from a kibbutz of one hundred or less, in terms of its social relations and the active participation by members in community affairs. Obviously both social control and cohesion are more difficult to maintain in a large kibbutz, and the danger of some social disorganization occurring is much greater in a kibbutz of one thousand or more members. This is well recognized in kibbutz theory, which holds that a kibbutz should be small, no more than a few hundred members, to ensure that every one of its members is part of the "in" group. Also a kibbutz that is less than ten years old is very different from one that is thirty years old. But even then, all are strangely similar as far as child rearing is concerned.

Differences exist not only between movements but within one and the same movement. One finds kibbutzim where a young mother is forced to leave, or is threatened with expulsion, because she will not leave her baby in the nursery overnight. But in some few kibbutzim of the very same movement, infants sleep in the rooms of their parents from infancy on and only spend their days, from morning to evening, with their peers. In a few other kibbutzim of the same movement, infants live in the children's houses day and night, but at an older age sleep in their parents' rooms for a few years.

Such internal differences are not permitted in the left-wing movement, because policy is uniform for the movement as decreed by a central ruling body. But even in the left wing there are differences from one kibbutz to another in the speed and rigor with which central policy is implemented.

How then, with such differences between the three socialist movements and within each movement, do I say that for purposes of this study all kibbutzim are more similar than not? Because despite the differences among them in regard to politics, and some economic and other arrangements, the inner attitudes of kibbutzniks are most similar. This is particularly true of the founding members, whose influence still dominates in all essential matters that shape the impact of the kibbutz on its children.

Most important of these similarities, as Stanley Diamond (1959) points out: all kibbutzim share a like way of organizing the life of the child—irrespective of whether or not he sleeps with his parents or how many hours he spends with them, or where—in which "the collective idea has triumphed over the concrete person" and where "the family no longer serves as a mediator between society and the child."

Diamond also remarks (in my opinion correctly) that the kibbutz is neither an extended family nor a folk society because "the 'child of the kibbutz' has been reared in a peer group of his own, sheltered, so to speak, from the parental generation. . . . This primary emphasis on the peer group in the socialization of the kibbutz-born child, beginning in the earliest weeks of life, functioned as the most effective way to break the psychic link between the generations." This is true for all kibbutzim, and in terms of child development, by far outweighs any difference between kibbutzim.

Though I had read Diamond's report, I could not be sure that the different kibbutzim were indeed all that similar in regard to child rearing. So I had to decide *a priori* whether to try to sample as many settlements as I could within my limited time, or to concentrate on only one, making intensity of study compensate for wideness of sample. I decided on a study in depth, because emotional interactions need to be explored in detail, at least when the frame of reference is psychoanalytic.

❧ Ethos for a Nation

WHILE THIS IS NOT A REPORT ON THE KIBBUTZ MOVEMENT, but only on its child rearing methods, no educational system can be understood apart from the society it serves. I myself have no firsthand knowledge of the system itself beyond what can be learned from living in one of them for several weeks, from visiting a few other settlements, and from studying one particular aspect of life within them. Those readers who wish to understand the framework in which kibbutz education proceeds will find it in a growing literature which is readily available. (For the reader's convenience, the salients of kibbutz structure, and of Atid in particular, are sketched briefly in Appendices C and D. Further sources of information are listed in the bibliography.)

At the same time I shall have certain things to say about kibbutz parents pertaining to their attitudes toward children. These may be viewed by some as critical—though I have tried to report and not to pass judgment. Therefore certain facts about the kibbutz must be stated as a minimum. For example, it must be understood from the outset that kibbutz mothers never viewed their being mothers and the raisers of children as their main function in life, as do many or most middle-class American mothers.

From its very inception the purpose of the kibbutz movement, for both sexes, was first and foremost to create a new way of life in a very old and hostile land. True, the raising of a new generation to this new way of life was soon of crucial importance, but of necessity it took second place. Because unless the first generation created the society, how could it shelter any new generations? It was this older generation that subjected itself to great hardships and dangers, that first reclaimed the land, wresting harvests from a barren soil, and later fought the war that gained them statehood.

Today, apart from the still pervasive problem of making fast their new statehood, there is still the war for social ideals to be waged. But those ideals are harder to maintain when the problem is no longer one of creating a homeland, but of maintaining themselves as a splinter group in a land swept up in a booming economy. Such ideals are specially hard to preserve when the surrounding population is by now so largely concerned with acquiring the more convenient life that goes with a higher standard of living. The kibbutz parent, in his devotion to ideals, may be likened to our own early Puritans; except that these latter-day Puritans are not surrounded by a wilderness but by modern city life, which makes things a lot harder.

Kibbutzniks have never been more than a tiny minority in Israel. Nevertheless they have played a critical role there, both as idea and reality, out of all proportion to their numbers. For example, in 1944 Henrik Infield, in his book *Co-operative Living in Palestine*, placed the total membership of all kibbutzim at about sixteen thousand. Twenty years later their numbers had grown to about eighty thousand, living in about 250 kibbutzim, but they were still only about 4 percent of the population of Israel. Yet this 4 percent accounted for some 15 percent of all members of the Knesset (Israeli parliament).

Even if the kibbutz stood for no more than a small sect, living by its esoteric convictions and trying to raise its children by these lights, their devotion to lofty ideals would command respect. But for Israel they do much more than that, since they still provide much of the national ethos, and the best part of it. As many thoughtful Israelis told me: Were it not for the kibbutz dream of a better society, there would be nothing unique left about Israel. Having created a refuge where Jews can live free of persecution, Israel would be nothing more now than just a tiny new nation.

(Though written before the 1967 war, I see no reason to change this statement. The Arab-Israeli conflict is no longer a matter of the majority group persecuting a minority of its own citizens, but of two or more nation-states at odds over territorial rights. That one is smaller than the others does not make war and persecution the same thing, which they are not.)

It is also a nation with only one tenuous claim to the land: namely, that some two thousand years ago it was occupied by the spiritual ancestors of those who again hold possession now. This is not much of a claim compared to the uniqueness Jews felt, and which kept the Jews going during the two thousand years they were homeless.

All this has, in fact, led to many contradictions from which kibbutz life still suffers: In reclaiming the land, as in creating the state of Israel, kibbutzniks displaced Arab neighbors and fought them, though violence was contrary to their socialist convictions. Kibbutz founders wanted Israel to be an ideal state, free of all exploitation, where life would proceed in peace close to the biblical land. But the realities of the Middle East force Israel to be a garrison nation geared to defense, if not to war; a capitalist nation with many of the unpleasant features of a new nation trying to industrialize in a hurry.

I know that they also suffer from another contradiction, because they are keenly aware of it: Since they are atheists, they cannot base their claim to the land on the biblical promise that gave it to the Jews. The Jews needed a homestead. How desperately they needed it was made clear first by Hitler, and then by the plight of the Jews in Arab countries. But no other land was acceptable to the religious group, and no other land offered asylum to areligious Jews. So it had to be Israel, whether for political or emotional reasons.

In the face of all this contradiction and conflict, then, is where the kibbutz ethos makes a difference. It stands for utter devotion to the idea that once again Jews in Israel must not only create a new model of the good and just life, but actually live it—when need be at the cost of great personal hardship—or die for it if they must. Certainly the six-day war vindicated kibbutz child rearing methods and made it once again a symbol of all that is best in Israel. Not only did the kibbutz provide an inordinate percentage of the officer corps, it also suffered staggering losses. Some 4 percent of the Israeli population lives in the kibbutz, and kibbutzniks thus accounted for some 4 percent of the fighting force. But while about eight hundred soldiers fell in the war, two hundred of them came from the kibbutz (most of them born and raised there). Thus the 4 percent kibbutz segment of the Israeli army suffered 25 percent of all casualties. This was the true measure of their heroism, courage, and devotion to duty. Once more, as in the settling of the land and the war of liberation, the kibbutz ethos gives special meaning to the lives of Israelis today.

It is in this context of self-elected mission that the entire phenomenon of the kibbutz must be understood, and flowing from it, what the parents do or do not do in raising their children. It means that everything I shall say in this book must at all times be related to this background.

🌷 An Afterthought

How did the kibbutz way of raising children come about? First, it seems that kibbutz founders did not trust themselves to raise their own children in such a way as to become the carriers of a new society. To quote Diamond:

> The collective method of child rearing represents a rejection of the family, with particular reference to the parental roles. . . . It was felt that the family itself has to be banished, in order to rear the "new Jew." . . . [Kibbutz founders] were moved by the desire to create a new generation

that would be "normal," "free," and "manly," unsullied by the exile. . . . They did not think themselves worthy of rearing such children within the confines of their own nuclear families, and they dared not trust themselves to the task."[4]

Thus the realization of their larger dream depended on this new and uniquely brought up generation. But the new generation, and the unique way of bringing them up, were an afterthought, an accident. The kibbutz—a society that devotes its all to the future, and hence to its children, that has turned upside down all traditional modes of child rearing to realize its goals—started out as a society that had no interest in children whatsoever and no room for children in its life.

While this in no way invalidates the educational method, it accounts for many contradictions that cannot be understood except from its unplanned inception. We are faced with the anomaly that what started as a nuisance, because it stood in the way of the founders' main purposes—to execute an idea—has become a central feature on which the idea's survival now depends.

As Joseph Baratz (1954) tells the story of Degania, the first kibbutz, the original kibbutzniks (of whom he was one) wanted no children in their community. Most of the settlers did not even want to marry, because "they were afraid that children would detach the family from the group, that . . . comradeship would be less steadfast." Therefore it was seriously proposed that all members should oblige themselves not to marry for at least five years after joining the kibbutz, because "living as we do . . . how can we have children?"

When the first child was born in the kibbutz "nobody knew what to do with him. Our women didn't know how to

---

[4] This wish to create the "new" Jew, and some of its consequences, form the essence of Yael Dayan's novel *Envy the Frightened* (New York, World Publishing Company, 1961). Though the picture she draws is extreme, and hence distorts the reality I observed, some of the tendencies she describes are real enough among some groups.

look after babies." But eventually "we saw it couldn't go on like this. . . . By the time there were four children in the settlement we decided something must be done. It was a difficult problem. How were the women both to work and look after their children? Should each mother look after her own family and do nothing else?" The men did not seem to feel strongly either way.

> But the women wouldn't hear of giving up their share of the communal work and life. . . . Somebody proposed that the kibbutz should hire a nurse . . . we didn't hire a nurse, but we chose one girl to look after the lot of them and we put aside a house where they could spend the day while the mothers were at work. And so this system developed and was afterwards adopted in all the kibbutzim, with the difference that in most of them the children sleep in the children's house, but with us [at Degania] they stay at night in their parents' quarters. . . . Only recently have we built a hostel for children over twelve where our own children live.

This is how the famous communal education of children began.

I myself questioned the founding generation: I wondered why the original group, so intent on creating a new way of life, had given no thought to their own continuity by planning for the next generation. The answer was always the same as the one given in published accounts by the earliest settlers: "Founding the settlements, cultivating the land was so arduous, so much a grownups' task, that we could not think about children." I cannot help feeling that part of the original attraction of a thus-defined task might have been that it left no place for children. Because if one does not think of having children, it is because one has no wish for them at the time, and not because the task at hand is so arduous.

If my speculation is valid, one might carry it a step further and say that the founding generation knew they had no wish to replicate the family as they knew it, and of this they were entirely conscious. But despite their rejection they could not think of how else to raise children. Hence to them, the decision not to form families meant not to have children. If so, then kibbutz life was attractive to those who for this or other reasons did not wish to have children. My assumption seems supported by the incredibly low birthrate in the early days of kibbutz history, which contrasts sharply with other settings in which a people live in hardship and danger and nevertheless produce many children.

It would seem, then, that chance and a desire for quite other things, dictated the child-caring arrangements made hastily, piecemeal, and with little plan or thought; arrangements that were later formalized into dogma, as is probably the origin of most dogmas. Or as Murray Weingarten (1955) put it, "This system, at first merely a pragmatic arrangement . . . has assumed the flesh and blood of a very definite educational philosophy [because] the purpose of the kibbutz is not only . . . to set up a new economic framework for society [but] to create a new man."

But when the first of these new men arrived on the scene as a newborn infant, he was a nuisance to everyone but his mother and possibly his father. The reasons for this strange contradiction lie in the psychological origin of the movement.

❧ Kibbutz Origins

ESSENTIALLY THE KIBBUTZ HAS TWO MAJOR SOURCES. FIRST, there was the founders' desire to repudiate their ghetto existence. And second was the desire to create a new way of life in what had once been the homeland of the Jews. But the particular form taken by both these desires owed a great deal to the adolescent revolt of a small "elite" group in Central Europe at the turn of the century, namely the *Wandervogel* movement.

Wandervogel means *migratory bird* in German, and its young adherents wanted very much to migrate out of the world of their parents—an idea most persuasive to ghetto youth at this time. The *Wandervogel* movement was a revolt against the authoritarian families in which these essentially middle-class youth had been raised, and against the authoritarian schooling of the German *Gymnasium* most of them had attended. What they sought was a more authentic, more nature-bound way of life (Walter Laqueur, 1962).

All these ideas appealed to Jewish ghetto youth who rebelled at the even more binding traditions their parents lived by, and a system of religious education that was vastly more oppressive than any German school. In addition, it must be remembered that things German held a particular attraction for Eastern Jewry. Their ideas about emancipation had reached them from Germany, in the form of German enlightenment; socialism in its Marxist form had come to them from Germany; their very language, Yiddish, was based on medieval German. Nevertheless, while kibbutz founders were deeply influenced by *Wandervogel* ideology, the manner in which they combined it with socialism, Zionism, and a Tolstoyan emphasis on the virtues of life on the land was uniquely their own.

In any case it was the first of their desires, the wish to escape, that was dominant, or they would never have left home, and their second dream could never have been followed.

Once in Palestine, their daily lives and their work had to bend to the harsh facts of politics and economics. But they were freer about how to shape the inner life of their community, including the rearing of their children. Or to put it differently: Once there were children, they had much greater freedom about arranging the child's experience in such a way that he would grow up to realize their dreams.

To quote Diamond again, "the kibbutz served as an arena for the over-reaction of its members against *Shtetl* [ghetto] life and as a mechanism for adaptation to the socio-economic realities confronting them in Palestine." True, quite a few of the founding generation came from the cities of Central Europe and not from the *Shtetl*. But in most cases their parents had grown up in the *Shtetl* and perpetuated many of its features in the lives of their children. Others, for whom this was not true, had come from youth movements very much like the German *Wandervogel*.

One might add that at first, and for some time to come, whether they came from the ghetto or a more Westernized type of youth movement, their background equipped them very poorly for a pioneering agricultural life; so poorly, compared to American settlers who went West, that they could not make a go of it as single family units and were forced to rely much more on each other. (The difficulty of making a success of farm life as an individual family seems universal. Reflecting on his own childhood on a farm in Indiana, for example, Allan Nevins [1967] recalls the severe limitations imposed by individualism in a farming community, compared to the advantages of kibbutz organization as he observed it on a visit to Israel.) Be this as it may, what I did not find stressed in the literature was how their poor preparation as colonizers forced kibbutzniks to repeat, though in a deeply different way, the close unity that had characterized the ghetto, and for similar reasons: because it helped them survive in a basically hostile environment. Not only that, but as in the ghettos, they survived through deep devotion to a creed, though again a far different one. In place of their parents' religious creed, they chose a socialist-atheist work morality closely tied to a return to the soil.

Part of the ghetto existence to which kibbutz founders reacted, and possibly overreacted, was a closeness in family life that to them seemed devoid of freedom. (And here things were not too different for the lower middle-class Jewish family in the big cities of Central and Eastern Europe.) To begin with, since all life in their homes had centered so exclusively on the family, there would be no family as such in the kibbutz. Next, since the roles of men and women were unequal in the families they came from, the sexes would be entirely equal in the kibbutz. What was stressed here, according to Spiro, was " 'the biological tragedy' of women. Because woman must bear and rear children, she has had little opportunity for cultural, political, artistic expressions. If she could only be freed from this time-consuming responsibility, as well as from such other domestic duties as cleaning, cooking, and laundry, she would become the equal of men."

As Weingarten (1955) reflects, this philosophy of sexual equality was often carried to comic extremes. They "went so far as to print a pamphlet [whose] theme was that the only obstacle in the way of achieving true equality of the sexes was the unfortunate physical difference between men and women."

Again: Since the often poverty-stricken ghetto family was immensely concerned with both religious values and earthly possessions, neither religion nor materialism would exist in the kibbutz. I could extend the list indefinitely. But doing away with the family structure and striving for utter equality between the sexes was part of a larger desire for equality in all things.

The exploited worker of Europe, in his devotion to early socialism, strove for economic, political, and social equality.

The socialist Jew, who felt ready at last to break the chains forged by centuries of social, economic, and political inequality, knew it was not these alone that had kept him in his degraded position. He knew he was equally constrained by his Jewishness, by the crippling demands of his rigid religion, by his parents' strict adherence to Jewish ritual and traditions. And if the Jew was a woman, she felt even more degraded by a religion that required men to thank God each day that He had not created them female.

Beyond this I have a feeling which I cannot substantiate. But few religions have been as rejecting of womanhood as the Jewish one. It was a religion that viewed her very femininity as a curse, that condemned her to apartheid in its places of worship, that even forbade her to wear her own hair, and required her to shave if off at marriage.

It was this ritual rejection of femininity by their parents, and their own glorification of masculine pursuits, that may have influenced the first kibbutz generation to view man's work as preferable to woman's, including the work of rearing children. If so, then it may explain why women of the second generation who were reared areligiously show little preference for typically masculine work. They wish for important work, but only a minority take this to mean the hard physical labor of men, and few feel deprived if they lack it.

Thus the kibbutz movement was also a particularly Jewish revolt against debasement of the female and in favor of equality. It was therefore the women of the kibbutz, much more than the men, who insisted that their child bearing and child rearing functions must not interfere with their absolute equality with men. The phrase quoted earlier about the "unfortunate physical difference" cannot fully be savored apart from this context of the biblical curse upon woman *qua* woman.

But if the founding of the kibbutz was in large part a reaction to the ghetto existence, what kept it going thereafter was not what its founders wished to get rid of, but the positives they found in their new life. It is true that living as their ideals demanded, even at the cost of great hardship and self-denial, gave them deep satisfaction. It greatly enhanced the ego to be able to live up to (ego) ideals that were so difficult to achieve, that were so largely self-chosen, not imposed. But this alone gave no primary emotional satisfactions, did not satisfy the id. And without that, life is empty and cold, however virtuous. This necessary warmth and this meaning they found in their deep emotional ties to the peer group.

Kibbutz is the Hebrew word for *group*; it has no other meaning. All the satisfactions that in the ghetto had come from the family, and many more, came to kibbutzniks from their peers. Hence their greatest fear was that if men and women were to stop sharing the same life activities, if women were to turn again to a preoccupation with pregnancy and child care and the men to competing for a living, then the group would cease meeting their emotional needs.

Again and again I was told that if the children were again to live and sleep with their parents, then the parents could not so freely be part of the communal doings of their peers, and that these are what give meaning to their lives. In this sense it is true: The kibbutz woman seeks her deepest satisfaction not from her children (as her mother did) but from her contemporaries, male and female. And so does the kibbutz male, who finds in his fellow kibbutzniks many of those emotional satisfactions the ghetto father sought from attachment to his children. But this deep peer attachment depends on full participation in the common enterprise, requires equality in how one's everyday life will be spent.

As one old-timer put it, who for more than thirty years had worked as a metapelet with infants, "Let's face it, the kibbutz wasn't built for children, but to make us free." And by this she meant nothing abstract, but the freedom to live in such a way that no kibbutznik, male or female, would lose any of the emotional satisfactions gained from a life devoted essentially to each other rather than to their children.

A more extended example may suggest the degree to which kibbutz institutions must be understood as having grown out of both: the necessities of the agricultural pioneer and the overreaction to a ghetto past. I quote from Diamond's analysis of the meaning of the communal dining rooms, which I found to be fully borne out by my experience.

In the kibbutz, the communal dining hall discharges multiple functions. It is a social center from which all roads radiate. It is a ceremonial center in which most community affairs are held. It is a political center in which the general assembly meets. And, of course, it is the place wherein all adult members take their meals. The communal dining hall, then, serves as a significant symbol of the whole collective undertaking. Indeed, we would contend that the communal dining hall is the heart of the collective. Should it be abandoned, the kibbutz would, viewed from within, turn into a strikingly different kind of society.

Now the communal dining hall, approached historically, serves as an expression of the deep rebellion against the old Jewish family structure, with particular reference to eating customs. The family meal in the Shtetl was a religio-psychological sacrament. It was religious in its prohibition of non-kosher food, and the ritual emphasis on cleanliness; psychological in its function of binding the family together, while refreshing and clarifying the relations of its component members. The father sat at the head of the table and usually uttered the benediction; the mother spent a good part of her time in scrupulous food preparation; and the children, ranged around the table, witnessed the continuity of Jewish tradition symbolized in the family meal, while consuming Mama's dishes, and recognized Papa's authority. Moreover, the relation of the Jewish mother to her child was strongly expressed through over-attention to feeding as an aspect of over-protection, a reaction, in part, to the dangerous encircling environment. Bottled up, as the energies of the Jews were in the Shtetl, the Jewish mother could hardly express her love and fear for, her insecurity concerning her child in any more effective way than making sure that her offspring's immediate physical wants, as she conceived them, were satisfied. As we have indicated, the family structure of the Jews functioned as an armor against adversity, and eating habits were bolts in that armor.

Now the communal dining hall represents a massive psychic rejection of the former eating customs. Family members do not necessarily sit together, eating is regarded as a bare physical necessity, little value is put on the careful preparation of food, and meals are consumed in a hectic and unceremonious atmosphere. Further any special attention by one family member to the food wants of another is regarded as an abuse of cultural ideals. Indeed, the consumption, and, of course, the preparation of food in private rooms is still reckoned a cardinal sin against the Kibbutz. It was, and is to a lesser extent today,[5] considered almost obscene, an activity which people literally engaged in behind closed doors and drawn shutters, precisely because it recalled the shameful past, and reawakened memories of the old discarded family relationships which had produced what was conceived to be the weak, unmanly, fearful, incapable Jew of the *Galut*.

Now, obviously the communal dining hall served a utilitarian function. Given the woman's desire to engage in

---

[5] This has changed still more since Diamond wrote his analysis, but much against the desires of the leadership. Left-wing kibbutzim in particular have built elaborate "coffee-houses" at considerable expense so that kibbutzniks will congregate there for their afternoon tea or snacks. This is meant to wean them away from having tea in their rooms, which is still felt to violate the communal spirit.

"productive," that is, non-domestic or non-"service" work alongside of the men, some such communal dining hall was a necessity. Also, in the pioneering period of the kibbutz, building thirty or forty individual kitchens and dining areas was hardly feasible. Moreover, given the work training function of the collective, and the concomitant high population turnover, central kitchen facilities were indispensable. Yet, neither these material factors, nor the functional imperatives dictated by other Kibbutz institutions, can explain the inner meaning of the communal dining hall. To comprehend the latter, we must view the communal dining hall in functional-historical perspective, and that we have attempted to do.

To this astute analysis of the origin and meaning of the communal dining room as a central institution, Diamond might have added another factor. While stressing that much of parental authority in the ghetto was exercised at mealtime, he does not stress that in reaction to this, kibbutz children do not eat in the communal dining room. They eat with their peers in the children's houses or (as adolescents) in their own dining-assembly room, not with their parents.

At the same time, and having said this much about the origins of child rearing in the kibbutz, I would like to stress again the obvious: Whatever the social and psychological origins of an institution, they have no place in evaluating its merits.

❧ The Women

LET ME TURN NOW TO THE OVERREACTION TO GHETTO LIFE among women in particular. In talking with those who joined the movement as young girls, both foreign-born and Israeli-born women (but *not* kibbutz-born), it became apparent almost at once that kibbutz life had offered them a much desired chance. It enabled them to reject all of what they felt to be antiquated female roles except childbirth itself, and even then many delayed having children till later in life.

Partly this sprang from a devotion to what seemed the more important and immediate task: to conquer the land and to build the good new society in Israel. Just as some American girl might postpone having children because she does not want to interrupt a professional training she finds more important at the moment, so did many of these women set motherhood aside for what was the essence of their lives at the moment: to live a life that was free of inequality between men and women, and in the process to build Israel and the kibbutz.

But just as they dared to live out their conviction that what was needed was a life very different from their parents', so in a way, they also dared to admit to certain commoner anxieties and to act upon them, as a more conventional woman might not feel free to do. I refer to their anxiety that they might not make good as mothers. While this anxiety may not be universal, it is certainly widespread, at least among our own middle classes. The difference is that, as in their wish for equality between the sexes, the kibbutz woman acted on her anxiety. More than that, she shaped universal policy (universal, that is, for the kibbutz) on the basis of such anxieties, and convinced the men that they should follow suit.

But by so arranging for child care, the kibbutz woman rejected what, in the eyes of the world, was good mothering, the kind she got from her own mother. And just as any child who rejects his parents expects to be punished for it, and fears it most in regard to what was the essence of the rejection, so she may have feared she would be punished for rejecting a mother she found wanting, by turning out to be an even worse mother herself.

After all, we learn our sexual roles through identifying with the parent of our sex. Now the ghetto parent, the typical Jewish "mamma," gives her all to her child, but expects a great deal in return. Her life in the ghetto, so miserable in its external conditions, gets meaning only from the promise of the future, and this is embodied most of all in the child bearing function of her daughter.

According to orthodox Jewish doctrine, only that person is a Jew who is born of a Jewish mother; on this score, at least, the man counts for nothing. So even religious tradition enforces the mother's demands by making the daughter responsible for perpetuating Jewishness. True, the son is expected to give in return too, but less by raising children than by his devotion to religion, and by what he does out in life in a variety of ways. (I was amazed, in my discussions with American-Jewish mothers, at how intensely they still feel that their daughters [and daughters-in-law] hold the power to grant or withhold happiness by "giving" or "not giving" them a grandchild. No such feelings seem directed at their sons or sons-in-law.)

Deep in the Jewish girl's unconscious, from earliest childhood, the idea was imbedded that the good daughter is the one who grows up to be a good mother. She is the daughter who repays the mother's outpouring of love by giving her a grandchild. And at this the daughters rebelled. Knowing, however, that they never wanted to give to their children as exclusively as their mothers had done, left them with a sense of unworthiness and betrayal. Clearly they seemed ungiving, compared to their mothers. Certainly they felt themselves ungiving to the older generation, and feared they would be just as ungiving (or not giving enough) to the next generation, to their own children. Much as they were ready to cast off their mothers' role in practice, psychologically they remained beholden to an image of their mothers who had instilled in them the unconscious feeling that only giving all is enough.

That is why, in rejecting the role of the parent, things were very different for the women than for the men. Among the founding generation, males too rejected the parent, but only in part. True, they could not identify with their fathers in the religious role of the male, nor with the ghetto Jew's acceptance of a miserable social position. But at least they could identify with the father's role of provider, the one who must make a living for himself and those dependent on him. Things were very different for the women. The essential female role in the ghetto was one in which the woman's entire life was swept up in caring for husband and children, and in nothing else.

To the founding woman, her mother's life seemed so overwhelming an example of giving to children, so much all of one piece, that she could not imagine herself identifying with part of it, and not others. These mothers of theirs, in their single-minded devotion to family and children, seemed most powerful figures to their daughters. To be free of such an image, one had to be free of it *in toto*. The daughter could not conceive in her unconscious of being able to take care of husband and children and still be an equal companion to men. She felt she could not do that much better than her mother. But she felt she could do things entirely differently. If her mother's life had been all of a piece, all wifely and motherly, so would her life be all of a piece. She would be solely man's equal companion at work and in her whole daily life.

Toward their own generation, however, kibbutz women felt anything but ungiving. If they saw themselves as bad children, they felt they could be excellent comrades. Since their comrades had helped them—as a matter of fact had paved the way for their revolt—they could be loving comrades to their age-mates, including being wives to them in the new way of the kibbutz. This they could do because they felt their husbands expected no more of them than they were ready to give. Motherhood they dared not attempt, because there was nothing in their experience to assure them that what they were ready to give was enough to make them good mothers. And here we should not be harsh on them for being thus misled by their conscious and unconscious anxieties. Even today, and in spite of kibbutz evidence, leading experts insist that mothers who work or are otherwise active in society, do indeed cheat their children out of good mothering.

Some of what I deduce here as the inner source of woman's fears about her own mothering abilities is speculation. But many statements made to me, and also reported in the literature, suggest it to be an essentially correct interpretation of motives. For example, I was told again and again that kibbutz rearing protects the child from the evil effects of bad mothering, and this by parents and educators who insisted that the mother is greatly important in the child's life, even in the kibbutz.

Even more telling is their view of what causes emotional disturbance in kibbutz children. Always they insisted it was the mother—or occasionally the father—who was responsible.[6] Not once was I told by kibbutzniks that the disturbance was caused by kibbutz rearing, though they were ready to discuss possible imperfections of the system in general—for example, that they might be starting too late in their education to cleanliness, etc.

The insistence that kibbutz rearing protects the child from bad mothering (and by implication that some kibbutzniks

[6] See also pp. 189 ff.

are just such bad mothers) combined with the insistence that all emotional disturbance is caused by the parents and none by kibbutz rearing, suggests that bad mothering, or parenthood, is viewed as the only possible cause of emotional maladjustment. It shows how fearful the kibbutzniks are of their potential for being bad parents to their children.

Such a dim view of their ability to be good parents is in stark contrast to how readily they assume that all comrades are good comrades. That is, they seemed convinced that comrades are good comrades, until there is obvious evidence to the contrary. But there seems an almost equal conviction of the potential in these good comrades to be bad parents to their children. (This, the kibbutznik's profound conviction that the parental impact is what causes emotional disturbance, stands in equally stark contrast to the tendency among us to blame the difficulties of our children on society.)

Here, then, is where the kibbutz found a way out: If mothers were not willing to give their children as much of themselves as their mothers had given, they would ask for much less in return. All the anxieties I describe here a woman could resolve in a single fell swoop by turning her children over to metapelets who would give less, but ask for even less in return. These metapelets would not devour her child as her mother had done. They would even protect her child from the danger that she, in her desire to do very differently from her mother, might be a bad mother anyway. And the children would not suffer but would gain, since they would have their satisfying life with their peers. Wanting the best for her child and feeling convinced she was unable to offer it, she either helped to develop or later eagerly embraced this new system of education.

Often it took little probing to elicit this feeling in some women: They had feared being totally inadequate as mothers, particularly with their firstborn. In some cases, where I could penetrate more deeply, the other aspect became apparent as well: They felt deeply guilty about the radical rejection of their mothers' readiness to make sacrifices for children. All this remained thinly disguised behind rationalizations: By true kibbutz values, only physical labor in the fields was worthwhile; they could not afford to neglect their labors by devoting too much time to their children; and last, but most often cited, in the early days of the kibbutz all manpower and womanpower was needed to keep the community going.

Again and again, when I raised the question of the origin and purpose of communal education, I was told in one and the same sentence, or else in statements made within minutes of each other, (1) that this is the best way to raise children, and the kibbutz makes great economic sacrifices to maintain such a system though it is extremely demanding and expensive; and (2) that from economic necessity nearly all women had to work in the fields and hence could not stay home to take care of their children.

So the system is declared at the same time to be much more economical and much more expensive; to have been forced on them by sheer necessity, and to have come about by deliberate decision. And so indeed it was, in my opinion: forced on them by unconscious needs as transformed into conscious decisions.

Because if greater freedom for women was truly their goal, one can only wonder whence the emphasis on economic necessity. Rapaport, whose kibbutz experience dates from the early days of the movement, remarks that of all the explanations tendered, "perhaps the only historically and factually incorrect one [is that] economic need demanded that women, like men, work in the field, and . . . gave rise to this economical, communal care of children."

If an inner psychological need or desire is clearly recognized as such, and is nevertheless and erroneously explained as a necessity, it means that somehow one feels the desire was wrong. But then one feels guilty for having yielded to such a desire and wishes instead to believe that one has been forced to submit. I believe that the kibbutzniks' purpose in claiming necessity is to quiet their guilt about refusing to personally care for their own children, while willing to do so collectively.

In all this there still is another contributing element. When the decision was made to entrust so many parental functions to the society they had built, the desire was to remove from those relations whatever might interfere with the children's love for their parents, whatever might create hostility in the child, or even ambivalence toward his parents. Then, because parent and child would have only good times together, there would be none of the deep animosity felt by the founding generation, as youngsters, toward their parents. As Spiro has amply discussed, these wishes were central in shaping their plans: All education should be entrusted to metapelets, and the time spent by children with their parents should consist entirely of what we in America would call "fun time."

An elaborate series of explanations are current among kibbutz educators and parents interested in education—and most kibbutz parents are—about how this system of child rearing removes the bad effects of the oedipal situation. True, these are explanations after the fact, since, as noted above, no one knew what to do with the first children who came. But here again, if a system is devised for reasons of one's own, and one is a conscientious person, then having created the system, one wishes to believe it serves higher goals—for example, that it does away with oedipal problems, particularly if one has suffered from them severely oneself.

There can be little doubt that these parents are serious in their wish to protect their children from the pain of oedipal conflicts. And whatever the psychological origins of kibbutz education, it certainly changes the oedipal situation.

I discuss this at some length because behind the great and sincere desire that their children should have very positive feelings for their parents, one again feels at every turn an even greater anxiety about the danger of the children's feelings being very negative. Out of this anxiety Freud's analysis of the oedipal situation was misunderstood to mean that parents should never have any but good times with their children.

What was overlooked was that no oedipal situation can arise without an initial deep attachment to the parents, and not because of how positive it is. Deep attachment implies strong feelings. And if Freud discovered anything, it was the ambivalence of human emotions; that our feelings never come singly but in their human admixture of opposites. Yet the kibbutzniks' hope was that by sharing nothing but pleasure with their children, the oedipal ambivalence of love and rejection would be avoided, indicating a fear of deep attachments pure and simple, of which ambivalence is a necessary part.

That all this accounts for kibbutz mothers' accepting separation from their children is further supported by how differently many, though not all of them, felt about their later-born children. These children quite a few mothers would have liked to keep at home, while their firstborns they were glad to let others care for, because they were afraid they would never do it well. It is borne out even more by the few mothers I interviewed who induced their unwilling husbands to leave the kibbutz after a first child was born there, so that their second or third child could live in the home.

The story is entirely different for the kibbutz-born mothers. It is true that quite a few of them leave the kibbutz because they do not want to be kept from their children. More often, however, they accept readily and with little inner difficulties the kibbutz method of child rearing. Not having experienced intense mothering care as infants, they are emotionally somewhat detached from their own children, and from mothering. None of the complex psychological problems I discuss above are pertinent in their case.

While as infants they probably wanted more from their mothers than they got, they learned from infancy what no child brought up in a middle-class family learns—that only the peer group comes close to giving them all they would like to receive but do not get. Unlike their non-kibbutz-born mothers, they do not fear they will be bad mothers; on the contrary. They are convinced they are good mothers who give their children everything a good mother should. But their own infancy was one of emotional semidetachment, not from their age-mates but from adults. It is all they feel their children need, since it is all they know of to offer, and they do not long for emotional intimacy, in our sense, with their infants. In this, too, they are radically different from their mothers, having been brought up in such radically different ways.

❧ *Pragmatism*

HAVING SAID ALL THIS, I MUST ADD THAT TO OVERSIMPLIFY BY explaining the kibbutz as no more than an overreaction to a personal background, or as an adaptation to a pioneering existence, would be to miss the point entirely. First, there was no need for kibbutzniks of either sex to reclaim barren soil in a faraway land, nor to embrace a particular view of the new man in order to counteract a home background.

These choices were uniquely their own and entirely spontaneous. So was their conception of the good and just life,
the one they embraced out of all those available from which
to choose. And while not unique in the history of mankind,
it is certainly rare that a group of people are so serious about
transforming themselves and society in the image of their
ideal as to create an entire new national ethos.

So while their educational system was not planned but
grew like Topsy and many mistakes were made, and while
the children were not exactly welcome, these communities,
once the children arrived, set about with determination to
reshape the educational system in accord with kibbutz
ideals. Originally it was a system that, if planned at all, was
designed not for the child, but against the child's robbing his
parents of their chance for freedom, and only later to also
protect the child from parental bondage. Since the children
were not to interfere with kibbutz life, the first solution was
to have their life organized as a replica-in-miniature of the
larger kibbutz. It would be a children's society of absolute
equality, with each individual subject to group norms.

To cite an early practice: In a few settlements each kibbutznik alike was given a comb, whether he needed one or
not, even those who were bald. Such a practice, though
never widespread, was soon given up since it contradicted a
central value of the kibbutz: that to each should be given
according to his needs. But the same was not true for the
children, who for some time were all treated alike. So all
infants were fed the same amount of food, a quantity suggested by the doctor as "normal," whether the baby wanted
it or not. Thus the children were expected to be even more
"equal" than adults, since of them it was assumed that their
needs were entirely alike. It took quite a while for such practices to be given up, for infants, too, who then were fed
according to their needs. (Here, as with us, the social mores

were more rigidly enforced on the child who could not defend himself, than on the adults who devised them.)

Since the adults did not trust their parental instincts and shunned the pattern of their parents, they at first relied entirely on the advice of their physicians, or so they now claim. If the doctor suggested feeding the child back his vomit, or tying him to the potty for hours, this is what was done. But soon they saw this was making their children unhappy. So as one eminent educator told me, "When my own daughter left the kibbutz because of her unhappiness about this kind of early experience, we changed the system."

That it was not a system they had planned for the children is again clear from the frequent explanations of why things were bad for the children at first. "We did not know what was the right way to do things, so we followed without question the advice of the experts, the physicians."

In this context I might mention how often the parents (particularly mothers) of severely disturbed children tell me how they slavishly followed the advice of experts, though the child's reactions showed clearly that the handling suggested by the experts was strongly resisted by the child. Often just a superficial inquiry would quickly show both: that the advice of experts was sought (though another person's silly remark is often taken for such an expert recommendation) because of a deep feeling that if left to one's own devices one would harm one's own child; and that it was slavishly followed for the same reason. Thus the kibbutzniks' asking physicians how much a child should be fed, or how early and stringently he should be toilet trained, and then slavishly following such advice bespeaks a deep distrust of their spontaneous ability to do right by their children. Yet so does the statement that: "nobody knew what to do with our babies."

But either a system is designed to avoid oedipal conflict, or it develops without plan and in the absence of guidelines follows slavishly the advice of the experts. For newer ideas, kibbutzniks now turned to an only partly understood Freud and tried to rear the children in relative instinctual freedom. Given such freedom, the children broke the basic law of fraternity and selfishly sought their own goals. As another leading educator told me, "Let's face it, they didn't obey, they took things and broke them, they went where they wanted and didn't play by the rules." This last, of course, was the cardinal sin against the group. So still another line was adopted in the rearing of children. But it was all done pragmatically, and this is the point I shall be stressing throughout.

Perhaps one example of how their pragmatism works in practice: Kibbutz parents do not want their children to sleep with them at night because they fear this will interfere with adult freedom. Yet they cannot bear the poorly suppressed knowledge that their children need them at night. So they instituted the night watch. But she (the night watch) cannot serve all the children in all houses at once, so in many kibbutzim they set up a loudspeaker system through which she could hear a child if he cried. Later still, they made it two-way so that she could also talk to the child. But this, they found, scared the child out of his wits—to hear a voice from nowhere in the middle of the night—so they gave it up.

Nevertheless, when a consultant psychologist suggested to parents in the left-wing kibbutzim that they should take turns sleeping in the children's house, if only with the infants, they refused. They wanted the best for their children, but not if it cost them their freedom.

In some right-wing kibbutzim, such as Atid, parents became worried enough about the infants' night fears to decide that everyone should take turns sleeping in the infants' house. This included, of course, the older bachelors of the kibbutz, but they were at a total loss when the infants cried, having no idea how to go about feeding or diapering a baby. So they solved their dilemma by pretending to be asleep and not to hear an infant when he wailed. Eventually this system was dropped, and it was more or less left to the parents what they wanted to do.

At Atid the practice now followed is that occasionally when things seem to be critical, some parents will sleep in one of the two infants' houses. This happens particularly when the weather is bad, since the feeling is that in good weather the infants do not need an adult in the house. But whether or not they will sleep in the infants' house depends on the metapelet's decision as to whether things are critical. The result is that in the second of the two infants' houses at Atid parents do not sleep in even occasionally. When I inquired about the difference, I learned that the metapelet of the first house thought that the parents' sleeping in was not a bad idea, while the other metapelet found it entirely unwelcome. So even here the feelings of the comrades for each other took precedence over what is considered preferable for the infant.

Given such inner attitudes, which are slow to change—and given the fact that birth control enabled kibbutzniks to decide when and how many children to have—the child population grew only slowly, and grew much slower in the left-wing which took communal life even more seriously. For example, Henrik Infield (1944) reports that in 1936, when the population of sixty-five kibbutzim was 6,988, there were only 646 children, or less than 10 percent—and this in a population that was young in years and contained only persons of childbearing age. For nearly ten adults, in the age group from about eighteen to thirty, there was only one child. And in the left wing there was only one child for every fifteen adults.

Five years earlier, in 1931, the over-all percentage of

children in the kibbutzim was only 4 percent. This, incidentally, may explain why even in 1964 I found so few kibbutz-born parents who had had children by then, a group I was particularly anxious to study. One gets the impression that kibbutzniks began to have children in larger numbers when their system of rearing was more firmly established and they could afford to have children without fearing for their own freedom. Thus more children began to be born in the kibbutz from about 1945 or 1950 on, though even now to have many children is the exception. And this, though having children has become very important for the survival of the movement, and though they are not an economic problem to their parents.

Nor can the low birthrate have been the consequence of economic hardship, as some claim who point out that as the kibbutzim became a bit more affluent, more children were born. Because neither poverty nor danger alone have ever been deterrents to setting many children into the world. Even among us, as in the rest of the world, the poorest, or the poor-without-hope, have the most children.

By now the kibbutz system of child rearing seems well established, though it is still undergoing changes, and will probably do so in the future. The early vacillation from extreme regimentation (to assure communality) to relative instinctual freedom (to assure freedom in adulthood) has by now settled somewhere between.

Implications

It soon became apparent to me that kibbutz child rearing, as I have described it, has important implications for our theories of human development. While supporting most psychoanalytic views, it certainly throws doubt on some quite significant details. But it also became clear that there was little to be learned from it that we could readily apply to our problems, at least to those of delinquency and the underprivileged child.

Partly this is because any comparison with our disadvantaged children is moot, given the uniform standard of living in the kibbutz. This prevents the devastating feeling that one is permanently at the bottom of the ladder, even if some kibbutz parents have little more of material goods than some of our so-called ADC families. (These are families receiving aid to dependent children, most often because the mother is unmarried or was deserted, etc. The aid is meant to enable mothers to stay home and care for their offspring.) And again: The difference in outlook is reflected in the birthrate, with rather few children per kibbutz mother.

First, then, what of the rearing of infants away from their parents? The kibbutz experience clearly demonstrated to me that children raised by educators in group homes can and do fare considerably better than many children raised by their mothers in poverty-stricken homes, and better than quite a few raised at home by their middle-class parents.

Second, what about communal rearing in a non-kibbutz culture such as ours? Kibbutz children grow up in a community of such cohesion, one where there is so high a degree of consensus on all essential issues that it is hard to visualize how we could duplicate it in our pluralistic society. The only exceptions I know of would be cohesive enclaves such as the Hutterite communities in America, for example, which indeed show much that resembles kibbutz methods in their rearing of children.

Strong cohesion, of course, also makes for repression, and much more of it than one finds in a pluralistic society. But repressive societies, since they do not so openly show signs of disorganization and dissent, often look as if they were mentally healthier—another reason we must not be carried away, either by the extent of delinquency in our society or by its virtual absence in the kibbutz. The question is: Does the kibbutz pay a price for its absence, and is such a price right or too high? Conversely, are there advantages we gain in our society from that relative freedom to act out, as represented by delinquent behavior? And if so, are these advantages worth the price we pay as a society, or that delinquents and their victims have to pay as persons?

Cohesion in the kibbutz is nowhere more evident than in educating the child. Kibbutzniks may argue apace and are often dissatisfied with metapelets. But even with the worst metapelet, and even in the worst disagreement between metapelet, teacher, and parent, they are in accord—as is everyone close to the child—on fundamentals. All agree that the life, organization, and institutions of the kibbutz are essentially as they should be, though details might be in need of improvement. Compare this, for example, with present dissension between many slum parents and the school system to which they entrust their children, and from which the children are supposed to benefit, despite parental distrust or indifference.

Consensus or a lack of it between parents and educational system do not reach the child's conscious awareness until he reaches the age of understanding. But there is no doubt that even the infant responds to the inner harmony or lack of it between his parent and the society in which he lives. No sooner does he enter school—be it day care center, nursery, or kindergarten—than he reacts to the slightest disagreement between parent and educator as to values or standards of behavior. While at best, among our own culturally deprived, we find the attitude that this or that teacher is a good person and teacher, they remain personal exceptions. There is a fundamental distrust of the system as a whole which even contaminates the personal exception. In the kibbutz, on the other hand, there is deep conviction that this is a good and just society, and rarely is there any doubt that the educational system is good for the child. Hence even with dissension between parent and a given metapelet, it is confined to a narrow circle of people and never extends to education as a whole.

Perhaps of equal or greater importance, the educational system is viewed as part of a total society that is fully accepted. Any educational system is a significant aspect of society, and to the child its most significant one. As such, it too is always tainted by parental views of society. Many parents among the culturally deprived, view society as an enemy that stands between them and their aspirations in life. Both kibbutz parent and educator see the educational system as an integral part of the only society that permits them and their children to satisfy their deepest aspirations. Individual quarrels with isolated features of the educational system, or with individual educators, pale against so high a consensus on all-important issues.

True, there are some slum dwellers who, while they feel outside of things, nevertheless strive for themselves or their children to belong. Such homes may be desperately poor, but their children are not culturally deprived. They are simply not able, for the time being, to participate in the culture. Coming from such homes they feel "unequal," that they got the wrong end of the stick, but that school offers them a chance to undo these inequities in our society. Hence for them, home, school, and society are still not as much "all of a piece" as they are for the kibbutz child.

The substantial cooperation to be found in the kibbutz, despite personal reservations between parent, community, and educator, can exist only where a consensus society is the universal ideal. This includes a far-reaching acceptance by the individual of the community's right to shape his own life and that of his children. And for kibbutzniks, the parental role of the community is accepted by child and adult.

This raises the question of whether, and to what degree, such consensus can exist in a society that is not fairly uniform in its way of life, and not of limited size. It is inconceivable how we in the United States could even strive for such a consensus-society when all our traditions, when our greatest social, economic, and political successes (though our contradictions and shortcomings too) flow from so deep a commitment to a pluralistic society.

Certainly among kibbutzniks there is a universal fe. 'ing that the kibbutz should not be too large; that much is lost when it is. The optimal size is a community of a few hundred members, perferably smaller than larger. So to broaden the question: can a consensus exist that is strong enough to support communal rearing, among groups that do not share an identical philosophy of life, where all members do not meet face to face almost daily, where they do not form in some sense—perhaps not a primary group or an extended family —but a system of peer groups, closely knit?

While the kibbutz is much larger than any extended family system we know of, and different because of any one parent's limited influence on his children, it resembles such a system in the sharing of property and mutual help in adversity, in the absolute responsibility felt by each member for the well-being of all other members, etc.

Still another quandary: Part of this consensus is that kibbutz children are educated with the ideal in mind that they will perpetuate the life and society of their parents. That is, they are raised for a closed, not an open community. I am unable to say if such an educational system would be possible where the ideal is that of an open society, as it is theoretically the ideal of the United States educational system (strong countervailing forces notwithstanding). The difference is that while the kibbutz ideal is conformity with little demand for essential change (an ideal not fully lived up to), here in the United States the ideal of nonconformity (though more honored in the breach) is deeply felt.

Hence no direct conclusions can be drawn from the kibbutz to our own situation because the kibbutz *anima* is too radically different from what prevails in our large urban centers. And it is there that such child rearing methods might conceivably modify what is currently misnamed the "culture" of poverty.

Perhaps a few further remarks on these differences may be added. They pertain not to the kibbutz as a social system, but again to the individual psychology of its members, particularly its mothers.

There are strong psychological reasons why kibbutz mothers are ready to accept the communal rearing of their children, while ADC mothers, for example, might resist.

Comparing briefly the kibbutz mother's situation with that prevailing in many of our slum homes, particularly those of the unmarried or ADC mother, the two emerge as distinctly opposite. The woman who has joined the kibbutz from the outside (but not the one born there) fears her damaging impact on her child. She feels also that mothering and its emotional obligations would interfere with her deepest aspirations in life: to be, live, and work as freely as a man.

For the ADC mother, handing her baby over to others is usually a deprivation. She finds her only, or most available, emotional satisfaction in mothering her newborn. Partly this is because she despairs of her chance to take her place in the community, in the work world. Thus while communal child rearing permits the kibbutz mother greater emotional satisfaction, it may do the opposite for the ADC mother. She may see it not as freeing her for a variety of satisfactions outside of the home, but as depriving her of the most readily satisfying experience she knows.

Finally, the kibbutz mother who hands her infant over to communal education does so expecting that the child will grow up to share this communal life with her and all her comrades. The ADC mother, much as she wants her child to have a better life, fears that handing him over to an educator means he will grow up and leave her behind; or worse, he will look down on her and her life with little understanding or compassion.

If one wished to speculate on these two situations, so different from each other, one might say that all parents share a desire to somehow perpetuate their existence through their children. Those who founded the kibbutz revolted against too excessive a desire of this kind in their parents. They felt they were being asked to turn their very lives into a "monument" to their parents' aspirations. And it had worked, too, for centuries, until the impact of Westernization broke the hold of religion.

But having broken the chain of generations, the founders are doing no different than their parents. Their greatest desire now is to see that their children should preserve the kibbutz intact, as a monument to their own past achievement.

Now the ADC mother, too, wants her child to perpetuate her life. But in her case this wish conflicts with her other desire—that her children should have a better life. What is true for both is that they do not want the child to interfere with what provides satisfaction and gives inner purpose to their lives. In the kibbutz this takes the form of wishing that the infant should not force the mother to give up her desire for a free and active life in the community. For the ADC mother, it is the wish that her infant's life should not be so different as to threaten her own adjustment to her present way of life, however precarious.

This is not to imply that it is better for the child of the ADC mother to be reared at home, when he could be reared in something akin to the communal settings of the kibbutz. As a matter of fact, I tend to believe that such a radical change would best resolve the problem of our slums, and in short order. I believe it just because the kibbutz example has shown me it is possible to create a viable personality type wholly different from that of the parents, in a single generation. What I wished to stress here was merely a radical difference in attitude that may make it easy and attractive to separate mothers from children in one case, and hard to accept in the other.

I can be much briefer about the relevance of kibbutz methods to others of our problems, such as those of the underachiever, the dropout, the delinquent. Underachievers, and later dropouts, usually start school too poorly prepared. All kibbutz children, because they share a common rearing, receive the same preparation for school work, so that in spite of great individual differences in native endowment, no one starts education with a handicap. The problem of under-achievers and dropouts (and nearly all dropouts were underachievers long before they became dropouts) stems also in part from our highly competitive educational system, and partly from the attractions of the adult world outside.

Many a dropout feels he has reached a point where he no longer wishes to sit on a school bench, but wants to go to work. In the kibbutz, work and academic learning are combined. As the child grows older, he works more after-school hours at the farm or in the shop, and is given ever more absorbing and responsible tasks. This goes a long way toward making it less onerous to stay in class for the rest of the time.

Most lower class dropouts leave school because the years spent there have made them more and more convinced that education as they know it does not meet their needs. They leave in self-defense. In order to spare themselves recognition of their deficiency, they turn on school as an enemy. The abyss between what they view as today's reality for them and what they aspire to for the future is what makes for their final break with education as a dead end solution. By contrast, kibbutz education is so much part of a common way of life, so embodies the youngsters' future aspirations that, however much they sometimes tire of learning, what they never feel is a split between them and the educational system.

Compared to the many who drop out in the United States because of their deep disappointment with education, those who quit in hopes of earning money (most often for a car) are by comparison few. In the kibbutz there is no chance at all to earn money, so there is no reason to drop school to earn it. Since there are no economic differences to speak of, there is no cause to feel economically disadvantaged. With every last one of a youngster's age-mates in school there would really be nothing for him to do with his time but to sit in the children's house doing nothing. (There is no TV and few distractions to enjoy.) Most of all, since there is no competition for grades, no being left back, etc., the youngsters feel little pressure. Some pressure is now beginning to come from parents and educators, but very mildly, compared to those in America.

Again, the kibbutz is a small society where everyone knows everyone else and where the consensus is high. Few turn delinquent in a society where delinquency and crime do not exist, where there are no differences in property and nothing to be stolen, and where hard physical labor is highly valued and offers acceptable discharge of some aggressiveness. Perhaps most important of all there exist no delinquent peer groups, and all the peer associations that do exist exert control over possible delinquent tendencies. The same is true for dropouts. Such examples are simply lacking in the highly work-oriented kibbutz.

Youngsters are made to feel they are a moral elite compared to the rest of the world. They are also steeped in the feeling that the kibbutz needs them badly, that they carry the kibbutz and its future in their hands. Never—except for unique psychological reasons—can the feeling develop that "there's no place for me" or "they don't need me." For all these reasons work orientation is a deterrent to delinquent tendencies, since those who shirk it are most effectively ostracized.

I have mentioned the absence of sex delinquency before. I might add that kibbutz attitudes toward instinctual freedom vacillate fully as much as they do in America. They merely differ as to what types of instinctual behavior are permitted or inhibited in these two radically different cultures. (At the same time, nothing said of a particular practice will necessarily be true for all kibbutzim.)

Thus while the stated philosophy is that sex is "natural," there is such great inner disapproval of extramarital sex relations that the contradiction makes sex a very difficult problem for young people. In general, as I shall later discuss, there is so pervasive a puritanical attitude that it restricts overt sex expressions and relations considerably. This plus the emotional semidetachment in which these children are raised tend to make for more flattened, less volatile emotions in adolescence than are typical of American youth. But it also makes for an absence of sex delinquency.

There is no open homosexuality, and even latent homosexuality is virtually absent, in part as a consequence of the same puritanical attitudes: If there is little sex, there is also little homosexuality. And since being "natural" is such a high value, to be so "unnatural" in sex is beyond thought. As for drugs they are not available, nor would the youngsters have the money to buy them if they were.

But in the final analysis these deviant behaviors are absent from kibbutz life because, despite its considerable tensions, it is again a society of high consensus where everyone sees the central issues of life more or less alike, and where everyone is under continuous scrutiny by nearly everyone else. Nothing can stay hidden. Asocial tendencies evoke immediate social counterreactions, and these are usually enough to induce their repression. Nor should it be overlooked that these counterreactions include a very deep concern by the community for all its members, including the deviate ones. For example they provide—for rural communities their size —psychological and psychotherapeutic services, particularly for their children, far above anything that America, the richest country in the world, provides in comparable settings.

My conclusion must be that despite published reports to the contrary the kibbutz system seems quite successful in raising children in groups by other than their mothers, and this from infancy on. But up to now this success has only been demonstrated for relatively small societies, where an unusually high degree of consensus exists, where there is very little differentiation in style of life or in property rights, and where the entire society functions like an extended family.

Larger Relevance

WHY, THEN, IS THIS METHOD OF CHILD REARING OF SUCH IMportance to us? Because, I believe, its relevance goes beyond the disadvantaged sector of our society, though I have talked mostly of them up to now. I believe that the present problems faced by middle-class parents in raising their children, even much of the malaise, the alienation of Western man, are caused by the growing distance between child and adult. As anthropologists have told us about other societies—and as Philippe Aries (1962) has traced it for us in the Western world before the industrial era—children and adults, in those times and those places, lived together with no gap, to speak of, between them.

Children, as recently as the seventeenth century, from the moment they dropped their swaddling bands, were not only dressed like small adults of their class, but lived much the same life as adults. Children drank wine and beer like adults and gambled for money at cards, while adults played with pinwheels and ran after hoops. All ages alike listened to fairy tales. Only in the seventeenth century did some difference begin to appear in manner of dress, and soon also in style of life. But even then, and for a long time to come, both child and adult worked at common chores, lived and slept together in a single large room and played the same games. Just as in the kibbutz, life proceeded within a narrow geographical space, and how adults spent their days was always known to and understood by the children.

Since life activities were far less specialized by age group than with us, children did not infringe on the life of their parents nor the other way round. But in the last two centuries, and ever more so in this one—particularly in the West —the life of adults has become so complex, so little accessible to the child, that despite our best efforts to bridge the abyss it continues to grow.

It is not that our children have grown much more childish but that we have become so much less so. As adults we simply do not enjoy childish games any more, nor do we feel comfortable when our young children enter our games as equals. No longer is our favorite literature fairy tales, as it was only a couple of centuries ago. No longer do our concepts jibe with theirs about what gives meaning to life. Our adult interests transcend the immediate surroundings, while the immediate alone is where the young child can fully share his experience with us.

Given the large amount of time the child now spends with his peer group, and his parents on their own adult pursuits, the time they spend together becomes more problematic. All too often it takes the form of the adult acting like a child or (worse) the child trying to act the adult. Both are artificial: The only natural way being for parent and child to enter a common activity in which the child can perform as befits his true age, and the adult as befits his. Chances like this seem restricted by now to leisure time only, as on fishing or camping expeditions. But even for these to be truly meaningful, they would still have to be central to the well-being of the family as a whole.

Interestingly enough, the adolescent's alienation from adult society was recognized some fifty or a hundred years sooner than that of the child, though the child's alienation began it. Consider the current wave of adolescent revolt, starting with young adults in Berkeley and Watts, or their counterpart in European cities. If we compare it with the first adolescent revolt—that of the *Sturm und Drang* by a small elite group about a century and a half ago—this form of alienation seems to become more devastating to the individual and society as time passes.

Although the *Sturm und Drang* phenomenon appeared at the beginning of the nineteenth century, adolescent alienation as a distinct phenomenon in Western society appeared only at the beginning of this century, and began to engulf an entire age group only very recently. Far from being confronted with the so-called "vanishing adolescent," he is just coming into his own as a distinct and estranged group. But since adolescent alienation inspired the kibbutz as a possible solution, it becomes understandable why a so-conceived movement created a setting in which there is little cause for adolescent alienation. The kibbutz satisfies the adolescent's longing for simple, radical, unequivocal solutions to life's problems—including the adolescent's need to feel superior to the surrounding society, for assured and equal status, and for a life closer to nature, to mention only a few.

Only with affluence did several age-groups in our society (first among them the adolescent) develop a special style of life, the leisure to deal with special age-group problems, and then to become a separate subgroup of society—all of these making for social alienation.

Before the twenties, most young people were full-working members of society as soon as public schooling was ended; that is, at about fourteen. While they were not technically considered adults, they lived a considerably more adult life than do our high school students. And by college age, most of them were married and had children. There was neither time, nor occasion, nor leisure for questioning one's place in society, for adolescent revolt. Nor was that other precondition present: the higher education that permits an objective detachment from the traditional fabric of society. Youth was too caught up in the struggle to feed himself and his family.

Far from the adolescent's vanishing, it was only the affluent society—permitting extension of public schooling till eighteen, plus the vast increase in youth going to college—that created the problem of adolescence. Because it meant the postponement of earning a living, and the postponing of adult sexuality till well past the age when sexual maturity is reached. Actually the adolescent's estrangement, the struggle he has in order to find himself and his place in society—these exist because he has only so recently come to be and not because he is vanishing. The problem is most acute for the lower-class adolescent, because for him the life of relative leisure—and his ability to speculate about his place in society and what alternatives there are—is most recent of all.

At the moment we see the same thing happening to the pre-teen group, which is in the process of developing a separate language, style of life, clothing, and special ways for dealing with boy-girl relations that are different from those of either childhood or adolescence.

One shudders to think what the revolt of children and preteeners may be like some fifty or a hundred years hence if no accommodations are made. With the increased drawing apart of the age groups because of the specialization of tasks assigned to each of them, they will have become further alienated from their families and society. They will also have grown fully aware of it, and suffer from it, as they are now just beginning to do.

Though the kibbutz is more fortunate than we are in having the life and work spheres of children and adults much closer to each other than with us, it has not been enough to really close the gap. The "sacred hours" when kibbutz children "visit" with their parents create specific dilemmas, as I shall later discuss at some length. In the kibbutz, too, somehow the two generations have for long stretches of time and in many interactions grown uncomfortable with each other, a situation that is painful to and regretted by both. That they tend to blame this on each other—though in the kibbutz it is largely the consequence of how differently the new generations are raised, and with us it results largely from social and technological development—merely aggravates the disappointment.

Let me cite only one such development, which alone made possible the woman's role in the kibbutz, and with us accounts for the change of woman's role in society: Thanks to modern medical science woman can now plan her pregnancies at will. How recently she was freed of the burden of many pregnancies may be seen from the fact that my own paternal grandmother bore twelve living children, remembered several other pregnancies that ended in miscarriage and possibly had a few others that she did not recall because she aborted too early. So nearly all of her active life, her years of full health and vigor, were taken up with pregnancies leaving little space for anything else. She had no chance to fill any other place in society than the one tradition assigned her. The conditions then affecting female psychology determined that her place had to be in the home, and regulated how her days there would be spent.

All this has changed now. Given her new freedom from necessity, many a middle-class American mother wants more of a life for herself than her mother enjoyed. But because of it, she fears (like the early kibbutz woman) that this means she is not a good enough mother. Thus what is new in the relation between mother and child, and what was acted on so radically in the kibbutz, is the woman's resentment that her life should be swept up entirely in her wifely and motherly roles. But by rejecting these as the sole purpose of her life, she betrays the image of her mother, which she so early and deeply internalized—so much so that her rational fight against it is still felt unconsciously as betrayal. And of this betrayal she feels guilty.

The solution many a middle-class American mother selects for allaying this guilt is the exact opposite of the kibbutz woman's solution. She works doubly hard at being a good mother, with the result that she pushes her child, often beyond his endurance. He must perform well and thus prove her a good mother, though she worries that she is not. The kibbutz mother, on the other hand, feels she is protecting her child against her fear of being a bad mother by handing his care over to the kibbutz. Since the kibbutz is the source of her greatest emotional satisfaction, she is convinced it will be the same for her child. Therefore she asks the kibbutz to raise her child, no longer (as her mother did) for her sake, but for his. With us, though, the relation between mother and child suffers from the still shifting role of women, from the new importance of life outside the family in the mother's existence, and from her conflicts about it.

While kibbutz founders were not necessarily aware that their conflicts with their parents resulted from any such developments, it affected them keenly. They had wanted to be close to their parents, and their parents to them; this they both knew. But neither one had any use for the other's way of life. Thwarted in these mutual desires and recognizing that in the modern world, whether they liked it or not, the life of the parent is encroached on by that of the child and the other way around, kibbutz founders reached for a solution to an impasse.

What they did was to separate most of the child's and adult's life from each other, while providing the child with enough adult leadership to make him secure, and to arrange for the necessary growth experience that children cannot provide for themselves.

Each generation would have a life of its own, arranged as much as possible to accord with what comes natural to and is desirable for one's age. Adults would live a life unimpeded by children, and children would grow up without having to bend themselves and their lives to parental desires and needs. By not getting in each other's hair, they would salvage all that was positive in the parent-child relationship, and only that; or so they believed. To this extent they are further ahead than we are: They have not only realized that parent and child have been pulling further apart, but have acted on their realization. Here in the West we do not lack for sug-

gestions by sociologists, psychiatrists, and what not. Sometimes it is advised that the mother should stay home and
devote all her energies to child rearing and that fathers
should do the same as much as possible. Or the opposite
panacea is offered: Mothers should stop hovering over their
children and have more of a life in society. I do not see that
any of these remedies offer much hope of undoing the gap
between the generations. And we might as well realize that
at a later age the so-called adolescent revolt, or the alienation of youth, is found only in industrialized society, or in
societies that move towards industrialization.

We see also that children are being sent to school at an
ever younger age. And it was only some years ago that kin-
dergartens were added to our educational system, to be followed later by nursery schools for ever younger children. All
reflect the fact that because of changes in family and society
the home becomes ever less suitable for the child, while associations with his age-group grow more and more important to him. Even the age groupings in school are more
"specialized" than the wide spread of age associations the
family used to offer its children, and which once provided an
easy and natural transition from infancy to adulthood.

It is not by deliberate arrangements that in our society,
too, the peer group becomes ever more important as the
socializing agent. And no system has taken the child's socialization by the peer group more seriously than the kibbutz.

So far as I can see, our solutions are as yet far from
purposeful. Worse, they are contradictory and hence un-
workable. They consist on the one hand of advising us to see
that our children should grow up and get out of the nursery
the sooner the better, should be serious and behave like
adults when they are barely in their teens. But we expect
youngsters *not* to assume the adult's responsibility of work,
sex, and parenthood till they are well past their teens. The

training bra is a symbol of this contradictory push, a bra to be worn long before it serves any purpose than to make the girl feel and act older than she is. Commercial efforts like this to push for precocious maturity succeed only because they meet with a parallel desire in the parents.

I believe the unacknowledged wish of middle-class parents that their pre-teen or barely teen-age children should already be and act like grownups is a clear reflection of the gulf between child and adult I have just been discussing. Since the generations no longer have a common ground to live on together, both child and adult wish to be free of each other, the sooner the better. Despite which, parents are most astonished, for example, when their push for early dating leads to an early mating which they then find inappropriate.

At the opposite pole, we hear it advocated (by those erroneously labeled progressive) that far from pushing their children, adults should make no demands on them—which satisfies neither child nor adult and deprives the child of both the experience he craves and the adult leadership he needs.

With all this and more going on in our family relations, which seem considerably less than satisfactory, we might learn from kibbutz experience what is good and what is questionable in their far different arrangements for socialization. Most of all, since theirs seems the direction we are heading for ourselves in some measure, it behooves us to find out what happens at the end of such a road.

In its own way kibbutz child rearing seems to reflect many needs of modern man in regard to the parent-child relation, and stands for one way of meeting them, if tradition is disregarded and if procedures are chosen on purely pragmatic grounds.

Out of deliberate efforts to create a new way of life, the kibbutz has simply gone much further and faster in directions toward which we all may be headed. Since traditions counted for nothing, were in fact deliberately cast off, there were no brakes on going all the way toward what Riesman has called the "other-directed" (here, the peer-group-directed) man.

The rest of this book reflects my opinion that I found their system not entirely successful, or at least not from our point of view, but certainly not a failure. More important, it suggests that we should carefully and without bias examine the kibbutz method of education to learn what it can tell us about child rearing and personality formation.

I am convinced, for example, that we must reexamine the timetable by which our children are presently raised. In order to build our society of affluence it became necessary to replace the pleasure principle by the reality principle in more and more areas of life. More important here, it became possible to arrange the life of the very young in ways that require them to give up the pleasure principle sooner and sooner in life. But everything has its time and its place. And it never occurred to Freud, when he said "where there was id there ought to be ego," that this would be applied to the age of two or under. Certainly he did not dream that children would be encouraged to learn to read, or study math, at an age when he was convinced their main task in life was to enjoy oral pleasure.

As the study of other cultures has shown, the niceties of cleanliness, tidiness, and such things as table manners are only very small steps toward the socialization of the child who does nicely without them. But these niceties, where insisted upon, are very big steps toward the child's alienation from his body, since it is not he, but his parents who command what he should do and not do with his body.

Why do I stress this when up to very recently most children were brought up far more strictly in many respects, and with far less "autonomy" than today? Because while it is true that yesterday's child was not allowed to talk back to his mother, this was a mother who had breast-fed him skin-to-skin during his first years of life. The instinctual satisfaction came first, along with the physical and emotional closeness —and the distance and restrictions only much later. Later, too, his work on the farm or in the shop was not an alienating one. Nor did we overstimulate his desires at the same time that we unduly restricted his autonomy over his body. We did not keep him from work achievement at an age when it counts, and overregulate his life through the straitjacket of a competitive educational system.

An entirely new balance is needed now, between the pleasures and autonomy enjoyed, and the restrictions and alienation imposed. Because in regard to this balance the situation in the Western world has changed radically in the last few generations. To put it on the simplest level: We cannot, in one and the same breath, demand high achievement and a high repression of instinctual desires. We cannot at the same time want our children to read and enjoy books, and also forbid them, as toddlers, to soil and despoil these so valuable books by building toy houses with them.

By now we can more or less decide for ourselves at what age the pleasure principle should yield to the reality principle, and at present we advise it the earlier the better. Certainly before bottle feeding, mothers had no choice but to let the infant suck pleasurably from her body, and in the absence of "baby foods" this tended to go on for a considerable time. Bottle feeding became possible only with that progress in hygiene which made it safe from bacterial infection. (It also made a fetish out of cleanliness, and maybe all the washing and scrubbing has further reduced the pleasure we take in our body and in life.) But while we are now free to arrange things in time, we have not learned to arrange them at the right time. More exactly, we have not learned to ask what results we hope to achieve, and if our new arrangements will bring those results.

A great deal of modern drug and sex behavior has its roots in the desperate effort to set things aright—to give the pleasure principle a belated chance to assert itself, after denying it too early. The trouble is that the timing is incorrect and sets nothing aright. Normally the infant or small child derives pleasure and a sense of competence first of all from his body and its organs. If drugs are used, the hope is that they will bring about those sensual enjoyments that the body and its organs have failed to provide and that one failed to experience at the right age.

But if drugs are needed to make life a worthwhile experience, what worse indictment of one's body than its failure to provide them? Much of what passes for sex freedom, from promiscuity to experiments like naked parties, is nothing but a desperate cry: "Show me, by coming physically close to my body, that there is nothing wrong with it." Only this does not work at so late an age, because nothing others may do can overcome an estrangement from the self and from others that is first of all an estrangement between us and our bodies.

Perhaps what is needed is a timetable based on a better appraisal of what the affluent society can afford. And it can well afford to let the infant enjoy living for pleasure over a considerable span, so that when the time comes, he can easily relinquish it, step by step, for more exacting demands. If a ready discharge of aggression or bodily freedom is no longer possible or desirable, then the child needs from the very beginning much greater autonomy and a chance to develop inner mastery of his body and emotions. He needs much less alienation from his body and from physical closeness to others at the earliest age.

If we are to learn anything from the kibbutz experiment,

we must avoid measuring their ways against ours, as if ours were eternal standards, which they are not. If, for example, Diamond states that the kibbutz child "is prematurely socialized," the question that is begged is "prematurely for what?" Or if, as others have remarked, the kibbutz child sucks his thumb too long, we must ask "too long for what?"

Whether something is too early or too late in child rearing depends on what goals are being striven for and what results are produced. These do not depend on how a particular step in socialization compares in timing with our own culture. Because our own—though deservedly valued—is hardly the most perfect of all possible worlds.

2

Infancy and Early Childhood

THE MOST IMPORTANT THEORETICAL QUESTION RAISED BY the kibbutz method of child rearing is: What exactly constitutes the love and tender care a child needs for developing well? The view that institutional rearing creates severest pathology is so uncritically accepted by now that some observers of kibbutz children have seen the evils they expected to see where this observer did not (Bettelheim, 1960, 1967). Does it follow then that love and tender care are not necessary, as Harry Harlow believed at first (1958), only to find, in the end, that even monkey babies cannot grow to be viable monkeys without it? (Harlow and Harlow, 1962). Or does something else take its place in the kibbutz which is just as effective as our type of mothering? And what of the fact that such mothering exists only as an ideal with us, since we often fall short of it in practice?

🌱 *Basic Security*

INFANTS DO INDEED NEED LOVE AND TENDER CARE FOR DEVELOP-
ing well. But the kibbutz example suggests that our view of
what ingredients go into love and care are maybe parochial
and not universal. According to Erik Erikson (1959) the
infant needs love and tender care because it creates in him a
sense of basic trust—both a trust in his own competence and
a trustfulness of others. As he puts it:

> the general state of trust implies not only that one has
> learned to rely on the sameness and continuity of the outer
> providers but also that one may trust oneself and the capac-
> ity of one's own organs to cope with urges; that one is able
> to consider oneself trustworthy enough so that the pro-
> viders will not need to be on guard or to leave.

What Erikson has in mind here are the "sameness and
continuity" the mother provides for her infant at this earliest
period of his life. His example of why the infant has to cope
with his urges to keep the provider from leaving is that of the
infant who wishes to nurse at the breast and must therefore
control his urge to bite the nipple.

Clearly this is pertinent for our nuclear middle-class family. But the kibbutz example suggests that the infant can
achieve basic trust even if there is much less sameness and
continuity of the outside provider than we assume is needed,
so long as continuous providing is guaranteed. It suggests
that trust in oneself can develop even if there is no threat of
the outside provider being on guard or leaving; that self-
control over one's asocial urges can develop out of a desire
to keep the willing companionship of the peer group.

Maybe we can better understand what is needed for basic
trust if we focus less on what specifics the environment must

provide, and more on what the inner experience of the infant must be. Here we might also consider Erikson's important warning against an undynamic view of basic trust. It concerns what the child needs, at any given stage of development, if he is to master it successfully and hence be prepared for the next stage of growing up. And this need, according to Erikson, is for "a certain *ratio* between the positive and the negative which, if the balance is toward the positive, will help him to meet later crises with a better chance for unimpaired total development." Thus what counts at the very earliest stage of development is the ratio in the infant's experience of basic trust, versus basic mistrust.

I suggest that the inner experience of the infant leading to trust is that of security, whatever the outer experience that creates such a feeling, and whether or not it is based on any sameness in the person of the provider. And security derives from the feeling that we can safely relax, that we need not worry—provided this feeling is not delusional, but is based on a correct estimate of reality. But since we can seldom relax altogether or be wholly free of worry, what is essential is the ratio between security and insecurity. The kibbutz example suggests further that security in infancy is made up of at least two different things: physical security and companionship.

Physical security at this age derives chiefly from the fact that adults provide for the infant's essential needs such as for food, shelter, rest, and other bodily comfort, a protection from excessive stimulation, etc. It is the necessary condition for survival but is not enough by itself to assure successful growth. To it must be added *companionship:* the filling of social and emotional needs, which imply age-correct stimulation and a responsiveness from others. But again: A companionship that in one setting (ours) may consist essentially of sameness and continuity of the outer provider may in another setting (the kibbutz) be built up of other ingredients.

The dynamic counterpart of this same-and-continuous-provider is separation anxiety—the fear of desertion, or its actuality. The more crucially the child's basic trust depends on the sameness and continuity of a single provider, the more devastating the basic mistrust caused by the loss of that person. Here, too, it is the ratio that counts, a ratio between the security derived from a single provider, and the anxiety of being separated from him on whom all security depends.

Basic security, then, is the assurance of survival. Only he who has the power to assure it can truly offer security. Only with him must we come to terms (or identify) if we are utterly dependent.

Freud, in his earlier writings, stressed the utter dependence of the infant on his mother. But psychologically that situation is very different from what is stressed in the psychoanalytic literature today. Margaret Mahler (1965) for example, speaks about "the decisive fact that . . . the survival of the human young depends on . . . the quasi-sociobiological symbiosis with the mother organism." Now a "mother organism" is quite a different thing from a mothering person. Perhaps Freud was more impressed by the infant's dependence on his caretakers, whoever they might be, than by his need for the mother's organism in particular. Because in Freud's time most middle-class children were not looked after by their mothers but by wet nurses and later on by nursemaids.

If we are less impressed by what (to me) seem somewhat mystical speculations about a symbiosis needed by the infant for survival, and more by his utter dependence on whoever can assure him satisfaction of his needs, then the kibbutz experiment may have something to teach us of what the infant must indeed have to survive.

It is true that nowadays the living-in wet nurse or nurse-maid is rare, and bottle feeding is widespread. Hence for most middle-class children all pleasure and displeasure originates mainly with the mother. But both are tainted by the fact that the child is in her near absolute power. So here, too, what counts is the ratio between care given in line with the infant's needs and care imposed to satisfy needs of the mother, irrespective of the infant's needs. (There simply are no kibbutz parents who beat up their children. The phenomenon of the "battered child"—that is of children so abused by their parents as to need hospitalization—is unthinkable in the kibbutz.)

Whatever has been said of the omnipotent beliefs of the infant and his convictions about power over his mother, such beliefs begin to break down very quickly, as soon as the mother is needed but is not there, or as soon as she fails to relieve pain or frustration. From then on and with every step he takes toward independence, the infant grows more keenly aware of the mother's power, and so does the mother.

To be dependent also means to be in the power of the one on whom we depend. And since the infant's dependence is not only physical but emotional and social, he is in another person's power on all counts. The normal mother is aware of, and afraid of misusing this power. It is this, the parent's power over the very life of his infant, that set the tragedy of Oedipus in motion. Had the father of Oedipus not had (and used) the power he held over his son's existence, his son would never have slain him. We cannot separate the receiving of dependent care from the power relations within which they are given and received.

The story in the kibbutz is entirely different. There, through a conscious act of will, parents have transferred their power to the community. All children are viewed and cared for as "children of the kibbutz." It was a strange experience, for example, to have a child introduced to me as Dalia, the daughter of Atid, and a few hours later to meet Dalia with her father, this time to be told with pride, "this is my daughter." There is no question in her father's mind that she is his daughter. But neither is there any doubt in his or her mind that she is also in a very real sense a daughter of Atid.

It took me some time to respond differently to a parent who claimed a youngster as "my" child, and another who claimed him as "ours." Each kibbutznik feels his parenthood of every kibbutz child in a deep and parental way. They are proud of the children of their kibbutz. There is deep feeling when they claim this or that child as "ours." In many ways, like an uncle, they are more straightforward, less ambivalent in their emotional attachment to such a child than in the attachment to their own child, which may be much more complex.

The difference between an American uncle's feeling for his nephew, and a kibbutznik's for a son of his kibbutz, is that the latter knows for sure, and how much, his work contributes to the well-being of all the sons and daughters of his kibbutz. He is also secure in the conviction that many of them, his sons and daughters once removed, will carry on the work of his life, as no American parent can be sure that even his own children will.

Children, for their part, do not refer to individual kibbutzniks as their parents. But to them, in an emotional sense, the kibbutz as a whole stands for the providing, controlling, and educating parent. Again and again they refer to the kibbutz as giving them all they need, and as shaping and planning their lives, just as an American child refers to his parents in this context.

In all the countless ways that a parent educates his children—from how they should spend their time, arrange their day, to how they should eat, sit at the table, talk, play alone

or with others, and including such extremely intimate matters as their toilet training—the kibbutz, through its metapelets and the peer group, will educate the child. Though
children refer to no one but their real parents as parents,
they are intensely aware, both consciously and unconsciously, that all these extremely important functions are exercised not by their parents but by the community. With the
important difference that to them these are not parental but
community functions.

To kibbutz children, then, basic security is provided not
by their parents but the kibbutz. How early in life this is
realized I cannot say. Here, unfortunately, my observations
may have been hampered because I do not speak Hebrew.
But my impression is that the children realize it even before
they can talk. And this holds true not only for physical
needs, but for social and emotional security, though we do
not know as yet when and how the two blend, or when and
how they separate at last.

Even in our complex world—and kibbutz life is here so
much simpler—man's basic needs are still for food, shelter,
and clothing, along with stimulation and companionship. All
these are provided for the kibbutz child either entirely, or to
a very large degree, by the community, not by his parents.
He sleeps in a separate house built just for him and his age-
mates; he is fed in the presence of others from the first, and
soon only with them; his clothing comes from the communal
supply.

Most of his stimulation comes from the metapelet and the
infants he rooms with, since his mother spends at most only
a few hours a day with him (and none at night), and these
few hours are broken by absences. That is, she comes about
four or five times a day and usually spends about half an
hour, occasionally up to an hour or so, with her infant.
Nevertheless, kibbutz theory holds that his emotional needs
are met mainly by his parents. And this radical separation

between providing for his physical and emotional needs was meant to ensure that the pleasures of the latter would not be sullied by resented controls surrounding the first. (One may wonder about the outcome of such a separation, and I shall return to this again later.)

In the nuclear family the closeness of child-parent ties depends largely on what parents do for and with their child, both materially and emotionally. That the direct emotional giving of parents to children is important for the relation between them is recognized in kibbutz theory and practice. But there is great ambivalence about material giving. While all basic material giving is to come from the kibbutz, parents in most kibbutzim get a food allowance so that they can have goodies in their room to offer their children when they visit. In quite a few kibbutzim, children and adults may also receive small presents from persons outside the kibbutz. But there is widespread dissension about this, both because it reduces equality, and because it injects economic considerations into human relations where they are not supposed to exist.

Much more crucial is the ambivalence to be seen around breast-feeding, that earliest giving of the mother to her child.

🌿 Early Weaning

BREAST-FEEDING IS HIGHLY APPROVED OF BY KIBBUTZNIKS AS the "natural" way to take care of an infant. At the same time it is controlled and interfered with by community values, if not by express regulation. That is, while most infants are breast-fed, they are weaned by six months, an early weaning that seems contrary to the emphasis put on the importance and desirability of breast-feeding.

The contradiction seems to parallel kibbutz attitudes toward the dining hall which is viewed as "the heart of the collective" but where no efforts are made to make the eating together enjoyable since it is viewed as "a bare necessity." Obviously a person for whom eating is just a necessity will be ill equipped to make the same experience enjoyable for another person, even her own infant. (Perhaps in consequence of this attitude, working in the kitchen or dining room is a much disliked job assignment and carries no prestige. So much so that high status persons—members of the central administrative bodies, the school principal, etc.— choose to work an occasional shift in the kitchen or dining room, to show that they do not shy away from sharing with their comrades the least desirable activities of the community.)

When I questioned the practice of early weaning it was explained by what (to me) seemed strange and forced rationalizations. At their simplest they took some form of the circular argument that since the infants are "through" with nursing by six months, the mother is expected to be back at work full time by then, and since she is supposed to be working full time, she no longer has the time or the patience to feed her infant. Even if she were to try to nurse the baby, she would do it in such a hurry that it would not be good for the child.

So nursing is stopped at six months because the child is through with nursing, and he is through with it because the mother does it impatiently by then, and she does it impatiently because she is supposed to stop it, because the infant is through with it. As in all rationalizations there is a kernel of truth: namely that many mothers find their work, and the associations around it, more satisfying than time spent with the infant. But this did not seem true for all mothers, though I would not presume to guess what percentage they form.

The argument that weaning at six months is no problem appeared in other forms too. I asked what would happen if a mother wished to nurse her child beyond the six months and was told that it would not be allowed. "We just feel that some six months of nursing are enough. But since the mother knows this ahead of time, there's no problem."

Another argument was that since the infants begin to get solid food at three months, and since the mother works part time by then, she begins to hurry the feeding. The metapelet, who has no other work assignment, has more time to feed the infant slowly with a spoon, which is better for the child. To quote one mother: "The metapelet told me 'Half an hour is over. Enough now, you better go. I'll take care of the child.' And so I went."[1]

Here again the arrangement proves self-validating. Starting with the conviction that feeding by the metapelet is preferable, the mother is hurried on and the feeding by the metapelet therefore becomes preferable, which seems to prove the point. But it hardly answers the question of why, if the mother had enough leisure, were not hurried by the metapelet, community pressure, work assignments, or a combination thereof, she might not take as much time as the metapelet in feeding her child and do as good a job or better.

When I asked why, after the infant is weaned from the

---

[1] A word about patterns of speech in this and other direct quotations. If it seems abrupt, even harsh, it must be realized that for the vast majority of my informants English was neither their native tongue nor the one they now used. And even when I spoke with them in their original tongue, what they were reporting to me were conversations that initially took place in Hebrew; so again, what I was told was a translation. And in translation, one's difficulty in expressing oneself leads to saying what one has to say directly, without concern for nuances.

Even more important here is a rejection, in the kibbutz, of all emotionalism as being reminiscent of the ghetto. In its place is a desire for authenticity. And this is expressed through language by an avoidance of what we would consider politeness. No matter what language was being spoken, I found kibbutzniks so direct, with each other and with me, that it seemed a deliberate stance of shunning all efforts to soften bluntness, whether by politeness or by any other way of making their statements more acceptable to the other person.

Thus while their language stresses honesty and directness more than politeness, the reasons for it are doubly determined.

breast, he is not given a bottle to suck from, I was told: "Such a child does not know what a bottle is, so how could he want it?" To the question of "why not let him find out?" the answer was, "because it is better for him not to have a bottle." Here again was the circular reasoning or self-fulfilling argument: "We don't give him the bottle because he doesn't want it, and he doesn't want it because we don't give it to him." Since he doesn't know the bottle, the assumption that he doesn't want it seems borne out, and justifies the procedure.

Another mother told me that her child was not given a bottle when she stopped nursing him at about six months, because at that time of scarcity the kibbutz had no bottles. When I asked what they did then, if a mother had no milk in her breast, she said, "Of course there were bottles for those children whose mothers could not nurse them. But such children were weaned to a cup at four months." Since bottle-fed children were taken off the bottle at four months, it seemed reasonable not to give a bottle to a six-month-old child.

One mother, an educator in charge of infants in her kibbutz, had a different explanation: "It would disturb the child who's already feeding from a cup to also be nursed from the breast, or to also be given a bottle." When I pressed the point that I knew of many children who drank from the cup and even ate solid food, but who still liked to suck from the bottle, I was told that the doctors advise them that the infant is much better nourished from the cup.

Typical of the young mother's feelings are statements like the following: "In my case nobody told me 'you have to stop nursing.' But you got the feeling of responsibility."

And it is true, there is great community pressure to stop nursing at not later than six months, and this strongly affects mothers even in those kibbutzim where the weaning time is not centrally fixed, as in the left-wing kibbutzim. So much so that a psychoanalyst in charge of all child psychiatry for one of the movements told me (when I asked "why six months?"), "This is not so. There is wide variation." And when I asked what the variations were, he said, "I know of many mothers who stopped nursing after three or four months," which of course is quite true. Only such an answer suggests he was so immersed in kibbutz pattern that he could speak of wide variations though they were all in one direction.

This is not simply a puritanical attitude of depriving the child of oral gratification, as in the case of thumb-sucking which I shall shortly discuss. It is not so different from the pushing by middle-class parents toward an early independence, and it has essentially the same source: the mother's wish to have a life of her own, one not centered around the care of her child. For the kibbutz mother there is the added wish that her child stop being dependent on her so that he can sooner become part of his age-group. And it is true, there can hardly be imagined a deeper dependency than that of the nursing child on his mother. Hence, this period has to be cut as short as possible. That is why it is "wrong" to stay on the nipple longer than absolutely necessary, and "right" that the child should be fed from the cup (which is community property), by the metapelet (who is community-appointed to the task).

There is still another reason why early weaning seems imperative if emotional tangles are to be avoided. Were some children to be breast-fed up to eighteen months, let us say, and their crib companions had to watch them enjoying it many times a day when there was no breast for them, they would voice strong objections. Nearly the same would be true if they had to watch others being bottle-fed that long. Now six-month-old infants, while they observe and react, are not nearly so clear about conveying their feelings as they can be at one or at one-and-a-half. Hence all babies are weaned at so early an age that their reactions to the sight of others being nursed cannot be expressed very clearly.

First, this protects the mother from her infant's objections. Second, if all babies are weaned at the same age, she is spared any misgivings at knowing that her infant is being weaned when other babies his age are still enjoying the nipple. To protect the mothers then, if not also the infants, from an emotional onslaught of longing and guilt, it is almost unavoidable to wean them all at more or less the same early age.

While the breast-fed child is nursed only by his mother (wet nurses are not used), the weaning so closely related to nursing is not necessarily done by his mother, and rarely by her alone. In the left-wing kibbutzim the infant is weaned from the night feeding (with a bottle of weak tea, for example) not by his mother, not even by the metapelet who took care of him all day, but by the night watch, who is more or less anonymous to the infant since she changes every week. And this starts a few days after birth. It is so unsatisfying to the infant that within a few weeks after birth he gives up the demand for night feedings, which are then stopped. Occasionally a mother is permitted to nurse her child during the night—not when the infant cries for it, but only if the mother suffers too much discomfort from the pressure of milk in her breast. Matters are different in right-wing kibbutzim where the mother nurses her infant at night for some time. In some of them a temporary bell is installed in the mother's room, and when the night watch finds the baby crying for food, she rings for the mother to come and nurse him. But there, too, the metapelet takes part in the weaning process.

True, infants anywhere in the world may be given the bottle and later be weaned by a relative or hired nurse. But such persons follow the mother's wishes and orders and are thus, in their care-taking functions, extensions of the mother. In the kibbutz they are in the realest sense extensions of the community, not the parent. So right from the start of the feeding-weaning continuum the kibbutz asserts its role in the life of the infant.

❧ *The True Provider*

IF THERE IS ANY PLAN BEHIND THESE NURSING ARRANGEMENTS, it is based on the more or less conscious realization that if the child is to become a child of the kibbutz, the most basic event creating a sense of security, being fed, ought to come from the kibbutz as soon as possible. If so, it needs to come at a time when the mind of the child begins to comprehend, to "take in." Yet many mothers might be ready neither to let go of their infants so soon, nor to surrender to others part of the nursing and general care of the baby, did they not find their daily life at work and in the community so engrossing.

If it seems farfetched that at so early an age as the nurseling's, parental desires and community standards try to shape the barely emerging personality of the infant, it may be said that such attempts are probably universal.

For example, Jules Henry (1952) has demonstrated for our middle-class culture that an energetic grabbing for things (in this case, the mother's breast and her milk) and doing things in a hurry (drinking fast) are encouraged by the mother's attitude from the first feeding on, while slowness is discouraged.

Neither results from any conscious plan or desire. They are simply the result of the mother's valuing an aggressive getting of things, and of a culture that puts a premium on efficiency and speed; that sees little value in doing things in a relaxed and leisurely way. Hence the mother cannot help acting accordingly when nursing her infant, though many mothers would be appalled to realize they are already molding their barely born infant's personality.

Similarly the kibbutz mother and metapelet, being part of a culture that values nothing more than being true kibbutzniks, wish the child to be like all other kibbutz infants in this respect. A dominant kibbutz value is that all should have the same, eat the same, and not demand any special prerogatives, such as special foods. Hence the mother can accept that all infants are weaned at the same time, so that all will begin to eat the same solid foods at the same time.

If these thoughts seem farfetched, the kibbutz attitude to other types of instinctual pleasures seems to support them. Despite an original libertarian thinking, despite the original desire to ensure instinctual freedom, it soon became apparent that to encourage this ran counter to community spirit. And whenever the two philosophical positions conflicted— the one stating what is good for the individual, the other what is good for society—the collective won out.

As one educator told me in explaining kibbutz attitudes toward thumb-sucking: "We read Freud, and then Anna Freud too, and they told that if a child is sucking his finger, it's a sign he needs something. So we felt we had to give to the child this pleasure. But after a few years of that we thought that if we give only freedom, only pleasure, then we do not put them into a frame to be controlled [i.e., to accept control by the kibbutz, and to learn self-control]. So, in order to educate our children to accept their daily program, to enter their children's society, we had to change our attitude."

This development, after all, was not unique to the kibbutz. It happened to us in the West, too, when we were impressed with the devastating outcome of too much repression. In the early days of psychoanalysis a movement sprang up based on the assumption that the child who was given absolute instinctual freedom would become a particularly well socialized person. Experience soon taught us that without control over instinctual tendencies there cannot be socialized behavior. The real problem is where limits should be set, which tendencies need controlling and which not, and at what age.

Certainly few psychoanalysts believe that breast or bottle-feeding should be limited to only a few months, or that thumb-sucking should be forbidden. Because we have seen that the enjoyment of these instinctual pleasures, even to a very large extent, does not seem to interfere with a person's later ability to work or to form satisfying human relations. On the contrary, they seem to make for a more positive outlook on life as being more satisfying, on the whole, than disappointing.

While I cannot state it for certain, it seems to me that kibbutz restrictions on sucking in all forms, be it from breast, bottle, or finger, do not come from any deliberate wish to deny the child pleasure. They come from a wish that from the very beginning he should not seek satisfaction for himself or from himself (from his own body) as in thumb-sucking. This he should seek from the community. As one of them told me: "Since thumb-sucking is an overgratification because of a great need, we felt that if we do away with the outward sign of the need, we will probably also do something about the need itself. That is why, though years ago nobody would have dared to say it, we now tell the children 'take your thumb out.' " Thus while the restriction placed on aggression ("do not break things") seems only common sense from our point of view, the same is not true for thumb-sucking.

Among the charges leveled at kibbutz child rearing was

that its children are deprived, as shown in the greater incidence of thumb-sucking and enuresis. Thus the child sucking his thumb seemed to validate the critics. Still, the charge could have fallen on deaf ears. That it did not, suggests that kibbutz tendencies, too, favored the inhibition of sucking. For example, kibbutz rearing has also been criticized for not giving the children enough privacy, including private possessions (Peter Neubauer, 1965). But this criticism was flatly disregarded because the values behind it contradicted those the kibbutz wished to keep.

The laissez-faire attitude toward bed-wetting contrasts sharply with the inhibition of thumb-sucking. In fact it is rather an absence of attitude, since bed-wetting is neither inhibited nor approved, which it might be, were it viewed as an instinctual satisfaction. But neither is night wetting viewed as a satisfaction the child derives from his own body. While it may be that psychologically to the child, adults do not view it that way.

More important, it does not isolate him emotionally, as thumb-sucking may do, and hence does not violate community standards of behavior. And finally "visibility" is lower in bed-wetting. It does not so publicly proclaim, as does thumb-sucking: "I do not get enough from the community, and so I provide it for myself from my own body. I do not need you for satisfying my deeper emotional needs." Thus it does not conflict with kibbutz mores, which do not prescribe middle-class respectability and cleanliness, but do insist on doing things with the group. Since there is no group life for the children at night in their beds (or none that is recognized as such) bed-wetting defies no community values. That may be why it is ignored, while thumb-sucking is not. And essentially bed-wetting stops when the group starts to object.

That the group, the community, is the true provider, is one of the first lessons the young child learns, as soon as the metapelet takes over his feeding.

Very soon the child knows it is not even his metapelet who provides the food. He knows that it comes in a cart from the central kitchen which feeds the entire kibbutz. His home (the children's house), his toys (except for toys in his parents' room, in what are clearly after-hours), his bed, the mattress he sleeps on, the sheets that cover him, the clothing he wears, all these are not his. But they are also not his parents', and hence not in their power to give or withhold. They are all kibbutz property, and since he is part of the kibbutz, also his. Through them, the kibbutz provides him with security, or what stands for it symbolically.

While in one sense these things are less his than they are for a middle-class child, he feels more sure of having their use, no matter what. The middle-class child knows that what he has comes from his parents, who can also take them away. While the kibbutz child is not given these things, neither can they be taken away. His security against being cold at night, for example, does not rest on his owning a bed and a blanket but on their always being available to him.

Speaking again of the ratio between security and insecurity, it may be that while the kibbutz child is just as secure as is the middle-class child that a warm bed will always be available to him, he is much less beholden to a particular giver, and hence less afraid that the bed may be suddenly withdrawn. Unless the relations between parent and child are excellent, free of fear on the part of the child, one might conclude that the kibbutz child may feel a small security deficit because he does not own the bed, but a great deal more security that it cannot be taken away.

In short, if one looks at only one side of the owner-versus-user relation—as do many critics who feel the kibbutz child suffers from not owning things—then the kibbutz child seems distinctly less advantaged. But if one looks at the dynamic ratio between security and insecurity as regards the use of these important conveniences, it may well be that the ratio favors kibbutz children much more.

This is even more true of the most basic necessity, food. I have quoted Erikson before on the infant's need to impose self-control to keep his provider from leaving. The example used was the fear that by biting the nipple the infant might lose his supply of food. Implied, of course, is the infant's anxiety that the source of his nourishment may dry up. So here it makes a difference that the kibbutz child, from infancy on, sees that he and other infants are also fed by the metapelet. From the very beginning the kibbutz infant sees that his mother is not the only provider, not the only source of food. Because from the fourth day of life, both observations and personal experience teach him that if the mother does not provide it, the metapelet will.

Food is also much more his own to dispose of, for the kibbutz child, than for his middle-class counterpart. (I do not even speak, here, of the children of the poor, for whom there may not be enough food to go around, or for whom the fear of hunger tomorrow contaminates even those meals where he does have enough.) From quite an early age, the middle-class mother begins to teach her child how to eat, if not also table manners, either by open insistence or by her silent negative reaction to the infant's messiness. This means that in order to get his food, he must behave, must learn manners, must exert self-control in return for the nourishment he gets. And whenever we must pay a price for something, it is not securely our own. Because what would happen if we could not pay, or refused to?

Other reminders of proper eating behavior are at a minimum in the kibbutz too. Partly this stems from conviction, partly because the parents' own behavior around eating in the communal dining room is most casual when measured by our standards, and partly because the metapelet has neither the time nor the interest to teach table manners as she feeds the several children in her care. Also, since the children eat only with others their own age, no one is held up to them as an example to be followed. In an emotional sense, then, food is much more their own, to do with largely as they like, than it is for most children in the West.

True, the middle-class infant with older siblings also watches their being fed and derives some security from seeing them getting their food, no matter what. (Unless, of course, he sees an older child being sent away from the table.) But in the majority of families he also observes that the mother expects a great deal of the older child, even scolds him or threatens if he does not behave. Now in the kibbutz, too, a bit more is expected of the older child at the table. But since the younger child does not eat with the older ones, he does not see this and is not made anxious about food at an age when he might still be lacking in security about it.

Of course, when the infant begins to be taken to the parents' room daily for his visits, he too will see his parents with older siblings. But these hours with the parents are kept much more conflict-free than is possible with us. Far more crucial here: Such visits will not take place in the earliest months of life and by then the sense of security around feeding may be well established.

In the kibbutz too, both the general attitude toward food and the disregard for the value of private property preclude that any parent or metapelet will make a child feel guilty for wasting food or will anxiously urge him to eat more for his health. No such guilt or anxiety is created around eating, another reason why the whole mealtime situation is so relaxed in infancy and during the later stages of development. Added to this, the very earliest provider of food appears much less threatening, since the infant neither sees her in her inhibiting or criticizing function, nor has she the power, in his experience, to withhold his food. So again, on balance, the kibbutz child may feel more secure than his middle-class counterpart.

Certainly with each step he takes in understanding, he becomes more aware of existing power relations in the kibbutz and with it of his source of security. For example, he becomes much more attached to the children's house the kibbutz provides for his use, and much less to the persons who take care of him inside it, as I shall shortly describe. But he also becomes more attached to his age group than do middle-class children, because in innumerable ways it is the age-group rather than adults who help him with his fears, especially at night.

❧ Crib Mates

THIS IMPORTANCE OF THE PEER GROUP BEGINS IN THE VERY first days of life. We do not know whether, in the human being, something akin to the imprinting of animals takes place. But there is no doubt that the earliest experiences make a deep impact and are hence apt to shape all later ones in some measure.

Imprinting is thus nothing but an extremely important early experience. And in our own culture, at this most impressionable age, it is only or mainly the mother's image that is scanned by the infant as he nurses. In the kibbutz, by comparison, what greets the infant who wakens to feed, and looks around at his world? As likely as not, and from the very beginning, he sees just as much of the metapelets and other mothers tending their babies, as he does his own mother. She only emerges as separate and special when she puts him to breast.

Much more important in time and emotional impact are the constant companions who live in his room. Them he always sees and reacts to. Much of the waking time spent by the middle-class infant watching his parents, the kibbutz infant spends watching his roommates. As a matter of fact, so important may be the infant in the crib next to him, for example, that if his crib mate is moved to another room he may lose his appetite and get run down, a condition that improves when his "friend" or "twin" is returned.

Separation anxiety in the kibbutz is thus very typically experienced around the absence of a peer. And it can never be felt as acutely as by the middle-class infant whose mother leaves him, because however important the infant in the next crib, he is not the only one in the room, nor the only one life revolves around. At least two others are still left for companionship. And while the positive attachment to one person (the mother) seems diluted, when compared to our settings, separation anxiety is much less acute because of the continuing presence of several important others (metapelet, other infants). Thus again if we consider only the positive attachments, things seem to favor the middle-class child. But if we consider the ratio between security gained from positive attachment versus separation anxiety, it may very well be that kibbutz infants again enjoy the advantage.

While all children are "children of the kibbutz," and feel essentially like siblings, this is not just a matter of semantics. Those children who, from birth on, live together as an age-group, experience each other not only as siblings but as twins, since they were nurslings together and close crib companions. True, they do not share identical parents, and their heredity is radically different. But because of their otherwise "twinlike" existence they show some of the psychological features that characterize twins: the deep dependence and reliance on each other, the feeling that no one but their twin can ever fully understand them or share their innermost being. Only instead of one twin they have several, and of both sexes.

Because of this, though for other reasons too, the polarization, through which one twin often asserts his identity by being as different as possible from the other twin, I did not find in the kibbutz. I got to know one set of twins rather well. From all appearances (and from what I was told) they were identical twins, and by that time quite grown up. While extremely close to each other, they showed few of the characteristics I observe among identical twins in our setting. They were neither "half" a person without the other, nor did they show any need to develop in opposite ways to feel secure in their personal identity. My guess is that, having lived "like twins" from birth on with several others, and not just their own twin, they did not feel as dependent on each other as seems true of twins in our families.

Perhaps the difference in parentage and natural endowment gives enough real differentiation to those who from birth on grow up like twins so that there is no need to strive for any more on their own. It is not enough, though, to cancel out the strange situation that four or more infants share all vital steps in growing up and developing, as would be true with us only of twins or of infants growing up in institutions.

This is why the kibbutz child, in his relatedness to other children, feels closest to his very own age-group, in many ways more so than to his natural siblings, who come next, and third, to all other kibbutz children.

What does this collective life look like, for the older infant from the time he can crawl? These infants, when they wake, are placed in large playpens; then, as soon as they can walk, in rather large, fenced-in play spaces. For many periods of the day, even when the metapelets are supposedly taking care of a group of infants or toddlers, they are left to their own devices. Often this is for hours at a stretch, while the metapelets clean the house, fetch the food, sort the laundry, do the mending. During this time the infant, and later the small child, is never alone, as an infant raised at home might be even if the mother is just busy in another room.

In playpen and play yard the children crawl over each other, push each other down, and while at first the pushed down child may wail, he soon learns his place in the pecking order and adjusts accordingly. But life is not just bad times and getting pushed down; most of the time the children play successfully together. Since no parent interferes with the pecking order, and even the metapelet does so only rarely, each child stays in his given place and soon learns to play according to the hierarchy established. As long as he does, and soon they all learn to do it for most of the time, there is always someone to play with; they are never alone.

American readers will wonder what happens to the low man on the totem pole, to the weak child or the meek one who—were this a society based on nothing but the pecking order—would always come last, would never come into his own except by withdrawing or submitting. And this might well happen in our competitive society where winning is so highly valued. But things are not so in the kibbutz.

I did not see a single case of a bully or of bullying. I did see the weaker infants pushed over by stronger ones, but never deliberately—if one can speak of being deliberate in such things before the age of two—nor gloatingly. And thereafter such a child was usually picked up and comforted by another child, sometimes by the one who pushed him down. Depending, of course, on the relative maturity of the child, this stage may be reached anywhere between age two and two-and-a-half.

By toddler age, then, life is truly with the group; the children are comrades, not competitors. If one is stronger, he will use and occasionally misuse his strength, but not for long. Very soon the group spirit asserts itself, and he feels the disapproval and desists. The spirit of helpfulness among them is much more evident than the desire for dominance. Since there are no parents around for whom to vie, and since the competitive spirit is frowned on, the push is toward acting like brothers and sisters, where the stronger one exerts some controlling influence, but also feels called on to use it in the interests of his brothers and sisters. And this is well established by the toddler age. But even before then, they have all learned to be self-reliant to a degree most uncommon in our middle-class settings.

How early they are forced by the arrangements to learn self-reliance may be illustrated by two observations made in one of the oldest and wealthiest of left-wing kibbutzim. The first one concerns babies and occurred while I was interviewing an elderly metapelet, in charge of the infants' house there for many years. I was asking how many babies she had in her care, and she told me there were sixteen in the nursery, but that each metapelet was only responsible for four. "I work four hours in the morning," she said, "from 7:00 to 11:00, and then I return again at 12:30."

I wondered what happens then, between 11:00 and 12:30? (The time, then, was shortly after 11:00, and the babies were in a playpen on the porch, just outside the room where we spoke.) The answer was: "They don't need anybody, they're in the playpen during that time." Nevertheless, we could hardly hear each other at times because the wailing of the babies was so loud. So I said I could hear them crying right now so they seemed to need someone to look after them, and the metapelet told me: "If they cry too long, some other metapelet will look to see what's the matter. There is always one metapelet in the house serving all four groups."

The crying continued, and I went out to see what went on. I found seven babies in a large playpen out in the sun, with some nice toys in it. Two bigger babies crawled all over a little one and took a toy away from him. He cried for a long time while the one metapelet on duty was occupied with washing furniture. Finally she came out on the porch and picked up the crying one for a moment but without comforting him. He continued to cry, but more quietly now. So she put him down at another spot in the playpen and left. And soon he stopped crying and went about his business.

As soon as the being picked up may have raised some hopeful expectations in the baby, he was returned to the old situation to fend for himself as best he could. If many such experiences are repeated, as they are, it may force the infant (and all other infants who watch it) to give up hoping for comfort from a mother figure, or any desire for her presence.

It was not that the metapelet was insensitive. She was merely convinced that the baby had to learn to get along in his group, and not to rely on the intercession of someone outside it; that her comforting would only retard a piece of learning that was more important than temporary discomfort.

And a year or two later, when they are toddlers, they have indeed learned much: how to fend for themselves, how to get along with the group, how to find comfort there and satisfaction. One day, for example, I observed an entire toddlers-house group who had been playing for quite a while in the large play space in front of their house while the metapelet was away fetching their lunch from the communal kitchen and her adolescent helper was inside setting the table. On her return the metapelet called to the children to come in for lunch.

Scrambling to get there, one little boy fell and started to cry; he had obviously hurt himself. The metapelet very nicely went over to him, picked him up, but then set him down a moment later, before she had really discovered what was wrong, and long before he had quieted down or been reassured. She then went indoors because she had to, since there were now some fourteen children inside to be taken care of and fed by her and her helper.

Eventually after some hard inner struggle the boy fought down his crying. The others were too busy with their meal and each other to offer comfort at this moment, so the best thing was to join them as soon as he could. But first he took a knife from the table and went back outside where he sat down to scrape the dirt off his slightly bleeding knee. This took some time, and quite a few minutes later, he was still there and had not yet come to the table.

The metapelet could not have returned to him easily, even had she wished. Her other duties forbade it. But after some ten minutes the boy had got complete hold of himself and rejoined the group. He really had no true choice in the matter. Had he stayed behind, he would have gotten no comfort for his hurt and would not only have missed out on lunch but also the companionship of the children and metapelet.

During this same toddler age, though, the peer group also comes to be a source of comfort in lieu of adults. It was charming, for example, to see a three-year-old come up to an age-mate who was upset about something, inviting him to play, cheering him up, leading him back to the group. But because of it, the small child is more and more relieved of having to struggle by himself with an inner experience. Because even (or especially) if no other comfort is available, the group and its doings are always there to divert his attention to an external experience with them, and away from the one with himself.

At critical times, such as at night, small children have only their mutual comforting to rely on, since it may take quite a while for the single night watch to hear a child who wakes up crying, and a bit longer till he or she comes around. Though no one in the small community is entirely a stranger, the night watch rotates among members from day to day, or week to week. So even when the night watch is finally summoned by the child's anxious cry, the person who comes when the child thus awakens from a nightmare, deeply shaken, is more or less a stranger and can therefore give only small comfort. But as likely as not, when the night watch finally gets there, he finds that some other child has already soothed the anxious one.

Thus when in deep emotional distress, the kibbutz child soon learns to rely on the help of another child for comfort and security. Later on, too, it will more likely be a more advanced or a bit older child in his peer group and not the metapelet who will help him on the toilet, with getting dressed, and at all other times when he cannot manage by himself.

❧ Desertions

AGAIN, AS IN REGARD TO THUMB-SUCKING, WE MUST ASK THE question: Why do kibbutz parents, who like all other parents are very much concerned for their children, who want them to be happy and secure, then expose them to anxiety at night? Parents know the anxiety is there, or certainly they do from the time the children can talk, since several parents told me themselves how their own young child asked them to be a night watch so they could be there to comfort him when he woke up at night.

I have spoken before of the resistance met on this score by one consultant psychologist. The wish of the very young child to have his mother with him when he wakes up at night, afraid, seemed so obvious to her, that "all through my years of work I tried to get the parents of the babies to serve as night watch in the house where their baby was. They always, or nearly always, simply refused. I was totally unable to understand this. I began by explaining to them in great detail why it would be so good for the infants if an adult would sleep in the house with them. It would not have been more than three nights per month for each parent, but they were not ready to do it."

Why then, when their infants ask for it, when they themselves are uneasy about it, and their own psychologist advises it, do these parents refuse to be with their infants at night? The reason is the same one alluded to before. It is just as in many middle-class American homes where the parents want their children to be happy and secure but still push them academically beyond their ability and endurance, sometimes at an incredibly early age. It is not that they wish their children to suffer. But they are convinced the child will gain more lasting security and happiness from being pushed academically than from being allowed the lingering enjoyment of those comforts he may crave at the time.

In the same way, kibbutzniks refuse their infants a security derived from their parents, and force them to make do instead with whatever security the other children or miscellaneous adults can provide. They do it because they want their infant to learn early that security derives only from the comradely peer group of equals.

Strangely enough, this is not what they are consciously

aware of. Otherwise they would have explained it this way, both to me and their psychologist. What they are aware of instead is what old-timers expressed by saying the kibbutz was not created for the happiness of children, but to make them (the kibbutzniks) free. Yet it is not the night hours or the extra inconvenience they are unwilling to spend on their children. These people have subjected themselves to incredible hardships for their ideas and would not hesitate to do it again. It is the reestablishment of deep emotional family ties that they feel would enslave them and their children if they became the infant's main source of security. And this they avoid, even if it means the painful knowledge that their infant may be crying for them at night.

The importance of the peer group is intensified by moves from one house to another. Quite recently efforts have been made at Atid, and some other right-wing kibbutzim, to have children remain in the same house from birth until age four. But this is still the exception. And even at Atid the old type of infants' house is still in use, so that quite a few are still moved to the toddlers' house at about one-and-a-half to two years of age. The spread comes about because they are not moved until at least four to six toddlers are old enough to make the move together, as a group. In the left-wing kibbutzim all infants are moved to the toddlers' house at about two.

Even before the first move out of the infants' house, they may (and usually do) experience several changes of main caretaker. Metapelets get pregnant and have children; their work assignment may be changed; they are sent away for further education; etc. But these changes, though necessary, are not planned for, and not considered desirable. The two years the infants spend in this first house is a considerably longer period than in some other kibbutzim, particularly those of the left-wing movement, where there is an interim move. But even before such an interim move most infants experience a change of metapelet. Because typically one infant nurse (plus relief persons on her day off, vacation, etc.) takes care of the babies during their whole first year, after which another metapelet takes over. In the left-wing movement this change of metapelet occurs not at one year, but when the baby is six months old. In still other kibbutzim the change comes at about six to nine months of age.

In the words of one left-wing metapelet who had cared for many generations of babies from birth to six months: "As soon as I've learned how to hold him, and he's gotten accustomed to my way of doing things, he's moved to another metapelet." While this was said with some small regret, she did not doubt that the procedure was correct. And when the child is two, he is moved to the toddler's house and another set of metapelets; and still again at age four when he enters the kindergarten. Thus in the left-wing kibbutzim there is at least one more move and change of caretaker than in the right-wing, namely at six months.

It would seem that the left-wing kibbutzim are more radical in their wish to make the child beholden to the kibbutz and his peer group, by avoiding lengthy attachments to any one adult with his own unique ways. As a result of all these moves, from adult to adult and house to house, the child is much more dependent on the collective in general, and his age-group in particular.

This process of forming attachments to the peer group instead of adults, which begins as soon as the infant grows responsive to his environment, is powerfully reinforced by how undependable his attachments to adults turn out to be.

I do not know how early the children realize that day in and day out, year in and year out, only their peer group will remain with them, but it must be very early indeed. It is hard to fathom what goes on in the mind of a four- or six-month old child. But his experience is that however loving and nurturing a mother may be, she appears less and less in his life after the third or fourth month, as she eliminates one breast-feeding after the other. It is hard to believe that this fails to make an impact on his mind: that the mother is here for breast-feeding; and when it stops, her involvement with the child is reduced, at least in time.

The direct connection between mother and feeding, while it enhances her importance in one respect, reduces it everywhere else, since she seems to exist mainly as a dispenser of food. However important being fed is for the infant, it is by no means his total life experience. And the fact that his mother changes him and diapers him at feeding time (and also bathes him for the first few months, as she does at Atid) while the metapelet does it all the rest of the time, may suggest even more: It suggests that his mother is there for anything that happens around feeding, but is more or less irrelevant outside of the feeding experience. Because if the diapering and all the bodily sensations that go with it belonged to her, she would handle it all the time, and not just when she feeds him. It is one of the contradictions of the kibbutz that those who so strongly rejected the ghetto with its emphasis on maternal feeding should end by creating a situation where, although eating in general is underplayed, the maternal feeding of the infant is overstressed. This they do by relegating most maternal functions to the metapelet and retaining this one for the mother. While it may not be a return of the repressed, it certainly looks like an emphasizing of the rejected.

At any rate, the infant's experience at an extremely early age, compared to our middle-class settings, may be that "the more I grow up, the more I awake to the world, the less important becomes my mother." And soon it will be clear that his parents are basically daily and sabbath visitors in his life, and he in theirs.

To this sense of the impermanence of adults is added, in the left-wing movement, the change in metapelets at six (or sometimes nine) months of age. But six months is also the age when the infant is weaned. So it is not only the time when his contacts with his mother shrink radically in time, if not also in emotional intensity, but when he has to stop sucking his food. And just when all these losses and changes take place, he is also deprived of the initial metapelet, the one other person who best knew him, and how to satisfy his needs.

This double break in contact with particular adults may be what convinces him there is no permanence in human relations except with his age-group. Individuals are unreliable, but the community and the group are not, since the infants he lives with stay the same, and since the collective (a variety of adults) continues to take care of him and to satisfy his needs.

I doubt that those who set this policy know about "eight-month anxiety." Typically (or at least so in our culture) this is something that affects the infant between six to nine months, making him suddenly fearful of strangers whose presence meant little until then. It is the time when, according to Spitz (1965), the mother is selected out from a multiplicity of experiences and becomes an individual person to the infant, a unified object, or as much so as he can experience and conceive one. Thus it is the time when the infant becomes able to form attachments to particular persons, when it becomes important *who* it is that satisfies his needs, and the way this particular person does it. The familiar has now become exactly that. And along with it, by a process of polarization, the unfamiliar, the stranger, arouses anxiety. Hence familiar persons achieve new and even greater emotional significance, because they alone offer security when his fear of the unfamiliar is at its height.

Whether or not this time for the first great changeover was selected out of conscious or unconscious awareness that this is the time when deeper and more personalized relations are formed, and that this is the age when sensitivity to strangers is greatest, the experience is highly effective. Such a timing of the partial withdrawal of the mother and of the total disappearance of the baby's first metapelet powerfully forces him to fall back elsewhere for security—and my guess is on the physical surroundings and his age-group as the only factors that remain stable and familiar to him. What then become unified objects for the baby, as often as (or more often than) the mother, are the other infants, the members of his peer group, while in our middle-class setting it is the mother (or whoever stands in her place) who first emerges in the infant's awareness as a unified person.

No such radical separation from the first metapelet occurs at Atid, since matters are differently arranged in right-wing kibbutzim. True, even there children are weaned at just about the time the first unified person appears in their lives, and at the onset of this eight-month anxiety. But at least in their planning, right-wing kibbutzim seem to offer their infants a better chance of relating to their metapelets. That is why, when these children move on to the toddlers' house at two, one would expect them to feel strongly about the loss of the metapelets who took care of them for the whole first two years of their lives. But I was told emphatically by the metapelets—those of the first two years, those others who received them into the toddlers' house where they also stay about two years, and those of the kindergarten—that such is not the case.

One kindergarten teacher reported that "this year when a group moved into the kindergarten house, and on the first day their old metapelet came to dress them in the morning, a boy said, 'Why are you here again? I don't want you to be here any more.' " This was not just a fleeting reaction, since another metapelet complained: "My old children, when they meet me, don't even greet me [say *Shalom*]. It's me who has to say *Shalom* to them till it hurts. And still they don't say anything."

Such rejection of their old metapelets I tried to understand in terms of our prevalent notions about reactions to desertion: that by behaving as if they didn't know their old metapelets, they tried not to reopen wounds they had suffered at being deserted. And this is probably part of the story, but only part.

It is not that these children are unattached to their old life. But the nature of their attachment reveals itself in stories told me by kindergarten metapelets, such as: "A great many children who come from the toddler house to the kindergarten house go and visit the houses where they lived before, but on these visits they don't pay any attention to the metapelets who worked with them when they lived there, so much so that the metapelets feel insulted. When they visit the nursery home, the children like to play there with their old toys, the same way as they used to, and they say, 'This is ours,' and 'This is our house.' "

The same holds true when their next move occurs, from kindergarten to the house of the primary-school children at age seven or eight. (The kindergarten period in the kibbutz is longer than with us. It begins at about four, extends to about seven, and includes what we would call the first grade.) These new second graders (like the four-year-olds who returned to the toddler house) now go back to visit the kindergarten house and everything in and around it, but not their kindergarten teachers or metapelets.

The Impermanent Adult

In sharp contrast to the neglect of persons, the children resent very much having to leave behind them the toys and the furniture they grew attached to. Each time they move, they are allowed to take along with them some few toys they cared about most, but only for a very brief time. "After the children came to me from the toddlers' house," reports a kindergarten teacher, "the old metapelet came and took their toys away and returned them for the new group of toddlers to use. The children were disgusted, felt very bad about it, and said: 'She's taking away everything from us.' "

This kindergarten teacher, in telling her story, showed regret that the toddlers just coming to the kindergarten were thus robbed of their favorite old possessions. But she felt nothing wrong with the fact that the group who had just left her for the house of the grade school children were equally deprived of their kindergarten toys when they moved.

Now as far as she was concerned, there was no doubt that toys, furniture, etc., belonged to the house and not to the child. Yet she felt badly when the children coming to her house felt deprived of their favorite old "belongings." This was because the new group was now in her care, and their feelings were now her concern. It became her task to help them with these feelings, with accepting kibbutz values. In order to do so more smoothly, she would have liked some more time, wished the children could have hung on to their old toys a bit longer. But not too long, or they would get attached to what were, in the end, group possessions.

None of these wishes or feelings extended to the children who left her to move on to the next house. Once they were no longer her charges, the story was different. Then she felt it was only right that material things belonged strictly to what the kibbutz had assigned, and that ideas of owning them should not be acknowledged for even a short while. When I brought this to her attention, she felt there was by no means an inconsistency. When the children left her, she said, they were no longer toddlers, but grade school children. By that time they had learned that no importance attaches to private property. All the toys they had used were kibbutz property and remained so, as before. This they now understood and hence felt no loss.

Similarly, when I asked how come the children did not react with feelings of desertion to the loss of their caretakers, I was told, "To them it is not a desertion. They know that the infant's metapelet will go on working with babies, and that they will get a metapelet who takes care of older children."

This did not come from naïveté about the importance of the individual. Metapelets do not think so little of themselves that they assume they have no significance. But they are convinced that their essential importance rests on their social function, and that the children, because of their collective upbringing, understand and appreciate this. What the children need, in their opinion, are persons who do the best possible job of taking care of a particular age or developmental group. Importance and uniqueness, they feel, do not rest on who a person is, but on what he does for the community in general through his particular work assignment.

Trying to understand the emotional meaning to the children of such moves, I asked if they showed any night fears when, for example, they were moved to a new house and a new metapelet. "Frankly," I was told, "there are many cases of fear among the children, but we don't find these fears to be the result of moving from one person to another within the educational system, as the child is growing up."

I stressed that in like circumstances most children in the

Western world would feel anxious. To this a group of educators replied: "How our children react or do not react, and that this is contradictory to what happens in the rest of the world, is beside the point. Here things are different from anywhere else in the world, because our system of society is so different from all others. Therefore there is nothing so astonishing in the absence of fear or resentment among our children when they leave their old houses and metapelets. The transitions are clearly steps forward. The child feels that he grew up once more, like when a child gets long pants and a belt, and doesn't any longer wear suspenders to hold up his pants. He does not miss his suspenders. Though his pants may fall down, he does not mind. On the contrary he feels more secure because he now is more grown-up.

"In the rest of the world when children are moved to another room, or place, often it's not because it is good for them, but for reasons that are negative. Maybe a brother is born, and therefore the child is moved to another room. Naturally he resents it and feels it as a loss. It seems a stepping down to him, not a stepping up, as in our case."

That is, they were convinced that the children understood that all such moves were made purely for their benefit, were not for the convenience of adults, and hence felt no resentment. My guess is that they badly overestimated the children's ability to comprehend all this, not to speak of liking it. But half of the argument is true. Most normal children like acquiring the symbols of being now more grown-up. But this they can only enjoy to the full if they do not have to give up some of the advantages that belonged to the earlier stage.

If growing up means they cannot also hold on to the old satisfactions, then a lot of regret is mixed in, much longing for what they can no longer have. And this other half of the truth the kibbutzniks deny, fail to recognize. Nevertheless it is true that if the adults who arrange such moves are not conflicted about them, view them only as positive, it tends to have a reassuring effect on the child.

In part I pressed issues like these so as to better understand the educational system. But I was equally interested in knowing which issues the educators were sensitive to, and which not, by virtue of their working and living in the kibbutz world. Often what the educators of a system are insensitive about can tell more about the system than anything claimed for it on the positive side.

The insistence by so many educators that these many moves, and what I saw as many desertions, had no effect on the child was therefore of interest to me, because among the educators I spoke to were several whom I knew to have altered the course of these moves. They had been instrumental in changing the age-grading system, so that in right-wing kibbutzim the plan is for children in the toddlers' house to be taken care of by the same metapelet for at least two years. Since they themselves had brought this about, I knew they were aware that too many changes are upsetting to children. But while they had reached this awareness, they found it difficult to really accept it and to fully carry through on other changes it implied. Why else would they insist, for example, that "our children are not afraid of the dark," or "of being left alone," when all of us tend to be afraid at such times. Of course kibbutz children who wake up at night are afraid, and later on some recall night fears they experienced as young children.

But the dark was exactly what they feared, not the being alone. Fear of darkness is composed of many elements, the most important of which is that, first, one cannot see what may be lurking around the corner, and second, one fears desertion. Essentially, the kibbutz child's fear of darkness contains only the first, since from birth on he is never alone.

When kibbutzniks replied to my question by saying that

their children do not feel afraid at being left alone, they spoke from my frame of reference, not theirs. Kibbutz infants and children are always in the company of their age-mates. Hence to speak of them as being left alone is to apply a middle-class viewpoint which assumes that young children feel left alone just because no adult is around. Infants and children may need the help of a metapelet by day, or of the night watch by night for those things they cannot do for themselves. But what the conditions of loneliness are, or companionship, depends on one's culture.

David Riesman (1950) could rightly point out how lonely one can be in a crowd (perhaps even because of it), and many a child feels quite alone even in the physical presence of another who could realistically provide for his needs. In other situations he may have felt anything but alone, though with persons quite unable to look after him, realistically speaking. The kibbutz child, when in the company of those with whom he has spent his life from infancy on—and though they may not be able to care for him as only an adult can—may nevertheless feel less "alone" than we Westerners can fathom.

For some time I simply could not believe this and was convinced that the children's behavior was the result of repression; that they behaved this way in efforts to deny an unmanageable hurt. The longer I stayed in the kibbutz, and the longer I study the data and hopefully get a better understanding of their meaning, the more it seems that neither my views nor theirs tell the whole story, but that the truth is probably somewhere between.

Desertion is experienced most keenly if the person who deserts us is the person who has provided satisfaction and security. If, as a person, she has not, then the desertion is by no means so keenly felt. If security—apart from the age-group—is derived from the house, from the toys, and everything else there, then separation anxiety and a sense of desertion will indeed concentrate on them instead of persons.

Of course walls and even toys cannot satisfy the infant's basic needs. But these satisfactions can be projected onto them, and they can come to stand for what gives satisfaction and security: in this case first the house, later on the entire kibbutz. And indeed, in interviewing young kibbutz adults it was amazing to what degree they had forgotten their metapelets or declared them emotionally unimportant. But they remembered very well the children's houses, their toys, and how they and their comrades had played there together. And these memories, by contrast, were deeply invested with feeling.

For example, one group of young adults who had grown up together and were just about to enter the army at eighteen, told me they had no recollections of the metapelets who took care of them from babyhood through the kindergarten age. When I pressed them, insisting they must surely recall something of those early years, they all began to laugh. They remembered that when they were about six or seven and were being moved from the kindergarten to the primary-grade house, they had burned the doll house. It had not been a spur-of-the-moment thing but a well-planned arson. Because they recalled in detail how the boys had talked about doing it and how the girls had at first not believed they would dare.

Of course, this was an event they had spoken about often among themselves through the years. It was one of the many deeply meaningful experiences binding an age-group so closely together. But something could be made of the fact that this is what spontaneously came to mind when I pressed for memories about persons. If I am correct, the house had come to stand in their place, and they had vented their anger about the desertion against the doll house, since they could not rage at the metapelets. Or so I thought then.

By now I am not at all sure that my interpretation is the

full story. I now believe that the conviction develops very early, probably during the first few years of life that little of permanence can be gotten from adults. Security and a sense of permanence may then come instead from a house, and what it stands for. Hence when they moved out of the kindergarten, it was the house that disappointed them, so they burned it to retaliate. Their collective act also bound them more closely at a moment when they needed most to hang together.

By that age, with several disappointments in metapelets behind them, they seemed not to expect much from them by way of security anymore. One young woman in her twenties recalled that the metapelets of her first years of life had been very bad, had mistreated her and the other children. When I asked why she did not complain to her parents, she said, "The metapelets didn't have anything to do with us, [*i.e.*, had little emotional meaning to them] so we didn't complain about them. What I cared for were the children I lived with, but not the metapelets."

One of her age-mates, now a young mother, further emphasized the point both for herself and her little daughter. "The metapelets didn't do us any damage, because we didn't care about them. Though we had both a terrible kindergarten metapelet and teacher, we were not damaged by them. We [the group] were stronger than they; this is the strength of kibbutz education. My little girl is in the kindergarten now, and it isn't so good. If there were not the other children, she would suffer much. She knows that her metapelet doesn't love her, but she is in very good with the other children, and so it doesn't matter."

Neither do parents, for all their positive affection, offer reliable security. A mother tells of how her son, on being moved to the kindergarten, complained that he couldn't sleep at night. The beds in the kindergarten house did not offer support, he said, and he was afraid he would fall out of bed during the night. The mother asked the metapelet if her son couldn't have a bed in which he would feel more secure, like the one he had had in the toddlers' house. But the answer was "No, he will get used to it." So he had to suffer for a while till he got used to the insecure bed.

Situations like this can and do occur in any child's life, namely that the parent cannot or will not provide relief. What makes it worth retelling is that here the mother was very sensitive to her son's fear and discomfort, but did not act on her sensitivity, or not enough to get him relief.

This is what makes the children disappointed in adults very early. They know and could act, but don't. Such an attitude in adults is a very different experience from one where they don't know and hence don't act. In such cases the adult is less deflated as a possible source of security.

All this having been said about the role of adults in the kibbutz, it must be stressed that parents are, nevertheless, much more important in the life of the child than either his metapelets or teachers. They are one of the three centers around which the child's life revolves and whose impact will shape his personality. But in my opinion they rank third in a hierarchy of importance in which the peer group comes first, the kibbutz itself second, and the parents only last.

By the time the children enter kindergarten, if not sooner, they seem to have finished making the system their own; on the negative side by suppression or denial of their wish for adult comfort; on the positive side by turning to their peers for emotional satisfaction. Possibly they have done so as early as when they enter the toddlers' house. In any case, they seem clear enough by kindergarten age about where their security comes from.

To convince me that the children prefer these arrangements, a kibbutz mother told me that "a year ago there was discussion in the assembly whether the children should sleep in the parents' rooms. My son, who was then nine, knew about it and said, 'I should be allowed to take part in the discussion and I would tell them that the children don't like to sleep with their parents. They like it much better in the children's house.' I asked why? and he answered: 'In your room I hear the jackals, and I don't like that.' I asked, 'Are there no jackals to be heard in the children's house?' and he said, 'No, there I don't hear them because I'm not alone; there are other children with me.' So I said: 'But when you sleep with us, you also wouldn't be alone; your parents would be around.' So he said, 'But you would go to meetings, you wouldn't always stay with me in the room.' "

Thus the children feel that only the peer group provides that continuity and sameness that Erikson views as necessary for acquiring basic trust. And since kibbutz life has convinced the children that physical protection is assured them (though it may take a while in coming) emotional security comes first, and physical second, particularly when the anxiety is caused by a jackal in the distance. Perhaps with a jackal up close, physical security would come first, and a longing for the presence of the parent. But in general life for the kibbutz child is much more secure than is life in our city streets for our children.

Given also the kibbutz child's much greater competence in caring for himself in his environment, physical security is taken far more for granted than with us. Hence the emotional security provided by the peer group, because of its omnipresence and the many shared interests, becomes nearly all important, certainly more so than is true in our setting. (An exception would be our adolescent street gangs. At least they suggest that the underprivileged youth in our cities view the peer group as the only source of physical and emotional security. But then their reliance on the gang reflects the extreme degree of their physical and emotional insecurity, while kibbutz children feel very secure about their physical existence and build their emotional security with each other on this basis.)

Despite some exceptions, a kibbutz child's emotional involvement with his parents—and along with it his attachment, both positive and negative—is much less intense than that of an average middle-class American child. The emotional deficit, if it is such, is compensated by an incredibly strong attachment to his peer group, and by the much more diluted, but nevertheless very real emotional ties to the kibbutz as such and all its members. These are incomparably stronger than are an American child's ties to his cousins, his playmates, to other relatives and friends of the family, or to his community. (The only comparison might be an American's attachment to his religion, if it were focal to his life, as it is, for example, among the Hutterites or the Amish.)

❦ Bedtime

FEW KIBBUTZ ISSUES HAVE BEEN (AND STILL ARE) DISCUSSED SO assiduously as the sleeping arrangements of the children. For the present, children in a very few kibbutzim sleep in the rooms of their parents; but this is very much the exception, and I return to this issue later.

There is, on the other hand, considerable variety among the various movements—and sometimes among kibbutzim of the same movement—as to how the parents separate from their children at bedtime, after their daily visits. The visiting time is about two hours, and occurs at the same time of day for children of all ages. Thus it is not just the only time when parents and children are together, but also brothers and sisters. Still, as the children get older, they are more apt to spend all or part of the visiting hours away from their parents, on their own pursuits, such as those of the peer group.

In the left wing, when the visiting time is over, parents and children part in front of the children's house, and a metapelet takes over and puts the children to bed. In the right wing, the parents enter, spend some time putting the children to bed, and there is no metapelet available to the children at this time. In either case, it is at bedtime that the nightly separation between parent and child stresses the fact that now parents will turn to their grown-up collective life, and children to their own set of peers.

There are times when parents or child would like to extend the visit—and in the right-wing kibbutzim they have some freedom to do so, but not much. Essentially it is the kibbutz, through its committee on education, which decides when and for how long the parents may visit with their child. In this way it is an ever-present fact of life that it is the kibbutz that sets limits on their being together. Obviously if the parents wanted strongly enough to spend more time with their children, they would arrange for it through their vote in the general assembly. In fact, they accept the policy that exists, though there may be days when they wish it were different. And so the children know that their parents are not only in accord with, but have shaped the way in which their common relations proceed.

During the rest of the day, if work permits, parents also pass by the children's house, wave a hello, and the children as a group visit their parents at work. So there is flexibility and much chance for casual contacts. Nevertheless, parent and child are aware that limits exist, and if they were not aware and exceeded them, the metapelet would step in.

Where the parents themselves put the child to bed in the

children's house, this would seem to give the parent-child relations greater importance and thus would seem a good arrangement for both. But in a way it forces the child to rely even more on his peer group for companionship, because here, where the parent could (or should, in theory) be present, but sometimes is not, it throws the child on his peers even more. Because if the parent is absent, there is not even a metapelet around to turn to. In the left wing, there is no one but a metapelet present at bedtime, for a fairly large group of children. But at least she is predictably there, and in theory no one child is better off than any other.

Many parents have two, three, or four children, each one in a different house according to his age. This means, in those kibbutzim where parents put the children to bed, that they cannot stay long with any one child because they have to hurry on to bed down the next older child. Also, parents are sometimes away from the kibbutz and some have to work in the evening. In such cases, the child has to put himself to bed, deal as best he can with his disappointment, and he has no one to turn to but his roommates for human comfort in distress.

But even if the parents are free and present, and try to do a good job, it is the end of the day. After eight or more hours of hard work, and after the two visiting hours with their children, many of them are simply exhausted, physically and emotionally. Here it makes a difference that parents try to crowd too much emotion into the short span of time, because they feel the visit comprises the whole of their relations with their children. They want it to be so good and so meaningful, they want to concentrate on their children so exclusively, that they impose a heavy emotional burden on themselves.

So when bedtime comes round, to quote a kindergarten teacher, "the parents simply have no more patience. They want the children in bed and to get away as fast as possible. This is one of the things I find very bad in our kibbutz, and I do not know why. During the afternoon [visit], they want very much to be with their children. They go on walks and do whatever else they can. But then at bedtime they are tired of it all. As soon as they enter the children's house at bedtime, they want to be through with it, and this is a big problem."

These comments certainly tally with my own observations at bedtime, though I would cite one additional factor: the abrupt transition and the letdown. For two hours the parents and all their children are what we would call a family. And while too much of importance is kept away from these hours to make it a real family experience, it is a very serious playing out of family life. Now suddenly it is over, and kibbutz reality, which was denied for a bit, reasserts itself.

Precisely because these few hours together are supposed to be purely for having fun, the impending separation becomes a stark emotional contrast. In theory, the policy of putting children to bed was adopted in many right-wing kibbutzim to make for more intimacy between parent and child. But how can intimacy deepen at a moment when both partners know it has to end by official decree?

I found that most parents defend themselves by relating to it little. Most of them, from the moment they enter the children's house, feel very self-conscious, and so do the children. This is sharply different from how relatively comfortable they have felt up to then, as they walked to the children's house together. But no sooner do they enter the child's bedroom—incidentally, a very barren and unattractive room— than what intimacy they have had seems to vanish. This sharply separates the warmth of beforehand from the coldness in the room where they will tuck the child in.

And this is so when a parent has to put only one child to

bed. Matters are much worse if there are several children to deal with. Not that the distance between houses is great or that much time is lost in walking from one to the other. But putting a small child to bed takes time, even if parents do it fast. And if they do it too fast, it becomes more aggravating than comforting. Most of all the parent feels pressured and rushed; guilty as much about hurrying this child to bed as about keeping the other child waiting. It becomes an ordeal, even for the most loving and conscientious parent, and an empty routine for the parent less emotionally involved.

Matters are even worse for the children. The littlest one, who is usually put to bed first, suffers from the knowledge that his mother is rushing to get to the next older sibling. And the older child has to wait for his mother to come, knowing she is now with the younger siblings. But he does not know if she is already with the four-year-old, or if she is still with the two-year-old, which would mean it will take even longer till she gets around to him.

During this time the child must come to hate his mother and siblings, particularly since he has to watch two or three of his roommates being put to bed by their parents while he waits by himself in his loneliness—or he would come to hate them if he did not repress it. Finally the mother (or father, or both) comes, for at best half an hour. This half hour the child must now grab, because it's all he is going to get. That is why he cannot afford to hate the mother or to act on his emotions. Because if he does, the half hour will be gone, and nothing will be left.

Some parents try to relieve things by having one parent put one child to bed, and the other another. This at least prevents the child from having to watch in loneliness the others being with their parents. But it raises the question of why mother chose to spend this time with the younger one instead of with him, and so on.

Now in our families, similar waiting and hating takes place. But since we have the entire night ahead of us, the child can afford to balk and cry, to complain about having had to wait. Because after he has got his complaints out, there will still be time to be nicely together for a bit. The kibbutz child, however resentful the waiting has made him, must immediately repress what he felt up to the moment the mother appeared, or he is left all night long with his stressful emotions unrelieved.

Small wonder that some of the most sensitive, involved parents leave their children feeling very down. As one mother put it: "Every evening I leave the children's house depressed. The noise, unrest, the many people milling about. This quiet last hour together could be so nice, so close, and it turns out to be such a difficult thing, so unprivate, it's terrible."

And their disappointment, too, is not lost on the child. Whether he responds to it or tries to shake off his anxieties, there is only one source of ever-present relief to turn to: his peers. So the children look to each other for comfort, or at least the companionship of mutual understanding when a parent does not appear, or keeps them waiting too long.

For that very reason they must suppress any negative feelings they have about their peers. Every night some children are made jealous because they have to watch others being put to bed when their own parents have not come. These feelings the child must repress. It was sometimes pitiful to watch how very young children, jealous of others and feeling deserted, would cover themselves up or else turn to the wall so that they would not have to watch their more fortunate age-mates. Once the other child's parent was gone, however, there was the whole night and most of the next day when these children would have to rely for nearly all comfort, stimulation, and company on the very youngsters of whom they then felt so jealous. For this reason they cannot afford to become conscious of their jealousy, much less to act on it.

Nor is it only the children who turn to each other at this time of stress. Parents do the same, whether to avoid their own feelings of the moment, or because they are tired of their children by now, or for the simple reason that they find the other parent in the room more interesting, a better companion. With four children to a room (siblings never room together) there are nearly always two or more parents in the room, often five or six. And in every bedtime situation I observed, where several parents were present, some would be sitting on their child's bed with their backs to the child, talking with other adults about daily events. Often they became quite animated in what they were talking about, arguing over, or whatever. Others would get very involved in their talk with another adult, all the while taking off the child's clothes without paying any attention to him.

So now everything was different. Just a short while ago it was the child who was the center of attention. If, during the children's visit, another adult had tried to interrupt, he would have been told very nicely, "Not now, please, I want to be with my child." Now, by contrast, if the child should ask a question about the discussion, he will be told to keep out of it. Essentially the time has now begun when the adult belongs to his separate adult life with his comrades.

Even if only one parent is present, it does not mean things will be different. I have many times seen the one adult in a bedroom wander away to another room to talk to other parents. All the clearer to the child that now his time with his parents is over, and he must turn back to his comrades, as his parents have turned back to theirs.

Even if the child, on his own, makes special efforts to get comfort from his parents, the kibbutz situation often forces them to return him to his peers. If, out of night anxiety, a child runs away from the children's house to his parents' room, which is some distance away—and this happens occasionally—he is soon taken back, even by parents who feel badly about it. But to do otherwise would mean to be criticized severely by their comrades because they transgress the main law of the kibbutz: that children should be brought up as part of their group.

As one mother told me: "When my son left the kindergarten and was moved to the children's house, at first he couldn't sleep at night and ran to our room. I wanted him to be happy, but I knew he will get adjusted after awhile, so I did not mind taking him back." This again forces the children to seek comfort from each other instead of the parents. In many cases, I was told, the child would pick someone and decide that this one would watch over him and protect him. Then he would reassure his parents: "He will watch me." In the words of a mother who was also a metapelet: "I remember in the morning when we came to work, many times we found such a child who was afraid, in the other child's bed. He slept with the one that was his watcher during the night."

As the child grows older the importance of his age-mates increases steadily. Ever more important functions are taken over by his age-group, both in the giving and receiving of security, companionship, and satisfactions, but also as a source of emotional and intellectual challenge. If the community, as represented by his age-mates, was important to the infant because of what it offered to him, it becomes even more important to the toddler and later to the child of grade school age, that is during the latency and prepubertal period. Things change, and radically so, with the coming of adolescence, but this takes us far ahead of the story.

❧ *Emotional Input*

HERE AGAIN ONE MIGHT RAISE THE QUESTION: TO WHAT degree and in what sense is mother-love necessary? This time not only in terms of the child's need for security and all else his dependency requires, but of what might be called "emotional input." Good mothering seems to require that the infant receive a certain amount of emotional input from significant adults in his environment. But maybe it is less important than we think whether this input originates with only one, two, or (counting grandparents) three or four adults, or if it comes from a hundred or more persons of all ages. After all, the institutionalized children Spitz (1945, etc.) described suffered mostly from lack of affection, stimulation, challenge, and freedom to act, and not from being reared as a group.

What Spitz and others stress, therefore, is that it takes more than a lack of affection for the infant to stop developing, to waste away, even to die—as in those conditions known as hospitalism and marasmus (which are the often fatal consequences of a total withdrawal from the world at this age). Lack of stimulation is almost equally important. But on this score the kibbutz infant is much better off than many a middle-class child, not to mention most underprivileged children. Whatever a metapelet's shortcomings, it is still her full-time job to take care of the children. And while in my opinion she is much too occupied with routine cleaning, fetching, and doing, the fact remains that in theory at least she is there solely for the infants in her care, while not even the best middle-class mother is in theory there solely for her child.

Moreover, the stimulation around the infant's being fed is only part of his nursing experience. Many other sensations enter in, and constitute his experience with the world. The kinesthetic and tactile experience of being held as he nurses —but also when he is being bathed, cleaned, and diapered or played with, are at least as meaningful as the intake of food. So also are the stimulations that surround him. Noises and smells, familiar and unfamiliar, shape his picture of the world. Here the kibbutz infant is exposed to a much wider variety of stimulations than seems typical of the middle-class child, at least before TV became part of his world.

For example, in addition to his mother, the other infants in his room, and their mothers, there is the regular metapelet and her helper, all of them fairly permanent figures in his life. From an early age the infant is taken daily to the parents' room. In some kibbutzim this begins at anywhere from one to three months, depending on the infant's health, the weather, and kibbutz regulations. But in most kibbutzim, and in all those more rigidly organized, the infant does not leave his house for at least the first six months. At this early age, "visits" are very short; at first they last only about half an hour. But already his siblings and some of the family's friends begin to enter his life and also ministrate to him. Then there are the relief persons who take care of him on the metapelet's day off, and the ever-changing night watch, each with her own personal style of picking him up, holding him, talking to him.

The omnipresence of other infants plus all the comings and goings of the kibbutz offer a great variety of stimulation, apart from what his own parents provide in their hours together. Thus, on balance, and unless the American child has a very devoted mother, he may well experience less stimulation than the kibbutz infant. The real question is whether, and to what degree, the much and varied stimulation of many persons can replace the greater consistency and intimacy that comes of being cared for and stimulated mainly by one. Because the many of course cannot so easily gear the stimulation they offer to the needs and abilities of the particular child. Nor can the child develop as easily, when his development is not directed, first and foremost, toward mastering the one major relationship, with all others being secondary.

In the nursing situation, for example, typically three or more mothers will be nursing their babies at the same time. And while they will concentrate on their infant for some of the time, they will also chat with their comrades, watch the other infants, talk about them, etc. If an infant tries to gain more for himself by subtly adjusting to what he feels the mother wants, and she is more interested in what another mother is doing or saying, such an effort to model himself for a purpose will fall flat and will slowly be extinguished.

Since most of the infant's care is tendered by metapelets who have to change, bathe, and take care of several infants, they cannot subtly adjust to the way each infant feels best if he is held or moved about in ways specific to him.

While an adjustment by the infant may bring some extra attention from one metapelet, it may fail to do so from another, or may even bring a negative response. Then, since the infant at this early date cannot realize that different persons need different ways of responding to them, all his efforts at specific responding (or "to give in return" as Erikson puts it) will also be extinguished by non-reward. But by adjusting one's responses to the other, one does more than learn about others, one also learns about oneself. So from the very first the kibbutz infant has less reason to strive for individuation.

Still, it is not as simple as if kibbutz infants were to "get" less, and "give" less of themselves in return, during these early interactions. This would only be true if we were comparing kibbutz reality with an ideal of middle-class culture.

But most middle-class reality is very much at variance with such an ideal. The majority of middle-class mothers do not just love to adjust the way they clean and diaper their infants to the infant's subtle preferences. To some, cleaning up the child's mess is an onerous task, much more onerous than to the metapelet who has usually chosen, on her own, to be an infant nurse.

So while the kibbutz child may fare less well, compared with a child among us who has an excellent mother-infant relationship, he fares considerably better, for example, than the many infants in our society whose mothers, because of the nature of their own toilet training or for other neurotic reasons, find the child's excreta repulsive; or than those infants whose mothers make of bathing an essentially arduous task of getting the infant clean, a task often performed with compulsive rigidity, or else in a hurry because other things need attending. In the kibbutz the infant nurse has at least received some instruction on how to take care of infants.

Here then, from the beginning of life, we encounter some of the assets and liabilities of kibbutz child rearing as it affects personality formation, or so it seems to me. In the kibbutz, things can never get as bad as they may between a lone mother and her infant, because there is more than one person taking care of the infant. This has its price at the other end, because multiple mothering interferes with the depth of mutuality between two persons who interact in great intimacy at this earliest stage of personality development.

❦ Attuning to Others

WITH MOST OF OUR INFANTS, ALL THE CHALLENGES AND satisfactions originate mainly in one person and a very few others. Often too, the life pattern of even these very few persons contains much that is identical or parallel in ways of being and doing. This permits, often forces, even the very young child to attune himself, to respond, to react positively or negatively to the fine details and distinctions of such a life style of doing and feeling.

Many a middle-class child reacts to them unconsciously. He is so familiar with all his parents' normal ways of being and acting that he knows instantly when something is wrong because he senses even liminal changes. It is what sets him to worrying and wondering what might have caused it or what he might have done to bring it about—a mental habit acquired very early, which brings growing self-knowledge along with a deeper unconscious knowledge of his parents. But while such a limited variation in challenge may lead to much deeper and subtler responses, it is definitely a limited range.

In some of the older European cultures this is even more true than with us. For example, one investigator, who recently studied infant care in Holland, told me how astonished she was that babies there, during their first months of life, are kept in the crib with its nice and meticulously clean lace curtains drawn, are not played with, are essentially left alone except for when the mother comes to pick up the infant and feed him; and how this absence of play and companionship leads to a relatively late awakening of interest in the surrounding world. What she failed to see was how the mother's devotion to her infant when she is with him, compared to the lack of stimulation during the rest of the day, incredibly heightens the time when the mother does come; how it lays the basis for a one-to-one relationship, for the wish, later in life, to find fulfillment in the deep and concentrated relationship to one other person—in adolescence through the single great friendship, in maturity through the marital relationship. Thus in his earliest experience the Dutch infant learns to concentrate, to receive from and to give to one person only. And ideally, each adjustment to this person improves the one relation that (for him) is his central experience of the world.

Clearly recognized here was the absence of stimulation by things (toys, etc.). But the investigator, being a child of her culture, failed to recognize how this leads by necessity to a concentration on the one-to-one relationship between human beings. Then later in life (if nothing countervailing alters the pattern) things, and the external world, will be less important, while intimate relations to a few persons will be more so. With us, it seems, things (and in the kibbutz, the many comrades) interfere with the concentration on a few human relations and on the inner personal life. These the Dutch infant concentrates on, for want of anything else during the earliest period of his life.

Things are very different for the kibbutz infant who is never alone, who is always receiving stimuli from several other children, from his and their parents, from metapelets. No need there to concentrate on a single relationship to the exclusion of the rest of the world.

Exposed as he is to so many more people, around even the most intimate aspects of life, the kibbutz child knows an infinitely wider spectrum of challenges and reactions. He is not so attuned to subtleties in his parents' emotional reactions. Small changes of tone or inflection, of body tonus, choice of words or facial expression, are largely lost on him. But he escapes the middle-class child's risk of constraint to a single language and none other.

This, too, furthers the kibbutz child's independence, because he learns so early to interact with the many. Nor are the interactions empty, compared to a richness we are taught to expect and then do not receive. Such a richness of human relations is more an ideal with us than an everyday reality. So while kibbutz founders fear this subtle feeling for inti-

macy is absent in the kibbutz-born generation, it is a generation that never had intimacy held out to them as an ideal, as
it is in our society, which makes the many here who cannot
reach it feel doubly alienated.

Most kibbutz-reared children, then, are accustomed to a
bustle that pervades their whole life. If they are to make it
successfully in the peer group, they must develop a high
threshold against sensations, must screen out the finer
nuances, must respond to the essential, sometimes the cruder
message only, and let the subtler shadings go. Yet kibbutz
life offers them incredibly wider opportunities for all forms
of easy social interchange.

For example, it is important for the social and intellectual
development of these children that they are free at all times
to engage in what Jean Piaget calls their collective monologues. They chatter away *at* each other, rather than *with*
each other, which will come later and will easily build on the
first. At the same time they establish the level of their belonging to each other as one of simple interaction. Because the
collective monologues, while increasing sociability, lack emotional and intellectual depth.

By contrast: When the parent in our best middle-class
families responds to the young child's monologue with emotional depth, then the story of what develops is very different. Both speech and thought are enriched by how the
adult's responses lead the child to modify them both. But the
story is again entirely different if the parent squelches the
child's monologue, either by indifference or by expecting
him to advance to two-way dialogue, which is beyond him at
this point. It may easily destroy the child's confidence in his
ability to act and interact. None of this can happen in the
kibbutz because of group living.

Here again, comparing middle-class and kibbutz rearing,
there is both advantage and disadvantage. In the kibbutz

there is little talk that is over the child's head, since mostly he talks with his peers. And his parents, during their brief time together, gear all their talk to his level. The great challenges are avoided for good and for ill: Talk that is beyond his comprehension does not goad him to reach for an understanding beyond his grasp; but neither does it give him a sense of inferiority or defeat because of what he cannot comprehend. Life is always within easy reach, which is satisfying. On the other hand it demands no great mental exertion, which can make things seem lacking in intellectual zest.

If the foregoing seems a minus in the development of subtler sensibilities or in the challenge to intellectual curiosity, it is counterbalanced by the near-continuous challenge to master social interaction and the physical environment. And this is infinitely more so than would be true for the middle-class child. Doing, and particularly doing with others, is so much emphasized by the conditions of his life that the kibbutz child has little time or mental energy for thinking and feeling, particularly solitary thinking and feeling. For these he has virtually no chance, whereas many a middle-class child is alone to a degree that is just as unbalanced in the other direction.

Moreover, we cannot overlook that the kibbutz also protects the child greatly from the wrong kind of stimulation. Certainly this is so by comparison with underprivileged children, who must often live with overcrowding and all the fighting and shouting that go with it. In the kibbutz the children's night rest is interrupted only by their own discomfort or anxiety, but not by the comings and goings of adults or their doings. And if, in the right-wing kibbutzim, being put to bed by their parents inflicts painful emotions, this is mitigated by how briefly the situation lasts. Thereafter, sleep will not be disturbed by listening to, or wishing to overhear, the conversation of adults, or by their sexual activities.

Watching the ease with which these children go to bed, whether or not their parents are present, and observing the relative ease with which they let their parents go, was quite impressive. Particularly when I compared it with the battles royal I have witnessed in middle-class families, a battle between the parent who wishes to see his child asleep, and the child who wishes to stay up some more—the battle seesawing back and forth while the feelings of each partner get severely bruised. It brought home to me how much the middle-class parents' love and tender care has to make up for such bruising.

Of course the ease with which these children put themselves to bed has its price: They must repress the wish that their parents not desert them, must accept the demand that they give up ties to the parents at bedtime and replace them by those to their peers. I am tempted to call this a superego demand, but it is really the community's demand. So perhaps I should call it the collective superego's request. But thereby hangs a tale. Can there be a collective superego?

❧ A Collective Superego

CONSCIENCE, OR THE SUPEREGO, IS ESSENTIALLY A SET OF rules one has internalized by making them one's own without knowing anymore where they come from. To then break such a rule is to experience guilt.

At this young toddler age, conscience is still very much in a state of development, though one has already learned a great many rules of behavior. It is not yet in the form of a demand made on oneself, which by failing to live up to it creates guilt and hence threatens self-respect. It is rather an inner voice that echoes an original, external voice that tells us: "You should not have done that. You broke the rule and it will have bad consequences." Only barely is one also beginning to feel: "You are a bad person for having done such a thing." That is, guilt at this age is still very directly related to whose voice it is that one fears, and who the person is who will act on such disapproval.

In our middle-class family this voice is very much the voice of the parents, and it is strongly supported by that of all other authority figures. Some middle-class children fear the omnipresence of God, but nowadays not too many. More fear the policeman, or whoever else is viewed as the enforcer of law and order. In the kibbutz, as should be obvious, there is no policeman nor anyone like him; nor has religion any place. So there is no God who threatens retaliation, no policeman to arrest the evil doer. Fear (and later self-respect) does not depend on what the parents think, but what the group thinks.

A collective superego is derived from collective commands instead of uniquely personal ones. It is still an inner voice that echoes an original external equivalent. Only it is not a voice that shouts imperiously or angrily to me in particular, "Thou shalt not!" but rather a chorus of many voices where each individual voice is swept up in the group's telling everyone at large, "You (plural) must not!" It derives less from the threat of, "Unless you do right *I* will desert you" than the dreaded, "*We* will cast out the one who dares to set his personal wishes ahead of those of the community."

The crucial difference is that the child is very much part of this "we" that says what ought and ought not to be done. In a strange way it makes the voice of conscience much less awesome, much more familiar than that of a superego based on internalized parental admonitions. But such a voice is also more inescapable. We can try to hide from a parent, even from God, though their voices are more awe-inspiring, their threats much more dreadful. But we can never hide from a control system of which we are quite consciously a part.

This difference is due not so much to kibbutz philosophy as to kibbutz reality. The middle-class child is often alone, hears the parent's admonishing voice from the distance, can often claim "I didn't hear you." The kibbutz child is never alone, hence never unobserved. There is no escape from watchful eyes, though they are not those of particular persons, but of all kibbutzniks, everywhere around him.

In both cases the fear that sets the process of internalization going is that of being deserted, cast off, and hence— given the child's inability to take care of himself—destroyed.

In this sense the fear of transgression may be even greater in the kibbutz, since it is not a single overpowering person who threatens desertion—against which there is at least a chance of finding another who might not—but the group in its entirety. Though each of the voices is much less powerful by itself, no relief from someone holding a different set of values is conceivable. Here again there is both asset and liability: The source of the kibbutz superego is less powerful and awesome than for the child growing up in an authoritarian, middle-class family. But the commands are more inescapable because there is nowhere a dissenting voice to support one's own doubts or dissent.

What kind of an ego will go with such a collective superego? First and foremost there will be less of a split between ego and superego, since the superego demand is one that the ego (as part of the we) helped create. Secondly, since the child grows up in a consensus community, the task of the ego is greatly simplified—namely to mediate between the demands of the id on the one hand and the demands of conscience and reality on the other. Because in the kibbutz, to obey the demands of the superego is at the same time to meet the demands of the external environment.

Freud, in his last statement on the superego, wrote (1940) that "throughout later life it represents the influence of . . . not only the personal qualities of the parents but also . . . the social class in which they lived." He was thus aware that the contents of the superego have a great deal to do with the nature of the society the parents live in, and in which the child is brought up. Piaget, who studied children at the ages when the superego (or its surrogates) are developing, concluded that there seem to be two moralities in childhood—or at least so within the conservative middle-class Swiss culture his subjects were drawn from. Developmentally, the earlier one is a morality of constraint. It is formed in the context of the unilateral relations between the child as the subordinate and the adult as the dominant person. But soon the child develops, and becomes more than just a member of his family but also a member of his society. Then the morality of constraint is partially replaced by a morality of cooperation, and this is tempered and refined by the spontaneous give and take of peer interactions (Piaget, 1932; Flavell, 1963).

In the kibbutz, from the very beginning, relations between child and adult are not unilateral, and the peer group is much more important, and becomes so sooner than in Switzerland. This suggests that when conscience develops in the kibbutz, it is founded less on constraint and much more on the morality of cooperation. Or to use Piaget's central concept, it is based on having learned to obey the rules of the game.

In this respect, Western society, and particularly we in America, seem to be veering the same way. With us, too, the parent becomes less and less domineering in the child's life, the relation between parent and child less unilateral, and the peer group more important and much sooner in life—witness the earlier entrance into nursery schools, etc. If this trend continues, the superego in our society, too, may come to be based more and more on a morality that derives from the need to cooperate with the peer group, as is already true in the kibbutz.[2]

A conscience based on "obeying the rules of the game," on a peer group "morality of cooperation," is highly concordant with what in psychoanalysis are described as the separate and different functions of the ego and superego. So much so, that in many respects the two are identical rather than in conflict. This is quite different from a situation where obeying superego demands puts one at odds with the surrounding community and where the ego is hence split apart by trying to meet the opposing tasks of satisfying the demands of the superego and those of the environment.

With us, for example, the sex morality a child derives from the peer group is much more accepting of instinctual pleasure than is the morality of constraint he derives from his parents. Hence in regard to sex morality the child's superego is often more stringent than a good portion of reality (and hence the ego by itself) would require. Witness also the situation of many a middle-class child who has internalized the Christian morality with its demand for mutual

[2] On the basis of entirely different observations, David Riesman arrived at his dichotomy between the other-directed personality versus the tradition-bound and the inner-directed personality (both of the latter resulting from the "unilateral" relation between parent and child). But I believe that Piaget's developmental psychology permits us a better understanding of what is here involved. I would also refer the reader to Chassell's discussion (1967) of newer psychoanalytic concepts about superego development in which he questions Freud's superego concept in some detail. I feel, however, that in his criticism he pays too little heed to the difference in social conditions between those about whom Freud wrote, and those on whom his own article is based. Much has changed—since Freud's time and ours and between Central Europe and America—in the nature of parent-child relations, and the relative importance of the peer group. But these two, in my opinion, account for most of the difference between Freud's view of the superego and Chassell's.

help. This he tries to obey, while at the same time trying to make good in a highly competitive society, where success depends on getting ahead of the other, not on helping the other to keep up with oneself.

The kibbutz ego, being less torn apart, is by comparison a much stronger ego. But not having to fight a very complicated battle to satisfy contradictory masters (id, superego, environment), it will not need to develop great complexity or richness. While very strong by comparison, it will (again by comparison) be considerably less personalized. Because above all, the voice of such a collective superego is also the voice of the external environment.

This may have been the case throughout most of human history. But since the rise of individualism it was precisely the personal superego (or moral demand) that asserted itself. A personal stand was taken that went as much against the voice of the community as it forced the id and ego to get along with the superego. Luther's "Here I stand, I cannot do otherwise" rightly heralds the Reformation in which the individual conscience was set against community mores.

This highly individualized voice, or superego, came of having internalized some very particular and highly personalized figures, chiefly the parents. So while the ideal kibbutz ego sketched out here may have an easier time trying to mediate the person's relation to environment and superego, it is doubly hard for such an ego to go against superego and environment at the same time. Because such an ego, while strong in itself, is poorly prepared to fight both an inner and outer battle at once.

The question is: Will such an ego—one that is strongly swayed by a collective superego and in total accord with environmental demands—crave the intimate or the collective experience? The issue of intimacy is thus crucial for understanding the kibbutz. It is an issue on which kibbutz society is not alone in responding with deepest ambivalence.

Certainly it is a problem our own society has by no means resolved. But kibbutz society seems still more ambivalent about it, or at least devotes more official concern to it than we do. Let me illustrate from the ambivalence that marks the time parents spend with their children.

❧ *Children's Hours*

IT IS THE UNIFORM OPINION OF THOSE WHO REPORT ON THE kibbutz that this is a child-centered society. "In observing the kibbutz and from interviewing parents one receives the distinct impression that no sacrifice is too great for the children. Adults are willing to live in substandard housing as long as children may live in stuccoed brick dormitories" (Spiro, 1963).

And indeed in the early days of the kibbutz, when it had to defend itself from outside attack, the first permanent building, after the watchtower for defense, was the children's house. It was solidly built, of stone or cement, when everyone else was still living in tents. What would seem like an inordinate amount of labor power and the common income is devoted to the communal rearing of children. It is the kibbutzniks' first and for a long time only luxury, a real sacrifice in many ways.

This devotion to the next generation was also what attracted my interest in the kibbutz, above and beyond the fascinating theoretical problems their society presents. Therefore it was a distinct disappointment when I had to realize to what extent it is a giving of things—including the best possible housing, education, medical care, the giving of positive affection, even the "best hours" of the day—and to what a limited degree there is full emotional giving of themselves.

For example, as Spiro correctly observes: "The next two

hours [after work is done] are sacred; they are to be devoted exclusively to the children, and nothing is allowed to interfere. In summer parents and children spend their time romping on the grass, playing games, visiting the animals, strolling through the fields."

I should note that only Western observers call this time period "sacred." In the kibbutz parlance these are simply the children's hours. But the way parents devote themselves so exclusively then to their children struck Western observers as so remarkable that they searched for a special expression to indicate how seriously, or "sacredly" kibbutzniks regard it.

Indeed, these hours are truly devoted to doing a good job of being with the children and nothing else. If, for example, parents have important problems, anxieties, conflicts, these are kept for another time. And if there is a deeper intimacy between the parents, the children do not observe its consumation during the visit.

The children are terribly important, say the parents, and believe it. But anything charged with complex emotions must be kept from the children in the hours spent together. Since only what is emotionally positive is reserved for these hours, and since none of the more complex emotions are exclusively positive, children come to feel that whatever is emotionally complex in their lives must be kept in abeyance at this time. But the growing child, in his feelings for adults, is beset by all the complex and ambivalent emotions there are. And if these are to be kept out of their common relations, then the relations themselves tend to become emotionally shallow. In the eyes of the child this merely parallels the parents' leaving them for most of the day in favor of their preferred adult relations. Both behaviors suggest to him that what his parents offer is a very pleasant but not a very important relationship. Actually, children matter a great deal to the parents, but what "matters" to the two generations differs greatly.

Students of the kibbutz thus reveal a deep understanding of real attitudes toward these hours by calling them "sacred." It reflects how deeply important they are, but also the emotional distance that marks them. Because what is sacred is not profane; and in sacred relations emotional distance must be kept.

Most observers of kibbutz life have been impressed with how much the parents do with the children during their hours together. What I failed to see, or saw only rarely, was a truly relaxed being together. And if I found it, then strangely enough, I found it most often between fathers and their children. Perhaps the early separation of mother and infant, the many regulations imposed on their being together—all this interfered more with the customary mother-child than the father-child relationship. Even in our world the father does not spend many hours a day with his children. Hence the kibbutz imposes fewer restrictions on desires that come more naturally or traditionally to the father than the mother.

What also fascinated me as I first read of the kibbutz was that most mothers breast-feed their infants, and that they do this not in privacy, as if it were somehow indecent, but openly and with pleasure. I was convinced that a major cause of why so many American mothers are unable, or unwilling to breast-feed their infants, or can breast-feed them only for a relatively short time, is that they find it somehow vulgar or embarrassing. To feel as natural about it as I was told the kibbutz mothers do seemed to augur very well for emotional rapport between mother and child, and for the child's future ability to relate closely to others.

The reality I found did not entirely conform, and my views turned out to be erroneous. As described earlier, the nursing relation like all others is subject to stringent regulation by the kibbutz, though much more so in the left-wing kibbutzim, where the night feeding is eliminated immediately.

One is tempted to say that the mother withdraws when the child becomes mature enough to make feeding less a physiological and more an interpersonal experience. As relations tend to become more emotionally demanding and potentially more intimate, even the physical interactions are restricted. What is "natural"—the mother's breast and her milk—she is ready and able to give. But when the giving could grow into a unique one-to-one relationship, it is restricted in time and meaning. Otherwise it might interfere with the mother's collective relations, or even with the infant's relating to the peer group.

The same tendency makes for the rule that the newborn will enter the infants' house four days after birth, rather than several weeks later. The social organization of the kibbutz would in no way be interfered with were the mother to keep her baby a few weeks. But with every day the infant stayed with her, he would be so much more hers, and the separation more difficult for her, if not also for the baby. This was borne out by what a few mothers told me who, because of unique or emergency situations, kept their infants with them for a few weeks after birth. These mothers told of how much harder they found it to give up an infant who had spent his first weeks with them, as compared to others of their children from whom they separated soon after birth.

Similarly, there is really no other reason why the infant, during his first six months, could not leave the nursery he is confined to in most kibbutzim. Nor is there any reason why, in the few kibbutzim where he is taken daily to the parents' room before he is half a year old, the visit need be limited to only half an hour. The rationalization is the supposed danger of infection. But on the one hand, both parents visit the infants' house in their work clothes, and on the other hand the kibbutz (unlike our big city settings) is such a close-knit community that if a contagious disease were around, like as not everyone would instantly be exposed to it, including the infants' metapelets. Finally the weather is such that exposure is no risk.

If there is any reason for preventing the infant from being brought to the parents' rooms during these first six months, it can only be the wish to separate parent and child from the beginning, to break the attachment that begins with the mother's having felt the infant growing inside her, and to impress on the infant and his mother that the infants' house is his true home, as indeed it is. Once this has registered, so to say, on mother and child, then he may visit in the parents' rooms daily.

But during these visits I could observe repeatedly, and particularly in kibbutz-born mothers, a restlessness about spending time with their infants in intimacy. They loved to pick them up at the infants' house, they lovingly wheeled them or carried them to their rooms, showing them off delightedly to all comrades they met. Everything went fine, as long as the mother was doing something with or for the baby, preferably with others around. But once in the parents' room, and after she had fed the baby some goodies, she soon passed him around to be held by everyone present: older siblings, the grandparents, visiting comrades. The feeling was that this again was very much a communal baby; just of a smaller community this time.

At no point was the baby neglected. But the mother would turn now to this person, now to that, with the suggestion that he or she should now hold the baby. And he was thus handed around till it was time to return him to the infants' house.

Among kibbutzniks much is made of the fact that parents can and do also visit their children occasionally during the day. But then they are visitors, and every child soon knows the difference between parents one visits and parents one lives with. Also in the left-wing kibbutz (and some right-wing ones, too), even if the child spends much of a holiday or the weekly sabbath with his parents in their room, he returns to the children's house not only for the night but for his nap and his meals. Again it is impressed on him that the food, shelter, and rest, around which centers intimate care, are provided by the kibbutz through the children's house, and that the relationship to the parents involves only nonessentials, like play.

With us, too, it is unfortunate that it is often only at vacation time that the middle-class family really gets together. While I do not believe that intimate relationships can develop around vacation time associations, it is still an important recurrence of spending time together for parent and child. In the kibbutz the parents have an annual two-week vacation, which they may spend where they wish. Since they have very little spending money, they will typically take their vacation by visiting another kibbutz, or will go to the vacation places (rest homes) maintained by the kibbutz organizations for this purpose, or stay with non-kibbutz relatives in their homes. But their children do not go with them; they stay behind in their houses. This contrast of having two hours daily with the parents to enjoy together, but of separation when the parents could spend whole days with their children, is again not lost on parent or child.

Another factor may also play a role, though it is difficult to gauge its importance. Attitudes are certainly mediated to the child by his metapelets. But many metapelets have left the kibbutz for months or even a year during their own infant's childhood, to study to become a metapelet. How can they be deeply committed to the importance of continuity in mother-child relationships, and have taken off for many months or a year from their own children, or those others whom they raise? And how can this attitude fail to be transmitted to the children in their care, if not also to the children's mothers?

Even the parents' room where they visit together is a tenuous place for the kibbutz child. A place that offers a haven of closeness for a few discrete hours a day is not much of a physical or emotional haven. A warm hearth from five to seven in the afternoon, even with a few minutes leeway, cannot offer much security, however nice a time and place the parents try to make it. Because a place that offers the kind of security that stops by the hand of the clock merely rubs in how precarious a haven it is.

When we say "My home is my castle," we imply that home is a refuge, a place of security out of which (we believe) we can never be driven. How incongruous to even think of applying this saying to the kibbutz, where the parents' rooms are assigned by the community for their use. But how appropriate to the kibbutz as a whole, which is indeed a "castle" that protects and encloses the community and was a real enough castle when the first kibbutzim were surrounded by a hostile Arab world.

Many middle-class American parents are not exactly dying to spend all their free time with their children either, and most of them often feel and act on their strong desire to get away from their children, to have time apart and a life of their own. But most of their children have the almost daily experience (as when the father returns from work) that the father's feeling is: "Thank God I'm home now and can relax; that strenuous life on the outside is over for today." This feeling the parent emanates about home is what makes it such a good place for the young child.

Often the feeling may be as honored in the breach as the observance. But even in a family where there is tension, home is where the parents, so to say, take their shoes off, let their hair down, where one lowers one's guard—for better (if relations are close and affectionate) or for worse (if antagonism reigns). Even in a home of considerable dissension, the child observes that this is the place where one has least need of pretense, of caution. And this, too, is important for the feeling that home is where one can let go, be most truly oneself.

Kibbutz parents, by contrast, are so conscious of wanting the "children's hours" to be extra nice that they show only their best side, so to say, as a Western family might for an important guest in the home. While kibbutz parents too relax in their room and find respite there from work and from the omnipresence of others, the good life for them is still with their comrades, not in the room. Thus whatever the actual exceptions, for them and for us, the deep convictions about where one is most truly oneself differ sharply between us.

Kibbutzniks have argued apace about whether children should not spend more time with their parents, especially about whether they should sleep in their rooms. Yonina Talmon, when she heard of these discussions, had expected that parents would want their children to sleep in the parents' rooms during infancy. She was much surprised when she learned that this was not even considered, since it was not raised as an issue by any appreciable number of mothers. What quite a few of them wanted was for their children to sleep in the parents' rooms from ages six to twelve. This is the latency period, when the child makes the least emotional demands on the parent, is most pliable in adjusting his life to theirs.

As indicated before, I repeatedly raised the issue, in the

right-wing kibbutzim, of why—when many parents now have more than a single room to themselves, and when they themselves put the children to bed—it would not be quite feasible to have the children sleep in the rooms of their parents. The answer given me uniformly was that then it would no longer be a kibbutz.

Reasons varied as to why this would negate the kibbutz. But most frequent was the answer that if the children were to sleep with their parents, they would soon eat with them too, and this would be the end of their collective life.

I believe that the aversion to taking meals with their children, like their restrictions on the nursing relation, have the same unconscious origin: a rejection of how ghetto mothers tried to get emotional control of their children by pushing food on them. In citing the eating arrangements, I feel they have correctly assessed how important they find it to be with their comrades, unhampered, but also how difficult they find it to give of themselves to their children in ways that their parents gave to them. The first cause is conscious, the second is not.

Inner conflicts like these plague only the first generation. The second generation is much more down to earth about things: "That's the way we like it, and we can afford to go to extravagant expense for what we like or find important." Such a way of rearing children is for them not a matter of ideology but simply the most comfortable and sensible arrangement. That is why mothers of the second generation are much more at ease with themselves. They feel no need to pretend to themselves that they do what they do for anything but personal preference. This is not meant to imply that they do not love their children well enough; they do in their own ways, within the particular place they have assigned them in their busy lives.

Here again, as regards loving their children, and being

loved by them, what counts, I believe, is the balance between good and bad emotional experiences, and not any absolute quantity of love. Some children in the West may love their parents more than kibbutz children do, but only in special cases do these parents mean much to any other children. By contrast, I have spoken of the great pride and satisfaction kibbutzniks derive from the children of their kibbutz. Thus, while kibbutz parents may get less warmth and devotion from their own children by comparison with other societies, they get more of it from the other children of their community than do most parents in the West. On balance, the kibbutz parent may therefore experience, not less gratification than we do, but more, only the source of it is not just his own children but all youngsters together.

Spiro has correctly observed that when the children of the founding generation leave latency and become pubertal, something happens to their relations with their parents. "The intense parent-child relation lasts until the children enter high school, at which time it diminishes considerably and in some cases almost disappears. . . . Parents frequently complain that they seldom see their children now that they are in high school and that, when they do, they seem to have little in common." Here I cannot help feeling that things are not very different with us. But I am tempted to stress that there are good reasons why Spiro calls the relationships intense rather than intimate. And intense they often are, at least for the founding generation and their children. What must be noted is that "intense" has the same root as tense. Whatever is intense is also tense. These relationships are mutually intense because each wants something from the other that they cannot give, namely true relaxation in the feeling that they belong to each other unreservedly.

Things are much different, though, in the relationships between kibbutz-born and raised parents and their children.

These parents expect little intimacy with their children, do not hope or wish for a unique one-to-one relationship with them. Hence their relations with their children are more comfortably relaxed—neither intimate nor intense.

🌿 *Intimacy*

THERE ARE MANY REASONS WHY THE KIBBUTZ PARENT, BOTH of the founding and the kibbutz-born generation, is not intimate with his child, but one of them has again to do with the overweening idea of equality. Intimacy between adults—in paradigm, between husband and wife—is based on a sharing of emotions in ways that are essentially based on equality. That is, each one gives as much as he receives, though at different moments and in different situations he might give and receive in different degree. But if, among adults, one is essentially the giver and the other essentially the receiver, then we call it a dependent, not an intimate relation.

Things are very different as regards the intimacy between parent and child, because there an intimate dependency prevails. In fact it is this alone that will help us to be intimate in adulthood.

In the intimate parent-child relationship, too, both must be givers and receivers, but the nature and amounts of the giving and receiving are most unequal. The child remains dependent: that is he receives much more than he gives. He must *receive* from his parents, first, all that he requires for his physical security and comfort; second, affection, empathy, help in understanding the world and himself—most of all help in recognizing his feelings and acknowledging them for his own.

The parent must not expect to receive any such help from his child. And woe to the child whose parent expects to get help from him in recognizing and expressing his feelings. Nor can the parent expect more than momentary empathy from his child. It is only slightly less damaging to the child to be used by his parent as a safe context in which to unload anger and frustration, whereas the child should have considerable leeway in discharging frustration upon his parent.

The child also *gives* in a very different way from his parent. Essentially he gives to his parents through his steps in growth, through his social, intellectual, even his physical growth. He gives by proving them good parents. And he proves it by having a satisfying life of his own. He gives to his parents not so much by playing with them as by his learning to find enjoyment in play, most of all with his friends. He gives, in short, by the unfolding of his personality, by his coming to full flower on his own. This is obviously a very different giving than the parents' giving of dependent care.

Most kibbutz founders grew up in families where too much giving was expected of the child, where the giving was too little free to be spontaneous and too much dictated by parental demand based on rigid custom—the more so because this was a generation for whom the unfolding they yearned for was no longer one of resignation within ghetto walls. These founders, as youngsters, wanted a much richer and freer unfolding than their parents could encourage them toward or even help them attain. Instead they pressed their children to stay put. And this demand, the children felt, was the "much too much" they were expected to give. In the kibbutz they would change all this. They would make sure that their children got sufficient help in unfolding, and nothing would be asked in return.

This feeling—that one was made to give more than one received—is what makes for the anxious desire for equality, so that never again will one have to give more than one got. If

I feel sure of receiving whenever in need, I do not fear inequality.

It is the experience of having been given to for years in a dependent intimacy that permits us, in adulthood, to trust in mature intimacy. We can give freely because we are sure we will eventually be given to, in turn. But a child who has lived a life of equality receives no vast surplus of what I have called here dependent intimacy, and without it he cannot later afford to give it to others. He simply has not stored up enough to give of it freely, convinced that however freely he spends, his emotional storehouse will always be replenished.

The child who receives ample dependent intimacy from his parents, particularly his mother, can one day begin to spend it on his peers, who can give little in return. This deficit in peer life has to be replenished by the parents, until such time as the other peers, their emotional storehouse now over-stocked too, can give in return. And when the peer can freely give to his peer, both are fully grown-up.

This is why the kibbutz child who lives so closely with his age-group, fails to live intimately with any one of them in particular. True, he has more in common with his peers than with any other human beings. They are more important to him than anyone else, and emotionally closer. But for full intimacy, they have not exchanged their emotions enough, particularly their negative emotions, in a full give and take. Their emotional storehouse has not been filled up enough by their parents as they spend it in their life with their peers. And the parents have failed to replenish it because too much of the child's life was lived away from his parents.

One simply cannot belong to each other in intimacy for four half-hour feeding times a day. It is not that our middle-class mothers spend more time with their children but that the timing of emotional giving is not preset by the clock. It is exactly the unscheduled sitting with one's child through the night, when he is sick or afraid and needs it most—and not on the next afternoon—that makes for replenished emotions and allows the child to freely expend them on others.

The reason even intensity declines in kibbutz parent-child relationships, I believe, is that disappointment sets in, and eventually retreats, because the relationship is based solely on having a nice time together as equals. This may satisfy the child's need for a play companion, though the kibbutz child is less in need of one than most. But it fails the adolescent's need for adult examples that might have helped him in his struggle to know how to be intimate with another. And adolescence is where the lack of intimacy and the shortcomings of this educational system become most apparent, just as the latency period and adulthood are where its merits are clearest.

It is when the child makes little emotional demand on the adult that the kibbutz parent functions best. That is why mothers can and do breast-feed their infants during the first few months, and stop when the infant becomes more emotionally demanding. That is why they enjoy their children most when they are roughly between the ages of five and twelve.

On the other hand, if kibbutz children are not encouraged to make emotional demands on adults, neither are they asked to give in return. Demands on them are almost nonexistent from earliest infancy, and on through the latency age. With so little by way of emotional expectations, they can easily live up to those that are made. Hence in this respect they certainly enjoy a happy childhood, if not a happy infancy too.

3

The Latency Age

THIS, IN MY OPINION, IS THE HAPPY AGE IN THE KIBBUTZ. Demands are at a minimum, and what is expected of the child tallies largely with his own inclinations. The parents, because they are neither providers nor educators, do not loom so large or forbidding as they do in our middle-class families. Metapelets do insist on conformity to certain demands, but since they are less involved in the children and the children in them, their demands are much milder in emotional impact. Toilet training is not only delayed but undemanding, though like everything else, this has its consequences.

Interestingly enough, while it was the psychoanalysts who first alerted us to the harmful effects of a too early or too rigid toilet training, it was scholars of a psychoanalytic bent who criticized the kibbutz for what follows naturally from delayed toilet training: more frequent bed-wetting, or its persistence to a later age.

✥ *Bed-wetting*

SINCE THE CHARGE OF ENURESIS IS USED BY CRITICS AS evidence of neurosis among the kibbutz-reared, I would like to say, first, it is misleading. Enuresis refers to all urinary incontinence, but bed-wetting is something else again. If one is going to make comparisons about the incidence of night wetting, one must also consider how and where it occurs. And kibbutz sleeping arrangements are radically different from those of middle-class American settings.

In probing for childhood memories, I asked neutral questions, most of the time simply: "What do you remember of your early life?" or more pointedly, "How do you remember your early life?" More often than not, if anything negative was recalled, it was a fear of darkness at night, especially of getting to the toilet in the dark. To quote one young adult: "I remember one experience I was very much afraid of: when I had to go to the toilet down a long corridor which was always dark." Thus to compare bed-wetting in the kibbutz setting and ours, and to adduce from it a greater incidence of neurosis in the kibbutz, is tantamount to claiming that the same phenomenon occurring in wholly different settings is indeed the same thing, which it is not.

I have spoken before of the laissez-faire attitude toward bed-wetting in the kibbutz. Partly it is due to the fact that the ever-changing night watch does not care if the children go to the toilet or not during the night, and that even if she did care, she could not help them much because of her many other duties.

But this cannot be the whole story, since children do not become dry at night on the basis of whether or not they are taken to the toilet. The problem goes much deeper. First, night wetting (as discussed earlier) is not viewed by the kibbutz as an isolating activity or as one that gives the child too personal a sense of self-sufficiency. Therefore it is largely ignored, and from what I could learn was indeed much more widespread in the past. But if one wished to, one could rightly add: because the children were reared without any effort at training them. That is why the mere fact that children are not toilet trained at an early age cannot be used to adduce neurotic disturbance.

It took many years for parents and metapelets to realize that if one wishes a child to be toilet trained, one has to make some effort to teach him. The years of reluctance to do so were explained by the wish not to interfere with instinctual needs. While this was the consciously recognized reason, to me it was another indication of the parents' ambivalence about functioning as parents, individually. And a collective is not an agent that can effectively toilet train a child. (Toilet training in the kibbutz is generally taught by, and learned from, other children as much as from adults. Similarly, it is when the group objects that bed-wetting disappears almost immediately, excepting always a few children in whom it is a symptom of specific neurosis, just as with us.)

Bed-wetting in the kibbutz is thus due in part to the lack of effort to teach children to be dry, and for the rest to the ambivalence of parents and metapelets. As a matter of fact, parental ambivalence is so much a problem that when I spoke with one leading educator about the wetting she told me: "This is one of the problems we will have to discuss in our kibbutz. We have decided to do nothing about it until such time as we can thrash it out and know what our attitudes toward it really ought to be. In the meantime we just have to accept that we have eight out of twenty nine-year-olds who wet their beds every night." Given such ambivalence it seems miraculous that 60 per cent of the nine-year-olds do not wet at night.

Here I might digress on the strange ways in which kibbutz society uses (or misuses) psychoanalysis because it explains many seeming contradictions in their practices. Insofar as psychoanalysis is critical of middle-class Victorian repression, it is unequivocally embraced by all kibbutz movements (excluding always the very few orthodox kibbutzim), but there is little understanding of its essence. For example, when it comes to the irrational aspects of man, as opposed to the instinctual, then kibbutzniks proceed as if psychoanalysis had never been born.

That a small child prefers to eliminate where and when he chooses belongs to their acceptance of the instinctual teaching of psychoanalysis. But that an older child may continue to wet his bed because he senses that adults are ambivalent about asking him to stop, this they cannot see. (Obviously I do not speak here of the very few trained child therapists, but of the vast majority of educators and other kibbutzniks, many of whom are quite familiar with psychoanalytic writings.)

They are cognizant, for example, of Freud's ideas about the holding on to feces being related to one's holding on to money and other possessions. And if they were not, and the connection were at all valid, they would respond to it out of their unconscious, whether they also knew it consciously or not.

Since the essence of toilet training amounts to a deliberate holding on to one's excreta, and only secondarily of a letting go of them in a special place, the connection between toilet training and holding on to things is specific enough. And typically, kibbutz parents have little hesitation about telling the child where to deposit his feces—or so it seemed to me on the basis of what metapelets told me and what I observed.

Thus when a child wanted any help with going to the toilet, it was always freely given, though more often by slightly older children than by adults. What the parents seem to find hard about toilet training is telling the child to hold on.

Understandably, a society that concentrates on erasing all tendencies to hold on to things, whether to property, traditions, or children, would have great difficulty in teaching those children to hold on to anything at all. Hence their ambivalence about telling them to hold on till they get to the toilet. The wish to teach children not to hold on might even explain in part their reluctance to let infants hold on to the nipple (whether bottle or breast), just as they later do not let them hold on to toys or to the parents themselves. I might add that I did not observe a single small child holding on to, or walking around with, his baby blanket, or a similar security device, though the number of infants I observed for any length of time was small, and it may simply be chance that I did not see such behavior. When I inquired about this, I was told that some children carry a baby blanket or some other "transitional" object with them for security. But this they do most often, if at all, when visiting with their families, which suggests that these few need such a crutch to support them when they leave the security of the group. Within their group I did not once see a child of toddler or latency age depending on props of this kind, and I observed several hundred of them in several kibbutzim.

It is my conviction that kibbutz children beyond the age of three or four who remain enuretic at night (with extremely few exceptions) remain so in response to the ambivalence they sense in their parents and metapelets. As a matter of fact, where the parents were not ambivalent about it, then in all cases I could observe the child was fully toilet trained by a reasonable age, even where a metapelet was conflicted.

The unwillingness to recognize the ambivalent nature of human emotions is a pervasive problem in kibbutz child rearing. About this crucial tenet of psychoanalysis the kibbutznik has a blind spot. I could not convince any with whom I spoke that if the kibbutz has not yet decided if or how they want to influence their children's toilet habits, it betokens a deep seated ambivalence about the issue; that it pertains not just to the narrow issue of toilet training but to the basic one of whether or not to use their parental prerogative to mold their children's lives. Nor could I shake their belief that if the assembly voted to tell children to use the toilet from now on it would not legislate away the parental ambivalence; that children would keep on responding to both: the official demands and the ambivalence.

🌺 *The Casual Meal*

IN PRACTICE, HOWEVER, ALL THIS LEADS TO A SITUATION WHERE far less pressure is put on the child to achieve. There is much less pressure to be clean and neat altogether. There are few "Wash your hands!" if any, because when all children do, it requires little reminder. And while I was present at many meals in the children's houses, I did not once see a child being asked to wash his hands, nor can I recall that any did. They wash their hands when they get good and dirty, not because they are getting ready to eat.

There is no fine furniture nor any precious keepsakes to be careful about. Even their clothes belong to the kibbutz and are not their own to protect. In short, both the dos and don'ts are vastly reduced, compared to a middle-class setting. Behavior at meals in particular is most casual. And this is not just the case for toddlers or latency children.

The manners of adults in the communal dining room, as the children observe it on occasional visits, are most relaxed.

It is always noisy, with a continuous coming and going. At any given table each person eats at his own speed; no one waits till the other has finished with one course to go on to the next. Interestingly enough when the same adults have tea or snacks in their rooms, things are as "nice" as in our typical middle-class settings. Thus their behavior in the dining room speaks less of an absence of standards than a deliberate shunning of "niceties" when eating together. But when the children observe adults eating together, they see merely that mealtime is an unceremonious occasion.

This again is explained as a way to save labor. But things are never as simple as that, since the community puts a great deal of thought and work into matters they consider important. If they wanted a different kind of dining arrangement, they would create it. The dining room building, as discussed earlier, is the nerve center of the community and where the communal life unfolds. It is where the assembly meets, where work assignments are made, where the comrades get their mail and leave messages for each other, where all announcements are made, etc. Above all it is where the comrades get together around the common meal.

But then this central experience of the communal life— eating together—is one that is hurried through, the faster the better in the manner of *frère et cochon*. There is a spirit of careless fraternity about it, but it has also become something to hurry through in order to get to the nice, quiet room of one's own. Here again is the ambivalence: The one setting above all that was meant to symbolize the intimacy of all members together is the occasion most depreciated in form, and more often than not cut short in time. (Here, of course, I generalize from what is true for the majority. There are those, mainly of the founding generation, who linger around the table for long conversations, who move from table to table, chatting with the comrades, etc.)

What has happened, I believe, is that changes have taken

place, leaning away from an overstressing of communality, though the kibbutz does not wish to recognize it and hence cannot act on it yet. Once, this common eating together was a true communion. As a matter of fact, the dining hall was originally the best equipped place for adults in the kibbutz. It was a solid, well-planned building, while adults still slept under tents. Even now, as a symbol of shared memories, of the revolt against privatization, a great deal of sentimental memories are attached to the common meal.

Kibbutzniks may joke about the times when husband and wife would studiously not sit together at table (not to violate the communal spirit) and of what a foolish exaggeration it was. But emotionally they are still strongly committed to the past and feel nostalgic about it. The dining room, above all, reminds them of how bravely they once flaunted everything that smacked of respectable family life.

Somehow this dining hall, and their behavior within it, was so important to them emotionally, and as a symbol, that its character remained more or less fixed. Even when a kibbutz became more affluent and replaced the original structure by a better one, its flavor changed little. But without fully facing the fact, they now have and want both: They want their collective togetherness and a freedom from middle-class strictures, but they also yearn for relief from being always together, and this they hurry to seek in the privacy of their rooms. While the dining hall stayed more or less fixed, all change that evolved seemed devoted to the rooms, which became more and more invested with meaning and care.

But again, for the next generation, the kibbutz-born, these are just the familiar arrangements known from infancy: a hasty eating together from which one escapes to other things as fast as possible, be it to work or to play. This is the way they have eaten all their lives, have never questioned, and see no reason to question now as adults. For them, however, it is not that a relative privacy and intimacy in their rooms counterbalances a lack of them in their collective living; they neither expect it in the dining room, nor seek it in their rooms. What the room offers them is greater comfort, relaxation. It is a place where—unlike the dining room—one does not have to hurry or be with a multitude. But the absence of something does not by itself make for intimacy. There are just two ways of it all: One is simply how one eats and behaves in the dining room, the other how one acts in one's room. But for the latency child, the climate at meals is a boon.

Dinnertime is when the middle-class family comes together. But very often it is at table that the latency child is most pressured to mind his manners, to learn to eat and conduct himself by standards that to him are excessively demanding. There, he is supposed to enjoy himself and the food, though the meal is arranged to suit the convenience of adults, and their conversation takes precedence over what is interesting to him. For the kibbutz latency child, the freedom to rush through his meals with hardly a thought to polite manners makes them incomparably more relaxed than in our middle-class homes. There is no waiting, no postponing of gratification, no demand to be orderly, talk sensibly, sit quietly. All talk is on his own level. And things will continue in this fashion for the rest of his life in the kibbutz.

Comparing him once more to our middle-class latency children suggests that kibbutz children are particularly fortunate. Not so much because there is less pressure to conform, but because they are spared the underlying anxiousness of the parents that sparks the whole process of demandingness in the first place. It is not that middle-class parents exactly enjoy these daily battles, or like to impose on the child what he clearly resents. What drives them is the anxiety that they would otherwise be failing their child in his future struggle to succeed.

In most cases—barring a few overly compulsive parents, or those who act out other forms of neurosis on their child— the pressures for nice behavior, school achievement, and whatnot, have one central source: the parent's anxiety that his child will not otherwise make it in life. Such a fear does not exist in the kibbutz. Provided the child is a fairly good comrade, he will one day become a full kibbutz member whatever his manners, scholastic standing, or behavior in almost any other realm. He will fare no better and no worse in life than any other kibbutznik.

I believe it is this underlying fear and distrust that the middle-class child resents most of all. And his feelings are aggravated by his sensing that the parental demands are not meant just to teach him something, but imply doubt and anxiety about his future—which make him doubtful and anxious about himself. Worse, they imply that the parents are concerned not just for him, but for how his behavior reflects on themselves. And in our competitive society both are undoubtedly true.

In the kibbutz there can be no question of a child's behavior hurting the parents' standing in the community. The question of "what will people think if my child does poorly in school?" which inspires so much family conflict with us, hardly exists in the kibbutz, where a person is judged only on the basis of his own personal standing as a comrade.

❦ Living Quarters

DEMANDS MADE OF KIBBUTZ CHILDREN ARE FEW FOR STILL another reason: The sleeping rooms in the children's houses are virtually barren. Indeed this is so much so, that one cannot help wondering about it. When I inquired, the response was that there was no particular reason; "that's just the way the rooms are." The children spend hardly any time in the bedrooms, I was told; they play outdoors or in the common room, which is also their dining room. Actually, it is the kindergarten classroom that doubles most as a playroom, and this is always the biggest and most important room in the house.

The simple but very attractive way in which these two common rooms (dining room and classroom) are decorated contrasts starkly with the empty walls and barren furnishings of the sleeping quarters. (It is also in striking contrast to adult living arrangements, where things are just the other way around.) Essentially the children's bedrooms contain nothing but the beds and an occasional chair, if that, with perhaps a little shelf. There are almost no pictures on the walls, and if so, they are small and haphazardly placed.

The opposite is true of the children's classroom and to a lesser extent of their dining room, where there are many and well-chosen pictures on the walls, shelves with toys, attractive furniture, etc. Again things are just the reverse of what is true for adults. Stress is on what all children share, with a deliberate neglect of the personal, not to speak of the private.

The common rooms, unlike the children's bedrooms, are cared for by the metapelets, and entail no demands on the child. So, from infancy on, he is expected to learn that in space and furnishings very little is really his own. While we as adults would find such rooms empty and cold, they do not necessarily look so to the latency child. What may count for much more to him is their undemandingness. If there is little that is private, there is nothing he is bound to take care of.

And it is true that the nicely furnished room means less to the latency child and more to his parents as an expression of their taste, if not also their affluence. Certainly the latency child responds unconsciously to how his room is arranged. But consciously he is much more attached to his toys than to his pictures or his furniture. Much of the taste reflected in the room of the middle-class latency child is taste imposed on him. But so is the barrenness of the children's rooms in the kibbutz.

I have little doubt that most latency children would prefer a barren room to their nice rooms if it meant having to keep them looking nice. Or perhaps I should say, they would prefer a nice room if they could keep it cluttered with their clothing and toys, which to them makes for a most lovely mess; they are distressed by it only if they cannot find what they are looking for. Neither our nice middle-class children's rooms, nor the barren ones of the kibbutz reflect the latency child's own way of arranging his living space. Each is a parental effort at molding the child: in our society toward valuing private possessions; in the kibbutz toward a neglect of the private possession.

This I verified later, when I investigated whether the barrenness of the children's rooms had indeed simply come about by chance. I was speaking with a young kindergarten teacher who at that time was living in the kibbutz not out of conviction but because it was the only way she could support herself and her two small children as a divorcée. For this opportunity she was full of praise for the kibbutz. But at one point she remarked spontaneously that it was too bad the bedrooms were not cared for too nicely.

I asked her why, then, she didn't do something to cheer them up, and she said, "They don't allow parents to bring anything into the children's houses. When I tried to bring a picture for my children's rooms, there was a big affair. They don't want the children to have anything private. They worry what will the other children say." So I wondered (if this was the reason) why the children could not hang up their own drawings. "This they permit only in the dining room," she told me. "There were children in my group who occasionally asked me to put some drawing on the wall over their bed, and I tried it sometimes. But I had so much fear of losing my place in the kibbutz, that I stopped doing it."

I told her that most parents I had interviewed seemed to want the very best for their children, and it should therefore be possible to get their help. Why, I wondered, did more than two hundred parents allow their children's rooms to be treated with so little love? And she said: "I asked this question myself, and I still can't understand it. I guess nobody in the kibbutz has the courage to do it."

But this is not so; they are not afraid. The fact is that however badly they feel about the child's hardships, and however much they love their children, on balance they love even better the arrangements that free them of the day-long minutiae of child care. Likewise, however difficult the parent-metapelet relation may be (and it *is* difficult, as I shall later discuss), most metapelets are devoted to the children in their care and do a good job; but decorating the children's rooms is not part of it.

By contrast, most parents have fixed a corner of their room for their children which is arranged as nicely as they can afford, and to which great care is devoted. When this is discussed with them, they are quite conscious of wanting to make this corner as attractive as they can, because they want it to be nice for their children. When I queried why, then, they don't also want to make it as nice for their child in his own room, I met with a blank; or else, "the metapelet wouldn't like it," or "that's how it's planned for the children by the community; we don't want our children too involved with private possessions," etc., all of it directly contradicting what they do with the children's corner in *their* room.

As one might imagine, the reasons are complex. Certainly the parents do not want the children to learn to like private property. And certainly there is something to be said for having the rooms of preschool and primary school children uncluttered. But maybe the children's bedrooms symbolize the attitudes that still pervade the adult dining hall arrangements, while the children's corner is part of the trend toward putting more care into the rooms.

As implied earlier, kibbutzniks are aware of these contradictory pulls but not enough to act on them yet. There is presently a very strong feeling among them that all too much attention is being paid to having nice rooms, to the detriment of their communal gatherings in the dining room. Almost every kibbutznik was quite outspoken about this: As much as he liked having a nice room, it must not interfere with collective living. But most kibbutzniks fear that it does. And this ambivalence they fight through their children— another reason to try to prevent the child from getting too attached to the more private sleeping room (typically four to a room) and to try to make his common room the one he prefers. (Interestingly enough, when the children become full kibbutz members and have a little room to themselves, most rooms I saw showed great loving care in making this, the private sphere, as nice as possible.)

What counts too, I believe, is the metapelet's ambivalence about her own dual role as mother and metapelet. Like all other parents she wants her child to find her room more attractive than his place in the children's house. If his place there is too attractive, what will her room have to offer? Thus she is in a double bind: As a metapelet she should make the children's house attractive, but she should also not encroach on the attractiveness of the parents' room. As a mother she does not want her child's metapelet to lessen the appeal of her room for her child. In their combination these mutually supporting and contradictory desires stymie action, and the simplest way out is to do nothing.

Once again the kibbutz—which intends only to avoid teaching children to like private property—is powerfully supported by personal desires and conflicts. But once again life is simplified for the child.

❦ A Freedom to Roam

WHAT ABOUT OTHER LEARNING OR DEVELOPMENTAL TASKS OF the latency-age child? I refer to the mastering of motor skills, of language and thought, of his learning to understand the world around him. There is also the task of resolving the oedipal conflict. And finally, when that is achieved, what of his moving out from the immediate family toward wider social relations (becoming a kindergartner and then a school child)?

With respect to motor skills, the warm climate over much of the year makes for uninterrupted indoor-outdoor living, coops the children up much less than are most children in American cities, and enables the child to roam much more freely. There is little anxiety at his moving about. There are no strangers, and hence no fear of them. (Neither does he acquire any tools for dealing with strangers, which is a serious problem in adolescence. But at this age life is simpler in the absence of strangers.) Everyone the child meets is a friendly kibbutznik, which makes this a friendly world

There are no streets and no traffic in the living area, hence the child's freedom is not constrained by any fear of cars. There are no hot stoves that are not to be touched. With most houses one story high there are no windows to fall out of. Little that is dangerous can happen: There are no cliffs to fall over, and in most kibbutzim that I visited, no lakes close enough to fall into.

Almost every advance the child makes in mastering his

body and the external world reaps him further benefits and leads to no new constraints. Typically, when the middle-class child strikes out more on his own, as in learning to ride a bike, the parents worry about the new dangers entailed, and implant parallel worries in the child. Many steps that should add to feelings of competence are hence offset by new fears. All this is happily avoided in the kibbutz, as it once was in our small rural communities.

An eternal argument that plagues middle-class parent-child relationships: "How come I can't do (or have) it, when Johnny next door can?" rubs in the youngster's dependence and aggravates competition and jealousy. This does not exist in the kibbutz, where there are no playmates whose parents do (or own) things differently. The likeness of life for one and all, which may later be oppressive to some adolescents, is at this age pure blessing. The latency child wishes to be like all others, and in the kibbutz he has his wish.

Jealousy, which at this age centers so often around toys, is vastly reduced, since possessions in the children's house are communal. Some problems arise over toys kept by the parents in their rooms; there is some boasting about them, some jealousy. In this sense, time spent by the latency child with his parents is colored by the fact that there he does have his very own toys. Certainly it makes these hours special. But it also makes them unreal, compared with the rest of his day, because the time spent there is quite restricted. So, while the problem of jealousy exists, it is much smaller than with us.

Language development is fostered because the child is never at a loss for someone to talk to. I have referred to the advantages of being always free to engage in a collective monologue. The children chatter to each other continuously, are silent only when a story is being read or when they are napping or asleep. The scarcity of solitude, which will trouble them in adolescence, is no problem to children of this age who crave company and who, in their vast majority, shun solitude. (The extremely sensitive child may begin to suffer from the absence of privacy and solitude toward the end of the latency period. But for most of this age period it is not yet a problem.)

The often unbearable bone of contention between middle-class mother and child over "pick up your room," "hang up your clothes," "put on your boots," etc., hardly ever appears in the kibbutz. There are no rooms to be picked up, few outer clothes to put away, little need for boots or outer clothing. Again, if they must be put on, all other children are doing it too, which makes things much easier. And if the child neglects to, and the others are critical of him, their criticism, while it carries real weight, does not threaten or deflate. It comes from equals he can talk back to, as he cannot to his parents, or at least not as to an equal.

Another thing resented by the middle-class child is the being turned down when he wants the parent's company, because the parent is occupied and tells him, "I'm busy cooking"; or simply "leave me alone" or "don't bother me now." Conversely, demands are made on the child to run an errand or to fetch something, though it interferes with his pursuits of the moment. The impression given is that "It's all right with mommy to interrupt what I'm doing, but it's not all right if I interrupt her." There is none of this in the kibbutz. The child does not lack for companionship because he is always in the company of others; nor is he interrupted in his doings, because there is less that needs doing "around the house" in the kibbutz, where no cooking is done in the rooms, etc.

Not to give a false picture, I should say that, from an early age on, the children do have certain important things to do in their houses, such as taking care of their chickens or other animals, tending their vegetable gardens, setting the table, etc. But these are not chores done at parental request. Nor are they done in the parents' house, but in one's own. In doing them the children are not someone's little helper, nor are they being interrupted from important childhood activities they would rather engage in; they are going about the business of their very own lives.

The unfortunate feeling of many a middle-class child that his parents take his activities to be less important than theirs does not exist in the kibbutz. All things encourage the latency child's conviction that his way of life is as important and legitimate as that of other age groups, including adults.

To the middle-class child it is oppressive that so much of the important adult world is either beyond his comprehension or is consciously hidden from his view. But for the kibbutz child, if his parents keep their private affairs hidden, he does not know it, and even if he does know, or guesses, it carries less weight, because he has so much of a life of his own. If he suffers from having only limited access to his parents, or because his life is not so closely interwoven with theirs, I believe this is more than balanced by the fact that kibbutz parents cannot at every moment pry into the child's life with their questions of "What are you doing?" and "What for?"

It is this having to be ready at any moment to give account of one's doings to some superior person that keeps the middle-class latency child so dependent and resentful. This will show up just a very few years later in his defiant answer to the question "Where were you?" with the shortest possible "Out." The kibbutz child is safe from the prying of parents. For one thing they are simply not around for more than a brief predictable period. For another thing, they have no say over what he may do or not do for most of his day.

Secure within his own sphere of life, his is also an easy

world to grasp. Most of the community's work is devoted to the raising of food. As an economic activity this is eminently plain to the latency child, both as to the work it entails, and why needed and by whom. So is the preparation of food in the communal kitchen, the proceedings in the laundry, the building of houses, shoes, furniture. And while most older and larger kibbutzim now include some small industrial plant, these are comprehensible ventures such as woodworking plants, plastic factories or a small tool-making factory.

The child can watch the productive process from beginning to end and can understand and follow most of what is involved. Some are even suitable for the child (and later the adolescent) to take part in. For example, one kibbutz I visited got its main cash income from a "resthouse." This is a small resort hotel, where kibbutzniks or members of labor unions are sent for their paid vacations.

Much of the teaching is centered around these activities, and there are many visits to the work places of parents— both the parents of the child, and those many others who are parents by proxy. Since theirs is not a society geared to production for personal profit, all work is interrupted to explain it to the children when they come, and to give them a chance to try their hand. It is delightful to see how even the most important work tasks are interrupted while interest centers on explaining things to the children—always with pride, because "this is our kibbutz" and "we made it all ourselves." Everybody extends himself to the children in a situation that requires no intimacy with the individual child.

The raising of animals (cattle, sheep, chickens) is economically important to the kibbutz, often second only to the raising of crops. Even toddlers raise some animals at the children's house. Soon they also cultivate their own farms. Thus virtually all spheres of adult life are not only within the child's grasp, but from quite an early age he spends part of his day on exactly the same activities adults perform. Either he does similar things on a smaller scale, or has a try at the real thing when he visits adults at their work. Psychologically, too, these are well within his grasp, while only rarely does an urban child understand the how and why of his parents' economic and social occupations. The feeling that one understands all the things that count in one's world enhances beyond measure the feeling of competence, of security and well-being.

For the child one of the few drawbacks of having his life proceed so close to the world of his parents is having a mother who works as a metapelet. Usually great pains are taken to avoid assigning a metapelet to a group that contains her own child. But this does not stop the child from being keenly aware that his own mother devotes her work-a-day care to other children, and from finding it painful.

Sometimes this leads to serious complications, as in the following account by a metapelet: "I worked for three and a half years with a group very near my son's age. At that time my husband was away from the kibbutz most of the time, which made things harder on my boy. I worked near enough for him to hear my voice all day long as I worked with these other children. He tried to come visit me, but this didn't work out because he was very possessive of me. He wouldn't just come to visit, but would come with rocks in his hands and throw them at the children I was working with."

Things are not good for such a mother and child. They are even worse for the metapelet who, while at work in her children's house, can hear her own child crying in the next one but does not know what goes on and cannot leave to find out. Nevertheless, while a closeness to the parents' work world has its drawbacks, on balance I believe the advantages outweigh them.

Oedipal Relations

ANOTHER CONFLICT THAT BESETS OUR CHILDREN AT THE END of the oedipal period is spared the kibbutz child who has been part of a community from the start. He does not have to fight the ambivalent struggle about wishing to hold onto the parent, and wishing also to reach out to the larger world. The kibbutz child could never get that hold on his parent of either sex, nor his parents on him, which creates the deep oedipal involvement of our middle-class children.

The sexual attraction between parent and child—because it is that part of the oedipal relationship that shocks the conscious mind in our society—has become the center of our discussions about this conflict. But there is much more to the oedipal relationship than sexual attraction.

What provokes it is how all-important are the parents. And they are so all-important because the child's very existence depends on them. They are sexually so important because they are so important in general and not the other way round, as may be typical for adults where the over-all importance of the partner often derives from his sexual importance.

That is, the less the parent is the giver (or withholder) of all things, the less is he the only one who stimulates the senses and colors all experience (including the sexual ones). And the more it happens that others too become important to the child, the less will be his sexual desire for the parent. But the oedipal situation centers chiefly around the mother. The father enters only secondarily, as a rival for the mother. Hence the oedipal situation will be radically altered if the mother's role in the life of her infant is radically different from what is typical in our middle-class settings.

Above all there is the child's wish to have sole possession

of the loved person. Indeed, the root of the oedipal conflict is that this wish for exclusive possession is thwarted. But in the kibbutz all exclusive possessing is shunned. From an early age on, the kibbutz child learns that neither he nor his parents belong solely to another person. Exclusive belonging, one to another, is never part of the kibbutz child's experience.

It may well be that in our middle-class setting the very wish to possess the parent has already been shaped by other acquaintance with having and owning what never leaves one (the child's bottle, his blanket, his bed). Most of all the child hears in the feeling tone of the parent that to possess things privately is desirable.

To the kibbutz infant, by contrast, it soon becomes obvious that he cannot possess his metapelet, who has many other duties and several other children to care for. In our families, too, if there are siblings, the infant soon realizes that his mother takes care of them also. But except for twins, these others are older children who neither get nor require infantile care. The kibbutz infant sees other babies getting exactly the same baby care that he does, which makes it impossible for him to believe that baby care, and all the special attention that goes with it, is something the mothering person gives exclusively to him and no one else.

Neither can the kibbutz child come to think he possesses his parents, since his access to them is so restricted. And he cannot possess a friend, because the group will not stand for it, and the metapelet will try to break up the twosome, as I shall later discuss. Even his parents do not belong to each other exclusively. That they also belong to the community looms much larger in their minds and their lives than does any such awareness in our middle-class parents.

While marriage is now important in the kibbutz, this is rather recent. In the early days marriage was a grudging concession to the mores of Israel. Husband and wife would deliberately address each other by their surname, as they did all other kibbutzniks. Like their not sitting together in the dining hall, this was external, but it reflected an attitude. Marriage and the twosome it creates was not to interfere with the communal ties. This has changed. But while the externals are gone, the attitude lingers.

As a matter of fact there are other conditions that once made for the classic oedipal conflict but no longer exist in quite a few middle-class families. To cite an example: Once, the mother stayed at home all day and gave her undivided attention to her child (or so the classical example assumes, though reality was always quite different) while the father was gone. Then, when the father came home, he got the mother's full attention which was suddenly withdrawn from the child. The father must indeed have seemed an intruder then, who robbed the child of the mother's affection. But what about when both parents work and get home at about the same time every night? Can the father still be viewed as robbing his child of what he enjoyed more exclusively till then?

Much more important are those differences discussed in preceding chapters. To review them, in Spiro's words:

> The parents have little responsibility for the physical care or for the socialization of their children; the relationship between mates does not include economic cooperation; and parents and children do not share a common residence. Taking these facts, alone, into consideration, it may be concluded that the family, as characterized by Murdock, does not exist in the kibbutz . . . in a structural-functional sense, [but] it does exist in a psychological sense.

Unfortunately no one, to my knowledge, has analyzed the extent to which the oedipal conflict is predicated on the existence of the family in the structural-functional sense, and how much it derives only from what the young child would feel even if he were no longer dependent on the parents for meeting all or most of his needs. My hunch is that the oedipal situation as we know it has a great deal to do with the fact that the family in our setting is not just a psychological entity but also a structural-functional one.

It is the economic and social dependency of the child, and the mutual emotions that arise between parents and child through their intimate living together, that makes for the oedipal situation, and not the biological fact of parenthood. After all, there is good reason to believe that the origin of the family lies in the human infant's need for protection. But with survival assured by the kibbutz, it is hard to imagine an oedipal conflict that is played out around the hundred or so adults who enable the child to survive.

Parents are still important in the kibbutz: the mother because she nurses the baby, both parents because of the emotions that flow from them to the child. But with many other parental functions removed, all the feelings that center around them are proportionately milder. So while there are clearly oedipal involvements in the kibbutz, they are much lower in intensity and have a different content. Similarly, while there is some sibling rivalry, it is much less intense than is typical in our families. The main cause of sibling rivalry is the wish for exclusive possession of the parent. If no sibling expects such a thing because (as discussed earlier) the experience of exclusive possession was never part of his experience, then whatever rivalry exists between siblings is much more muted.

Oedipal involvements are particularly reduced between parents born and raised in the kibbutz and their children, as compared to those between parents raised elsewhere and the children they bore and raised in the kibbutz. In this, as in many other respects, things are very different for the first than for the second (or kibbutz-born) generation. Because the first generation, despite their conscious desire to do otherwise, cannot help repeating with their children some of what they experienced in their own infancy and childhood. Though they invest less heavily in their children, they expect an even greater emotional reward.

As they see it, their children, free of economic indebtedness to parents, should give even more freely of their positive emotions. This, the parental expectation of a deep and purely positive attachment makes for some oedipal (and other) difficulties. But the children still enjoy a childhood relatively free of deep oedipal conflicts. And by the time they reach adulthood there is no scarring to intrude on their relationships to *their* children.

Here, then, in the third generation, kibbutz theory seems to become valid: kibbutz child rearing, while not entirely doing away with oedipal problems, has significantly reduced them. Or so it seems, because few children of the third generation have yet grown to adulthood, and the few I met are too small a group to permit valid generalizations. If true, it is yet another reason why life in the kibbutz is such a sunny one for the toddler and latency child.

Later on it will make a difference that the child escaped deep oedipal involvement and the task of wresting free of it in a frightful battle with his emotions. This will be felt in adolescence and later in adulthood by those few who will strive—often vainly—to find themselves as unique persons. Let me use only one factor that makes for the difference.

❧ Empathy and the Introject

ACCORDING TO PSYCHOANALYTIC THEORY AND OBSERVATIONS, it is the felt (or feared) loss of important persons on whom one is wholly dependent that leads to the process of introjection[1] so that never again will one be left all alone and helpless. In order to fear the loss of a person in this sense, one must first have felt one possessed him—or what for the very young child is often the same: to have felt oneself in his possession. To possess and be possessed are to the very young almost synonymous. And should great imbalance occur here, it is likely to have severe pathological consequences. If, for example, the child feels that he is possessed by his parent without his also possessing the parent, it may lead to the kind of personality deviation described in *The Empty Fortress* (Bettelheim, 1967).

No such imbalance appears in the kibbutz, since the kibbutz child learns very soon that he is neither in any person's possession, nor does he possess any person. He is taken care of; he is always with others; but he does not really belong exclusively to any particular person, nor do his parents belong exclusively to him.

In the absence of such mutual belonging, in the deepest sense, there is considerably less feeling of loss. The child's always being cared for rather well and in much the same way, whether a particular person is present or absent, adds up to a situation where the loss of a particular person is felt much less deeply. At the same time, the omnipresence of caretakers (including all kibbutzniks) and the peer group, goes a long way to compensate immediately if a given person leaves.

I had no firsthand experience with children who lost par-

---

[1] Introjection, or the introject, is a somewhat technical term. According to the *Psychiatric Dictionary* (1940) to introject means "to withdraw psychic energy (libido) from an object and to direct it upon the mental image of the object." This happens "when an individual incorporates into his ego system the picture of an object as he conceives the object to be. Libido is then transferred from the object in the environment to the mental picture of the object."

ents through death, but I talked with kibbutzniks about it, and the impression given me universally was that the entire kibbutz extends itself to such a child. This surely makes it easier to accommodate to the loss—which may not have been too intense because of the more tenuous relationship to the parent, and because the death evoked no anxiety in the child about who would take care of him thereafter.

All this protects him against a loss felt so deeply that he has to undo it by introjecting. But in a strange way these introjects are what later endow the child in our culture with both a deep empathy for others (because he carries some other person within him), and a capacity for living independently (because with introjects to keep him company, independence is never again a being wholly alone).

If my speculation is valid, then it becomes understandable why the kibbutz-reared youngster seems unable to project himself into the feelings or deeply personal experiences of others—always excepting the peer group, since they are essentially alter egos. Of course, alter egos, too, protect us from feeling alone; but if they have not been made introjects because there was no fear of their possible leaving, then their physical presence is required to keep us from feeling all alone. This is quite different from the introject who is unlike the self but has become deeply our own. With him we can have inner talks of great richness.

It is doubtful that introjection can occur in normal persons much later than the beginning of the latency period, and certainly not unless it began in or before the oedipal period. I believe it is the kibbutz child's failure to introject his parents that explains much of his personality. And I refer here to an observation that made a deep impression on me: the difficulty or frank inability of kibbutz-born and raised youngsters to comprehend (much less respond to) a hypothetical question, when to answer it would have required them to step outside their own frame of reference.

Most middle-class children have to step outside themselves in order to deal with the problem of how one parent or the other would react to something, not to speak of brothers and sisters. From an early age, too, they are faced with the different social roles of boys and girls, which raises the problem: What would it be like to belong to the other sex? This is a hypothetical question, the raising of which makes a vast difference in our way of understanding the world. At a later age it is much reinforced by the question: What would I (or my life) be like if I'd been born of a different social class, of a different religion, or color?

Life is much more of a piece in the kibbutz than with us. Social differences between the sexes are greatly minimized. There are no social classes, no economic or religious differences, and the parents are in deep agreement on most issues. There are no religious differences between the parents, for example, nor about who earns the livelihood and who does not. Withal there is much less reason to wonder about life "if I'd been born different."

I asked repeatedly of second and third generation kibbutzniks, "How do you think you'd have felt about kibbutz life if you'd been born and raised in the city?" In the vast majority of cases the answer was "I'd be exactly the same and hold exactly the same viewpoints I hold now, because they're the right ones." And in a minority of cases: "I wasn't raised there, so I can't answer that." Not once did I get the answer: "Then I'd probably look at things very differently." To move outside the self and take a look at it was not a stance common to these youngsters.

While this was most marked in regard to hypothetical questions involving their own persons, it was almost as marked in less personal matters. Practically all questions I asked that took the form of: "What if things had been different?" brought the reply, "But they're not different, so what's the use of talking about it?" And talk about it they would not, much as I encouraged them to try.

I should say that this is true only for questions involving themselves as kibbutzniks, or some kibbutz arrangement, where pondering a hypothetical question might have brought them in conflict with group values. Being intelligent and well educated, they are well able to deal with hypothetical questions of considerable complexity, such as "How would kibbutz life and economy differ if industries were to be added to its basically agricultural economy?" But while they can very well conceive of things being different, what they cannot conceive is that they themselves would therefore be different, would think and act differently.

It could be argued that this comes of living in a community of "true believers," where all the existential questions have only one familiar answer. But I think the reasons for it go deeper—namely that these youngsters have not introjected persons with whom they hold inner conversations, talks that require them to recognize the introject's viewpoint and their own at the same time. I have mentioned the toddler's advantage in being free to engage in a nearly continuous "collective monologue" with his age-mates. This too has its price: There is no need and no place left for carrying on much of an internal, private monologue (or dialogue) within oneself. And since there is so much less explaining, correction, interruption by adults to be listened to, or to have to comprehend, there is also less doubt about the validity of what one says. Hence the greater inner security, but also, later on, the only limited ability to accept any viewpoint as valid but one's own, which means a limited capacity to deal with hypothetical questions that put in question one's own values or way of life. Not for kibbutz children to wonder "what I'll be doing when I'm grown up." When they grow up they will be kibbutzniks, good comrades in a cohesive group just as they are now, whatever their age. The difference will not be a different outlook or way of life or a different sense of responsibility, but only that they will wield a heavier or more complex tool, will work longer hours. Otherwise life will be just as they know it.

On the positive side, all feelings of exclusive or private owning are replaced in the kibbutz by feelings of belonging. The parent belongs to his group of comrades, though he does not feel he is owned by them or owns them. This is very much in line with how *A Dictionary of Contemporary American Usage* describes the sense of belonging as one "of having a rightful place."

Not so long ago, in the Western world too, each family member had his own rightful place—witness the specific place of the husband as husband, and the father as father, of the wife, of the mother, of the oldest son, etc. These have largely been obliterated. The result is a great deal of uncertainty about what is the rightful place of each family member in relation to the others. For example, the father is no longer to exact obedience from his son, but the son is still expected to be more or less obedient, at least up to a certain age. But nobody is sure what exactly this age limit is, and why it is set there. No longer is there a meaningful coming of age that frees the son of obedience; no special ceremony that changes the squire to a knight.

For the kibbutz child or adult there is no such insecurity about their relations to each other. Each has a place that belongs rightfully to him. And precisely because, as a youngster, he owns nothing, and in adulthood so very little, his sense of belonging to the group is sharply heightened. Exactly because the kibbutz youngster cannot fall back on other things that are his (his own room, his records, his books), the prospect of being excluded by the group is a devastating one. Without his rightful place there, nothing is left.

Conversely, being sure of one's place might explain another striking contrast to what is typical in our society, and why kibbutz childhood is such a happy age. Not once did I observe any physical fighting among kibbutz children. Not once—beyond the age when they push each other down in the playpen—did I see a child pushing another, not to mention hitting with hand or object. This does not occur in the kibbutz. I asked about it repeatedly, and the answer was always the same; while there are disagreements, they never go beyond verbal expression. There are no fights about things like who comes first, or who sits where. Compared with the frequent fighting that seems typical in our society among pre-school and grammar-school children, life in the kibbutz at this age is peaceful indeed.

Of course, it helps that there are no possessions to fight over and no social distinctions. But much of the fighting at this age in our society originates in the child's feeling that he has no place that is rightfully his. He must fight first to assert it and then to maintain it—whether the unending fight explodes in physical violence, or is carried on in more hidden form.

❦ Retreat from Power

AT THE SAME TIME, AND THOUGH BORN AND RAISED IN A SET-ting that has shifted the sense of belonging from family to collective, children of the second generation feel strongly that parents should exercise their prerogative to arrange and to influence their children's lives, and resent it deeply when their parents do not.

One kibbutz-raised young adult, because of her training as a social worker and her own psychoanalysis, was better able to put in words what had hurt her so deeply as a child. She expressed a resentment that I found to be typical for kibbutz children: They feel that the arrangement of their lives forces them to view their parents as theoretically all-good but helpless, and the metapelets as quite bad but very powerful. Within their own sphere, her parents never pressured her to do things she didn't like. But when she complained to them about demands by the metapelet that she felt were unbearable, her parents took no stand. They never said what they thought, but simply told her she had to obey the metapelets.

In her case, as in most others I could observe, the parents' loving attitudes were vitiated by their failure to protect the child against the outside—in this case the metapelet's demands.[2] Here again the question arises of what it does to the oedipal conflict if the parent is not the child's prime protector.

The Freudian discussion of the oedipal situation takes this protector role of the parent so much for granted as to hardly take note of it. But one may doubt whether a deep oedipal conflict can develop and be resolved around a parent who intends only good but shuns his personal respon-

---

[2] I vividly recall the story told by a prominent Negro educator of how all the deep positive emotions lavished on him by his minister-father became false in a moment, when, in boyhood, he was violently abused in words by a white man for a minor transgression. It was because his father, whom he had looked to for protection, had obsequiously joined in condemning the boy (and probably wisely, as he now knew, given race relations then, in the deep South). Not only did the security based on his father's love collapse on the spot, but from then on all further love he got was experienced as meaningless and shallow. While still pleasurable, it implied no security. This was not because his father had joined in the scolding. It would never have mattered if his father had really disapproved. Security broke down because the boy knew that essentially the father had approved the son's action but had turned against him at society's demand.

sibility where it counts. In the end he is felt to be no good as a parent, at least insofar as the essential parental function lies in protecting the child. And the proof that he is a good parent rests not with what he says or even feels, but with what he does. A parent who is well intentioned but unable or unwilling to act on it appears less of a parent without making the kibbutz more of one.

Here I should add that things have become a bit better in the kibbutz, or a bit harder depending on what one considers desirable. While power relations, and the respective roles of metapelet and parent have not changed, parents are readier now to tell their children if they do not like what the metapelet is doing, though the metapelet still has the last word. Before this, the parent had solely good intentions, but supported the bad metapelet. Now the parent still seems only well intentioned and has even stopped supporting the bad metapelet, but still does not act.

While the parent now seems more reasonable and more human, he appears even weaker than before. As I was told by the social worker just quoted: "Most mothers in the world would agree that work is indeed hard, when their children complain [in this case, about work on the children's farm]. My mother did not. Instead she always said 'Work is good. You must do it even if you feel you can't because all the other children do it.' Now kibbutz mothers tell their children, when they complain, that work is indeed hard, but they must nevertheless do it."

To my informant, this seemed like a great improvement. But though the change makes for a bit more pronounced oedipal problems, there is still nothing like the severity of ours. The powerful and demanding figure of the metapelet still detracts from the oedipal involvement with the parent, while the parent's loving influence prevents something akin to an oedipal conflict from developing around the metapelet.

With this in mind, a few examples may illustrate how much more diffuse things are for the kibbutz child, how the interplay between metapelet and mother prevents either one from playing so central a role in the child's life as to project him into deep oedipal conflict. But in reading these examples it must always be borne in mind that the peer group plays an enormously more important role and thus further dilutes the oedipal conflicts.

🌺 *King Solomon's Judgment*

LET ME FIRST SAY THAT WITH ALL THE DIFFERENCES BETWEEN kibbutz child rearing and ours, there are some relevant parallels. An obvious one is that if parents (especially the mother) and metapelet are in emotional accord about the child, then a happy situation exists. Its parallel in our families is where father and mother are in emotional accord about each other and about their relationships to the child. The same parallel holds when there is discord. Unfortunately the relations between mother and metapelet are more likely to be difficult than not.

Typical of their conflicts is that the mother wants the metapelet to raise her child, but doubts that the metapelet does it well enough. But she is also afraid her child may get too attached to the metapelet and lose interest in her. The metapelet (because she is usually a mother, or knows she soon will be) is often conflicted herself. She wants to be important to the child in her care, wants him to love her, but does not want to take his love away from the mother. Hence she must keep her emotional distance from the child. But the child feels both: the metapelet's reserve, and her wish for emotional closeness.

To complicate matters, the metapelet is often convinced, out of what she considers her professional knowledge or detachment, that the mother does not raise her child right and that she (the metapelet) not only does it much better, but must undo what damage the mother has done. Here again we have a situation very like what happens with us when parents disagree, or in more muted form, when parent and grandparent (or parent and teacher) are at odds about a child.

These conflicts may start at the very beginning of the child's life and of the parent-metapelet relation. One mother described such an instance vividly: "When my first child was born, there was some sickness in the infants' house, so when I came home from the hospital, I kept my child with me. During these two weeks I became very attached to my baby, and when the time came for him to go to the infants' house, I felt terrible. The infant nurse at the time was a very domineering person. One morning, as I remember, she stamped into our room at 6 A.M. (when work begins in these farming communities). She wore heavy boots and made a lot of noise. She came in like a policeman, took the child, and went away. I cried for a week; I was very unhappy. I used to run to the infants' house as often as I could to see if the child was all right. At the time I wasn't allowed to enter when I wanted; I had to try to look through the window. But when I saw he was all right, wasn't sick, developed nicely, I got used to it."

This, from a mother who was herself a kindergarten teacher, and a leading educator in her kibbutz. By the time her second child arrived, she had made her peace with the system. "This nurse was a very nice person. With him [the second child] I was much more at rest when he was a baby. Of course, by then I was older, much more mature."

It is the age-old story of King Solomon's judgment. Whatever the first nurse was actually like, to the mother she seemed an enemy—not a concerned caretaker, who may have felt awkward about taking the baby away and was trying to get it over quickly but was doing what she felt was best for the baby.

The mother wanted to keep her baby with her, tugged at him (by running to the infants' house, looking in, worrying how well he was doing), and so did the nurse who probably felt she knew what was best for kibbutz babies. As in the old tale, the true mother soon surrenders the baby so that he won't be torn apart. By the time the second one arrives she knows she must not even try ("I was much more mature"), and indeed things turned out better for this second child.

I had occasion to study both children, the older one fully grown by now but somewhat the worse for the battle that once raged over him; the second one, much better adjusted to kibbutz life. Interestingly enough, both parents are leaders in the fight to have small children sleep in the parents' room, though both are otherwise in full accord with the rest of kibbutz education. Those first two weeks together as a threesome in their room apparently made a difference to them for the rest of their lives.

As my informant's example suggests, the good mother is often the one who gives way to the metapelet for the sake of her child but feels guilty about it. At the same time she feels obliged to the metapelet who enables her to live a full life in the collective. Since the metapelet is only doing, in effect, what she asks of her, she cannot be too critical. This further explains why a bad metapelet may be retained, and there are some metapelets who do a bad job.

Maybe the worst example I encountered will illustrate the bind a good kibbutznik can find himself in, who also wishes to be a good parent. I had asked a mother if she had ever been critical of her children's metapelets, and she said: "To be honest, yes, quite a bit. My first daughter had a metapelet from the age of two to five who was entirely unsuited for this type of work."

I remarked that three years was a very long stretch in the life of a young child, and wondered how come the kibbutz, which knew of this person's shortcomings, let her continue for so long. She told me, "This is a difficult question. There are two reasons: The first is the conviction that if a comrade feels she's doing a good job, one simply cannot tell her, 'You're no good in your work.' So it often happens that the kibbutz has no choice. They simply cannot so easily replace a comrade, and what's the guarantee that the replacement would be any better?

"Now if a parent knows (as I did) that this metapelet is bad for my child, you're in a great dilemma. You know that this metapelet is bad, not only for your child but for some twenty or thirty other children. But you are also devoted to the general idea of the kibbutz. If you make too much of a fuss, or too openly, there might be a scandal. Feelings might be hurt for life. A family might even leave the kibbutz. Or you will upset parents who would otherwise not be upset. You destroy their contentment in life. Therefore you often have to keep quiet out of consideration for the common good."

Most often, in such cases, the child's interests are sacrificed to the collective well-being. But of this we should not be too critical, since it is true of any educational system that a few children will suffer personal hardship because of measures that seem justified by the general good.

Parents fear censorship for other reasons too, should they differ too strongly with the metapelet. Another mother relates: "My child was to get orthodontic care, but the dentist kept her waiting for her braces. One day she came to our room and said, 'Another girl has braces already because her mother said she wanted her to have them.' And I just feel in this one sentence she blamed me, that I didn't fight for her getting braces. You see, the parents aren't supposed to do that; only the metapelet. Maybe I was too much conscious of my duties as a kibbutz mother; I always went by what parents are supposed to be like. And sometimes I had the feeling that I didn't fight for my child's getting something when maybe I should have, even if it went against the metapelet or the system."

Now I believe the children are aware of how terribly they burden their parents by bringing them their central emotional problems—and I mean the problems they have with the peer group and metapelets. So they protect the parents by suppressing their own feelings. Time spent with parents is supposed to be enjoyable, even instructive, but certainly not burdened by heavy emotional problems—especially ones that throw the parents in conflict with their comrades. For example, one young girl received a bathing suit as a present from her grandparents outside the kibbutz, but she also wanted to get the one allotted each child by the kibbutz store.

As the father told the story: "My wife said, 'But you have the one you got as a present,' and our girl said, 'Yes, but I want another one, because some of the girls have two bathing suits; one they got privately.' Her mother said: 'But you know that if you want one from the kibbutz clothing supply, then you give back the one you don't want, and then you'll get another one.' But our girl insisted, 'No, I want to have two.' So my wife told her, 'I don't think it's right, but I'm going to talk to the metapelet and see if other children do that.' Our daughter objected very much and said, 'I don't want you to go and talk about it, but I want two bathing suits.'"

Much as the girl wanted two suits, she did not want to project her mother into a conflict with the metapelet, mostly because she knew who would win. But that is not the whole story.

The kibbutz parent stands least of all for the superego. As kibbutz philosophy states, this role belongs to the metapelet (and the peer group). The girl knew very well what the superego would say of her desire: It was wrong. So she did not want the conflict taken to this person who stood for her own superego, which she knew was conflicted. She wanted the mother to side with her against the superego, hers and the kibbutz's. When the mother refused, but was only willing to verify the facts, then the child preferred to drop the whole issue.

This small example will again have to stand for many others to suggest why both the oedipal conflict and its resolution are so different in the kibbutz. According to Freud, the superego is the heir of the resolved oedipal conflict, and so is identification with the parent of the same sex. But in the kibbutz, identification with the parent qua parent does not lead to internalization of the superego. Only identification with kibbutz surrogates does that—whether one identifies with metapelet, peer group, or the kibbutz at large, as here represented by the person in charge of giving out clothes.

My example also shows how the complex relations between metapelets, parents, and children force the child to suppress a great deal. It was not the girl's failure to get her wish that made for the need to repress, nor that her wishes set her in conflict with her mother and metapelet. It was that they set her mother against the metapelet in a conflict the mother could not face. This is what makes for so powerful a repression of emotions: the knowledge that even if the mother were to take up the fight, it would end in a defeat where the two could not even cry on each other's shoulder because the mother would still be defending the system.

The tangle of human relations the child gets caught in,

merely by having and showing deep desires, makes it seem hopeless to have emotions not supported by the group. It begins to seem best not to have any feelings but those. Otherwise one cannot look for support from any closeness to others, even a parent. For that, the parent seems too weak.

By the same token, the knowledge that all decisions of importance are not made by the parents—though they participate importantly—makes the parent seem less formidable, but also a bit less of a person. No doubt the very young middle-class child overestimates his parents' ability to shape their lives in society. In reality, many middle-class fathers have as little chance to arrange the conditions of their lives and their children's lives in society as the kibbutz father. They may even have considerably less say about their conditions of work. But as long as the child is little, he does not usually know this, and sees his father as an entirely free agent in society. And if the mother works, as many of the middle class do, then on the basis of prevalent notions, he tends to believe it is entirely her choice that she works.

Thinking then of how the young child sees his parents in society, the middle-class parent appears more self-determined, powerful, and hence dangerous, but for the same reasons more of a person. True, according to kibbutz ideology one is all the more a person, the more one is truly part of the collective. And this may well be a more rarified and moral view of personality. But as far as I could observe, such a rarified view is not the one held by kibbutz children. At least in those instances where the child asked something of his parent that went against a collective ruling, it was almost always my impression that the parent lost in stature for his child if, for one reason or another, he opted for the collective's decision.

On the other hand, all this has its positive aspects. While conditions are deliberately designed to weaken the personal influence of parents, they relieve the child of many anxieties that plague the middle-class child. Worries like "What if my parents separate? Or if one of them dies, who will take care of me?" do not exist to the same degree in the kibbutz. The child knows it is the kibbutz that takes care of him and always will be. He also worries less about how his parents stack up against other parents, since there are no obvious class distinctions, though a boy may boast that his father drives the biggest tractor.

The kibbutz child has still another advantage: He knows that his parent's work confers security and prestige and is very worthwhile, even if his father does not drive the big truck, or his mother is not in charge of dispensing all clothes. Certainly there are no occupations that seem devoid of value in the kibbutz, as many a middle-class child may eventually come to doubt the moral or social value of how his father earns a living.

Unfortunately I failed to explore in greater detail what it means to the latency child, and his relations to his parents and society, that all decisions of importance are made by the assembly. The children are quite aware of this, since they often tell their parents or metapelets what they wish the assembly would discuss, or decide. I heard several children complain bitterly to their parents about kibbutz decisions— for example, that the educational committee would not let them see a movie being shown to adults.

For a moment I envied the parent, thinking of how often I, as an individual, have had to defend such decisions and make them stick in the face of my children's objections, have had to take the brunt of their disappointment. But on thinking further, I realized how personal the fight had been on both sides; how much a clash of individuals it was.

Watching a similar disagreement between a kibbutz parent and her children, I realized how much decision-making is taken out of the hands of the parents, and how often what begins as a personal disagreement becomes a clash between child and impersonal collective. Watching the mother's response to her children's complaints, I saw how their anger was directed away from her (where they wanted to pin it) and turned toward the general collective. As kibbutz philosophy meant it to be, the parent could deflect her child's annoyance with her. But in so doing, something else happened to the relationship between her and her children.

Her daughter, with tears in her eyes, pleaded with the mother to "tell the metapelet how unjust it is. Tell it to the educational committee," she argued. As the pleading went on, and as her and her brother's personal desires were met only by general statements about the rules of community life, the two children became more and more disappointed at their failure to get a personal reaction, and hence at the effectiveness of close personal relations. But if difficult emotions are not to be conveyed but suppressed, things do not, unfortunately, stop there. Because soon the repression of troublesome feelings extends to the more positive ones.

Nor does the ever-present peer group, the daily full round of activities, permit any solitary concentration on these emotions. So again repression seems the easiest way out. The child's great opportunities, the great encouragement to do things with his body, with his hands, the appreciation given to all work achievement, always offer the chance to solve problems by acting on the physical environment rather than working them through in the inner, emotional life.

Here it must be repeated that the goal of kibbutz education is to change ghetto Jews into farmers who work with their hands, to prevent over-intellectualization. If this goal is to be reached, then little time or energy can be spent on the emotional life. The world is there to be manipulated through the activities of one's body. The mind is just another instrument for manipulating the environment; or if devoted to the management of human emotions, it should be in the sphere of social relations, not of the private inner emotional event.

🌷 Emotional Disturbance

OF COURSE, THE BREAKING UP OF WHAT (WITH US) ARE THE parental functions into two separate sets of experiences is felt to have many other and far-reaching consequences. One often cited in the literature, and by kibbutz educators and psychotherapists, is that the system of multiple caretakers prevents any one adult's pathology from inflicting unlimited damage on the child. That is, the effect of the parent's pathology is counteracted by the metapelet. Any one metapelet's influence, if pathological (and I observed a few cases where this was so), is kept in check by the influence of parents and other metapelets. And this seems indeed to be the case.

By and large, kibbutz-born youngsters seemed to show considerably less emotional disturbance, both in number of cases and severity, than would a comparable group in the United States. And I observed the most severely disturbed children in the treatment institution serving all kibbutz movements, and studied more intensively the very few such youngsters at Atid who were pointed out to me by its one psychotherapist and its educators.[3] What then became apparent to me was the much greater concern with what kibbutzniks consider emotional disturbance in terms of kibbutz aspirations. They worry about severe emotional disturbance, or claim it to be present, where we would not.

My judgment however rests on shaky grounds, because of

[3] See also Appendix B, pp. 326-327.

the uncertainty as to what would be a comparable group in America. A small rural community? But our small rural communities are much more shut off from the mainstream of cultural and intellectual currents than are people in the kibbutz. Is a comparable group one that shares the same cultural and social level? But such a group in America would not live on the land and be occupied so largely with farming. Comparisons being thus of doubtful value, I tried to fall back on evidence from within the kibbutz when making value judgments—such as about a relative severity of emotional disturbance.

Here it became apparent that those youngsters who showed severest emotional disturbance, and were so adjudged by the community (except for some where emotional disturbance was clearly the aftereffect of brain damage, etc.), were youngsters whose lives lacked the checks and balances of influence between parents and metapelets. With almost no exception, they were children who had no parents in the psychological sense, and who were forced to rely solely on the metapelets. Or else they were children whose parents were either "newcomers" to the kibbutz or for some reason were in violent inner, or even open, opposition to the kibbutz. This crossfire of diametrically opposed pushes and pulls from the parents and metapelets provided the framework for those few cases I saw of severe emotional disturbance.

On the other hand, where parents and metapelet were part of the consensus community, and the child showed emotional disturbance, it was not severe, or not at least by our standards. Thus, in almost every kibbutz I visited, I asked about youngsters showing emotional disturbance. In every case, at least one or the other youngster was pointed out to me as giving the kibbutz and his parents great concern because of emotional disturbance. But in each case I could investigate, it turned out to be a youngster in rather mild opposition to kibbutz society. For some, it was because kibbutz life did not indeed suit their personal aspirations. For others it was the consequence of an adolescent revolt against all adult values. Such revolt, to the degree it existed, would be considered normal, even healthy, by many psychiatrists in our society.

Here I might digress for a moment on certain other views of what causes emotional disturbance in kibbutz children. I have spoken before of how kibbutzniks wish to ascribe such causation to bad parenting, but never to kibbutz methods of rearing. An interesting parallel is the conviction, among psychoanalysts who have treated kibbutz-reared patients, that it is parents, and not kibbutz education, that account for emotional disorder.

These therapists are deeply committed to the theory of the all-important influence of parents, compared to which societal conditions are of minor importance. But they do not question how much this, their conviction, may account for their findings. And since (for very different reasons) both kibbutznik and psychoanalyst wish to believe that pathology results only from parental impact—the kibbutznik because his educational system is viewed as solely beneficial; the psychoanalyst because any other view puts his theories in question—they reinforce each other in respect to causation. For the same reasons they part company as to what prevents pathology. There the psychoanalyst is consistent: He maintains that only positive parental attitudes are the answer, while for kibbutzniks, only kibbutz life can help.

Reading or hearing the accounts of therapists, one is confronted with a very strange fact: Suddenly it is not the infant's utter dependence on his parents in the nuclear middle-class family that accounts for his conflicted attachments to his parents, and with it for emotional disturbance. Suddenly it is no longer the threatening power of the father that explains some of his child's crucial problems.

On the contrary, a kibbutz father—who at most has only a succoring role in the child's life—is viewed as having exactly the same impact on the child as the middle-class Victorian father. And infants whose basic tender care does not come from their parents, or only for two hours a day, who do not depend on their parents for food, shelter, and stimulation—these infants and their parents are assumed to feel exactly the same about each other as in a Victorian setting.

But insofar as a person's life experience accounts for normalcy or emotional disturbance, it simply cannot make sense that two sets of children whose experience with their parents during the dependency age are radically different from each other will have exactly the same responses to their natural parents (and hence suffer or not suffer emotional disturbance) for exactly the same causes.[4] (I do not speak here of so early and so severe a traumatization that it does not matter what its source, be it parent, metapelet, or peers.)

I do not doubt that what the psychoanalyst reports of his patients is correct as he sees it. But just as with kibbutznik and therapist, often the patient and therapist have the same wish to see the parent at fault. The kibbutznik, because of his attachment to the peer group, wishes to think it free of any damaging influence; so this he projects onto his parents. And the analyst, who is older or at least emotionally more mature than his patient, creates a transference situation

---

[4] I have devoted a separate study to demonstrate that it will not do to extrapolate from the meaning that a social practice has in one culture, to what it means in another (Bettelheim, 1954). Circumcision, for example, means something very different to a middle-class Jewish boy raised in a Victorian setting, from what it signifies emotionally to an Australian aborigine.

which evokes material pertaining to adult-child relations rather than those between peers.

Psychoanalysis, and all psychotherapy derived from it, uses a method especially suitable for dealing with adult-child and particularly parent-child problems and their derivatives. It is well known that patients in treatment with a Freudian analyst tend to dream Freudian dreams, while those in treatment with a Jungian analyst have dreams of a Jungian flavor. That is, the patient's unconscious responds in terms of both his underlying needs, and what he senses the therapist is ready and able to help him with.

Certainly the analytic situation, with the patient prone on the couch and the analyst sitting above and behind him, is more apt to evoke adult-child material than peer group material. But deep inner conflicts, because so all-pervasive, can be cast in almost any external pattern and worked through in many different ways. So it happens naturally that they are cast in the mold of parent-child relations, if both method and emotional climate are pushing in that direction.

When I talked with young adults, both those who considered themselves normal and were viewed so by others, and those who had received analytic treatment, I found in the normals little evidence of any powerful emotional impact by the parents, but always a full recognition of the tremendous impact of the peer group.

In those who had been in treatment I found the reverse. Many felt it was a parent (usually the mother) who had been the pathogenic influence, but just as many felt it was the mother who had saved them, in childhood, from the destructive influence of the group, and hence enabled them to seek treatment. Those who had undergone psychotherapy were thus convinced of the primacy of the mother in particular, both for good and for ill, and not just for ill, as the reports of psychiatrists suggest. This can be read as proving the overweening force of the parental influence, or as the result of a treatment method that stresses it.

My own conviction is that any educational system has potentials for the harmful and curative in personality development. If the parent stands at the center of the child's total life experience, then everything, good and bad, will seem to derive from the parent. If the institution stands at the center, even an institution designed to be as curative as possible, it will have potentials for damage which must be carefully recognized, constantly watched, restrained, corrected, and offset. And if, in the kibbutz, the peer group and collective stands at the center of the child's life, it too will be the main source of both normal and deviate personality development.

It was my own experience with a quarter of a century of institutional living that made me keenly aware of all this. How easy it is to fall into the trap of ascribing to parental influence those undesirable aspects of personality development that may actually have a great deal to do with institutional practice! One wants so much to see it as benign, without blemish. But how easy it is to find causation in parental rearing if one looks nowhere else. And how erroneous to find it there, as one can if one tries hard enough, when the true cause lies not in the parent but the institution. Just as staff members of the Orthogenic School wish to blame the child's parents for some reactions that belong to the child's daily life at the School, so does the kibbutz wish to blame on the parent what is actually born of kibbutz living.

❧ Multiple Mothering

How, THEN, DO WE EXPLAIN THE RELATIVE ABSENCE OF EMOtional disturbance in the majority of kibbutz-born children, though they do not experience mothering in our sense? I have said repeatedly that whatever the origins of communal rearing, a dominant wish was to be rid of the overly compelling attachment between parent and child with all its oedipal scarring and tensions. And it is true that being less dependent on one's parents for survival and even companionship, spending less time with them, not observing them in primal scenes—all these go to reduce oedipal tensions, though by no means are they absent.

The easy closeness to nature and—whether for lack of supervision or by design—the much lower emphasis on cleanliness, the late and lenient toilet training; these further ease tension and anxiety. (If other and severe tensions are created by early weaning, night-time anxieties and loneliness, they are not related back so directly to the parents and are diffused among many adults.)

All this and more reduces some of the traumata the loving mother must counteract by her devotion, in our society. Maybe quite a small amount of mothering goes a very long way, if large amounts of it do not have to counteract resentment at the many dos and don'ts of the mother who is also the prime educator. For the ego, for the personality to develop, the infant needs to experience satisfaction and challenge at his own pace. But nowhere has it been demonstrated that for survival or mental health the satisfactions, challenges, and frustrations must all originate in the same person.

Many children brought up by indulgent nursemaids experience a great deal of gratification, while the frustration comes mainly from parental demands. If this works out for the child, as it once did for many persons brought up by wet nurses, there is no reason to assume that an opposite arrangement would not also work out: one where the gratification comes mainly from the mother and most frustrations from the metapelet.

The inner unity of the personality comes with the internalization of figures who both satisfy and frustrate, who thus tell the child what is good and what is bad. In most cases the infantile experiences and the internalizations based on them, are originally far from consistent or unified. Most of the time, each parent is both indulging and demanding, both soothing and threatening. Such an absence of consistency and unity presents the infant with the enormous task of struggling for the unity and consistency of his own inner institutions in his own unique way—in the process of which he will achieve a rich, though complex personality.

At first, for example, the child tries to split the good aspects of the mother from the bad ones, and internalizes both: a good mother and a very different bad one. But since both in fact derive from the splitting of one and the same person, deep down the good and bad mother hang together. (Provided, of course, that she is a fairly integrated person; is neither very neurotic, or worse, schizophrenic.)

Though such a "double" internalized image lacks consistency—when compared with a situation where one parent is all good (the mother) and the other all bad (the metapelet) —much is gained in unity. Or I should rather say: If the good and bad mother result from the child's splitting the one mother into two images, then their eventual unification is predetermined, so to speak.

But if the internalized good image comes from one person, and the bad from another, then the split between good and bad are much more permanently established. Moreover, being so radically different from each other, they have nothing in common that forces the child to seek unity between them. No place there for subtle shadings, for questions, for an interplay needed to achieve unification—as the child may push for it where consistency is lacking in what is nevertheless one and the same person.

The same is not true for the example of the good nursemaid and the demanding mother who is the real boss. Since the child knows that the good nursemaid is doing the mother's bidding, it reflects back on the mother that the mother-substitute is less demanding. Matters are sometimes very bad when a seemingly giving mother hires a punitive governess. This is as contradictory as the "good" kibbutz parent who lets the community retain a "bad" metapelet, and hands the child over to her. Because it rends apart the image of the mother, who only *seems* good, but acts bad.

The somewhat demanding mother who retains an indulgent nursemaid seems to say: "I have to request certain necessary things. It is my task as your mother. But short of that, I want you to have it as good as possible." The indulgent mother who hands her child over for most of the time to a very demanding caretaker seems to say: "I don't want to dirty my hands with all these necessary frustrations, so I leave this difficult but important task to others. Let them struggle with you about it." But a parent who struggles with his child through difficult situations is very much a parent, while the one who leaves all these struggles to others is not.

This is not to say that the inner institutions of the mind could not function in their interplay if the mother were always "good" and the metapelet (or the father) always "bad." But such a personality would not function in a very unified way. That is, if the mother were totally indulgent and the metapelet were totally strict and demanding, then the one image would be internalized as the "good mother" and would stand for the id and the instinctually satisfying aspects of the ego, while the other image would stand for the superego plus the inhibiting aspects of the ego. The "good" and "bad" mother, while each consistent in themselves, would be permanently separated in a process that might even split the personality to the core.

The constancy of what is good and what is bad could still

be established. The child would know definitely what is right and what is wrong. But he would also have a rigid personality; a consistent one, but not a very complex or unified one. Because at any one time, the one image would be in ascendence and fight the other. Or else the child would end up with a split personality. This is prevented in the kibbutz because all internalized figures, however else they differ, have one very large thing in common: their commitment to the kibbutz as such. That is why I encountered no schizophrenics in the kibbutz-born and raised generation.

To summarize: If two or all three institutions of the mind (id, ego, superego) are represented by separate persons who play entirely different roles for the child, then either no unity of these inner institutions will occur, or only a precarious one. They may remain isolated from each other instead of interacting more or less smoothly. The more isolated they remain the more disorganized, or defensively rigid the personality; the more smoothly they mesh, the more complex but unified the personality.

A unified personality is built around the unity of the person or persons who serve as images for id satisfaction, superego demands, and ego achievement. If this is not so it leads either to a diffuse personality, or to a strong and stable defensive organization, a rigid defensive armoring. Typically, the latter happens if one of the two figures or set of figures becomes dominant, and the emotional experiences derived from the other are repressed or defensively dealt with. In both cases personality will not develop much further.

Fortunately for kibbutz reality, as I observed it, there is no such clear split between the gratifying parent and the frustrating metapelet, as kibbutz educational theory would have it. First, it is not a lone metapelet who takes care of the child, but several of them. Second, metapelets also provide some measure of instinctual satisfactions. There is some play and picking up, there is the feeding, little insistence on cleanliness or table manners, late toilet training, etc. And parents impose quite a few dos and don'ts. So the metapelets frustrate and gratify; and the parents gratify and frustrate. Most important of all, parent and metapelet are unified in their ultimate value: the kibbutz.

Nevertheless, because several persons both satisfy and frustrate, the children's attachments are not as deep, to any one of them, as if nearly all significant experiences came mainly or only from one person, or were experienced that way. For the same reason the children are not as ambivalent about any one of these adults as if there were only one person with whom to identify and depend on at so early an age.

So far so good. But there are other differences between the roles of parent and educator that I found no mention of in the literature or in discussions with kibbutz psychologists or educators, though I think them important.

I have said that both parent and metapelet offer instinctual gratifications, impose superego demands, and suggest ego development, though in differing ways and degrees. But as regards instinctual pleasures, the metapelet offers mainly the satisfaction of necessities. Once breast-feeding stops, it is she who provides food, shelter, rest, stimulation, clothing. The parent, on the other hand, provides important "extras" like a special warmth in handling the child (particularly if there is only one infant in the family), play that is less invaded by others, deeper emotional involvement, and so forth. (For all this the metapelet has too little time.) In addition, there is what the child gets from the all-important peer group.

This makes for a unique infant and childhood experience in the kibbutz. From the earliest age we see a separation between the person who provides the extras, and the one who provides the necessities without which the extras could not even be offered. It merely duplicates the broader kibbutz pattern where some "extras" in food can now be had in the rooms, but where the basic meals come only from the kibbutz.

The split, then, is not between the person who provides instinctual satisfaction and that other one who provides superego demands and frustration, as kibbutzniks like to think. In practice, the split is between a person (or set of persons) who provides what might be called the physical essentials for survival (while imposing superego demands and encouraging ego achievement—all of which together make for basic security) and the parent, who provides "love and tender care," or what we might call the pleasure satisfactions.

But even this is not the whole story. Because from an early age on, most of the push for ego achievement, and only a bit later some superego demands and emotional satisfactions, come neither from metapelet nor parent but from the peer group. Indeed, as the child grows older, he realizes more and more that security in regard to survival needs comes from that larger peer group, the kibbutz, while metapelet and parent become less and less important.

I believe that the puritanical character of the kibbutz-born with its relative lack of emotional leeway, is forced on them by some of these factors. It is quite different from the puritanism embraced by the founding generations out of choice. That was a reaction formation to the emotional hothouse they were raised in; hence it was often broken through—for example, by a certain sexual freedom not available to the kibbutz-born generation.

Character, among the kibbutz-born, is formed in part by the fact that the satisfaction of all the child's basic needs has become closely linked up in his earliest experience, and his internalized structures, with the superego demands coming from metapelet and peers. On the other hand, certain special emotional satisfactions have been relegated to a very different person and setting, and restricted to a few hours distinctly set aside for the purpose. The result is that "fun" (or pleasure) is restricted to a few hours "after work," and comes only from those who provide none of the essentials. And while I have stressed throughout that important pleasure satisfactions have come from the peer group all along, the peer group has always imposed ego and superego demands to go with them.

But because security is more basic, pleasure, greater emotional closeness, and fun, while nice, emerge as not really very important, and—what has vaster implications—they are radically separated from the rest of one's life. The result is the feeling that they are really unimportant, and not intrinsically connected with the more meaningful process of living.

✿ The Labors of Love

HERE, TOO, THE KIBBUTZ MIGHT TEACH US A LESSON ABOUT what may be in store for us. True, there is no such division in our middle-class families between who provides the essentials of existence and who provides what seem like the psychological "extra" satisfactions. But more and more the essentials are taken for granted by the middle-class child. Most of them need no longer worry—any more than kibbutz children do —about where the food, shelter, and clothing will come from. But there is a crucial difference.

While the child in both places need not worry about these basic needs, more and more with us the activities that provide for the essentials are hidden from the child's experience and seem to come without effort. The parent is viewed as the provider of love and tender care, but less and less as the one whose labor supplies what is basic to survival. Food comes from the supermarket, and since it is precooked, mother's time at the stove is much briefer. At an early age the child can even open a can and warm some food up himself. It has also been years since mothers bent over the sewing; clothes come from a rack in the store.

Much of the hedonistic outlook of our younger generation has its roots in this fact: The essentials of life seem to come without exertion. The kibbutz child's experience is very different because he is much closer to the very hard labor of adults who provide for his needs, and to the dangers of living in a world surrounded by enemies (another early experience that supports a later puritanic outlook on life).

The middle-class child depends on his parents for both the essentials and extras, but has no clear idea of what it takes to provide the essentials. Hence, those children whom all the extras do not seem to satisfy, because without a clear feeling for the essentials, they really are not enough. The kibbutz child has a clear recognition of where the essentials come from: they come from the kibbutz to which his parents contribute their labor. But whatever else a person provides, if he does not also provide the essentials directly, by this very fact he shrinks in importance.[5]

Marriage, for example, seems to work out much better

[5] This is a situation not entirely absent in our affluent society. Professionally I have dealt with quite a few children who inherited sizable fortunes from their grandparents. This, their economic independence of their parents, interfered often and very seriously with parent-child relations. The parents, but particularly the father, seemed much less than a father to himself and to his child, though the same was not as true for the mother. From her the child received infantile care that took visible effort. And this the child somehow sensed as a more personal giving than was the father's providing of a livelihood, when there was nothing he had done to provide it.

when the partners not only find emotional satisfaction in each other—this they can also do without getting married—but if their emotional closeness is supported by their providing for each other's physical needs. It is not love or sexual satisfaction that is lacking in many disorganized or fatherless families, but a father who provides.

I do not believe in the one-sided view that affectional ties between mates are a superstructure whose only firm basis is economic need. But neither do I believe in the kibbutz view that for husband and wife to have really good relations they must be freed of all economic necessity, and that the same goes for relations between parents and children. Such a separation of emotional from physical care—at least as I observed it in the kibbutz—far from strengthening emotional ties, seems to weaken them.

Actually, the ties between husband and wife in the kibbutz are by no means above economic necessity. That both of them work for the kibbutz and not just for each other dilutes the tie. Nor do they share economic concerns so exclusively with each other as a middle-class family might. Still, the bond is a strong one between them, and much of their interest and talk centers around it. The same is not true for the parents and child.

Perhaps at this stage of man's development emotions are not rarified enough to be very strong unless supported by the satisfying of physical needs. Once the Victorian separation of romantic love from its physical basis led to neurosis, hysteria, and worse. So also, if we separate the emotional attachment between parent and child from its physical roots, it may become insubstantial—like the Victorian lady's love for the husband from whom she withheld her body.

Before concluding this discussion of latency in the kibbutz, I want to stress again that I found it the happiest stage of kibbutz development. Never again will the whole of kibbutz life tally so perfectly with the needs of a particular age, with satisfactions so readily available, and with no demands being made except those that are also natural desires of the age. Watching latency children in class and at play, in their assembly discussion, at mealtimes, or when going so easily to bed and to sleep, one is impressed with the joy of living in them, how the day for them bubbles with interest, stimulation, excitement, and satisfaction. All of life seems at their fingertips, with none of it alien to them.

The only time of day one finds them somewhat subdued is when (toward the end of latency) they visit with their parents. It is as if they begin to sense the waning of attachment to their parents and feel nostalgic about it.

By this time their age-group has become so attractive that the youngster strains to be back with them, while his parents' wish that he prefer their company (and his own wish not to disappoint them) puts him under some stress. Also, the closer he comes to adolescence, the more he draws away from his parents, and about this, too, he feels a little sadness. Because his is not a defiant self-assertion or a "fighting for his rights," as is so often true of our preadolescents. His is not a stance that says "this is my world, and you adults keep out," which so often follows from the pre-teener's wish to deny his feeling that the world has no place for him yet. All this is spared the kibbutz youngster approaching adolescence. So while a withdrawal from the parent sets in, it is not a withdrawal from the world of adults. The preadolescent withdraws to his youth group, which is very much an integral part of the common kibbutz world. Even in the kibbutz, however, the strain of becoming an adolescent begins to cast shadows over an otherwise still sun-drenched life.

4

Adolescence

H OW STRANGE IT IS TO COMPARE THE ADOLESCENCE OF
early kibbutzniks with that of their children. For the
founding generation, adolescence was a time of glorious
dreams about creating a better society, a new Israel. Life for
these founders was hard, often dangerous, and comforts were
nonexistent. But their days were full to the brim, and fuller
of promise for the future. However backbreaking the work,
one felt acutely alive. Each person was the creator of a new
and better world, the carrier of great new ideas, a brighter
future. Even now—when they are well past middle age—an
added brilliance comes to their eyes as they talk of it, a new
tone to their voices. And this is no hymn to a shadowy past,
dead and gone.

It is strange to hear them tell of it—of the long hard day's
work, after which they would sing and dance through the
night or stand watch against Arabs till dawn—and then
compare such a life with that of their children who are now
the same age. These youngsters when they wake in the morn-

ing are tired already, are listless in class during the day and exhausted well before midnight. They feel that much too much is expected of them by this generation, their parents.

❦ *"They're All So Great . . ."*

IT IS PROBABLY TRUE THAT KIBBUTZ ADOLESCENTS ARE OVER-worked; certainly that they are overstrained. But mostly they are depleted of energy because so much of it goes into keeping up repressions. Their parents were spilling over with energy because the kibbutz gave them leave, for the first time in their lives, to throw off old repressions. Much of their new and contagious joy of living came also of having suddenly thrown off their sexual repressions. This new life in the new land was very much to be a life of new sexual freedom and fulfillment. Eventually it turned out that what many had embraced as sexual freedom was a sexual acting out, that promiscuity did not give them the greater sexual satisfaction they had hoped it would bring. But this they did not realize till later in life, when the bloom of exuberance was already receding with age and with the need to come to terms with reality.

It was this later experience with how a heedless promiscuity can breed disruption in the social life that led them to impose on their adolescent children a very high and repressive sex morality. And it is this that saps the youngsters of a great deal of libidinal energy. Repression in their case is especially hard to maintain, devours energy, because to these youngsters it does not grow out of an old and generally inhibited way of life, as it did for their parents, but of what is supposedly a new world of freedom. These adolescents cannot throw off parental inhibitions, because it is not true for them as it was for their parents that their elders seemed puny figures, willing slaves of the ghetto. To them, their parents seem true giants. The inhibitions imposed by ghetto parents were part of what had preserved a semislavery; good reason to throw them overboard. To the kibbutz-born generation, their parents loom as the great figures who brought freedom to the Jews in the face of a whole doubting world. How can one throw off repressions that seem part of what put an end to two thousand years of bondage?

This, in brief, is the story of kibbutz-raised adolescents. They must not only accept and admire their parents' epic achievements, but be grateful for all they inherit. They are expected to do as well as their parents, though there is no room to do it in at all. The first generation found its glory in successfully overthrowing the world of their parents, as they tell their children again and again. But now youth is asked to find equal satisfaction by doing just the reverse. They are expected to rejoice that no more glories are left for them to win, because their parents have reaped them, every one.

In America too, the self-made man tells his children that everything they enjoy is the fruit of his labor. He tells them how hard he had to work, and expects them not only to be grateful but to marvel at the ease he has made possible. And all the while he is really telling them that to become a person, you must win in tough struggle with the world. What makes the self-made American father pale by comparison is that the pioneers who fought to build America have been dead for generations, while these adolescents confront the founders of Israel in their living parents. As one youth told me: "They're all so great, so we're all so little."

The one revolt they permit themselves—and I sometimes wonder how they can afford even that, so oppressive and awesome is the image of their parents—is a total rejection of what they call their parents' "great ideas." Zionism, to them, is a term of ridicule, a concept out of the Ark; what our youth would call "hopelessly square."

I observed a group of eighteen-year-olds who tried to express this revolt in a skit they wrote for their graduation play. One of the songs in it told how their parents, who had broken free and escaped from the prisons of Europe, had forged a suffocating prison for them (meaning their classrooms and books).

Nominally, this theme is no different from a hundred others in our culture, including the rhymes children shout every spring when school is out for the year. In a way, too, these youngsters were trying to understand their parents by trying to understand the experience of their parents. Not having suffered in the prisons of Europe, they were doing their best to relate it to the closest thing they could think of in their own lives. But on a deeper level, it was not school that imprisoned them, but what their parents had done to end suffering, and how this paralyzed them (the graduates) from doing anything more dynamic than preserving their parents' achievements.

In this sense their skit was a healthy expression of adolescent revolt. It was also the adolescent's effort to assert that his life, too, was difficult and had its important happenings. If prison, and breaking free of it, was such a big thing in his parents' life, then he too had tasted confinement and was trying to break out.

In a way these graduates were also testing to see if their parents really believed in revolt, or just in their own past revolt. But they knew the answer, and so by equating ghetto and school, their resentment showed through. Still they were raised in a society where the personal aspiration comes second to that of the community, and they could not change now. When told by their adult leader that such a song was much too offensive to render in public, they quickly defended themselves. "We were only joking," they said, trying to save both face and their song.

Despite my account of this token revolt, there is no question but that adolescents are also grateful to their parents in a very real sense and admire them as the founders of Israel and of kibbutz society. Otherwise there would be less need to repress any wish to revolt. This, incidentally, is one of many examples suggesting why things may be different for the third generation. Obviously the second generation will not be able to tell their adolescent children about the revolutionary deeds that gave distinction to their lives. They will neither tantalize with any talk of revolt that the youngsters can never act on, nor make them guilty about how much was given up for their sake—another reason why proof of kibbutz rearing may well have to wait until the third generation is grown.

After all, adolescent revolt is not a stage of development that follows automatically from our natural makeup. For most of man's existence there was no such revolt among youth. Adolescents for thousands of years followed easily in their parents' footsteps. What makes for adolescent revolt is the fact that a society keeps the next generation too long dependent—too long in terms of sexual maturity and a striving for independence. When young people had to be self-supporting by twelve or fourteen, when girls married at that age or soon after, there was no place for adolescent revolt. Nor does it happen if the social attitude is that man since time immemorial has lived the same god-ordered existence, from which any change is inconceivable.

For adolescent revolt to be a more or less regular feature of growing up at least three conditions seem necessary: the cake of custom must be breaking down; a relative affluence must enable society to dispense with child and adolescent labor and keep its adolescents economically dependent; and society must want the young to stay sexually inactive beyond the age at which sexual maturity is reached.

All these conditions are present in the kibbutz: the youngsters are economically taken care of, and though their work is productive, their main task is seen as going to school. While the age-old customs have just been discarded by their parents, the young are asked *not* to discard any customs they inherited. They are supposed not to think about sex, and certainly not to act on their sexual desires, though they are taught to regard sex as a natural joy.

But now in adolescence, unlike the latency age—and while they still lack sexual freedom or an open hand in shaping their lives—the kibbutz begins to demand from them in earnest. There is still no great pressure academically, but great demands are made on them to work longer and harder on the farm or in shops. In and by themselves the hours are not too oppressive. But the youngsters are at an age when they grow fast. They are easily tired out by inner and outer pressures. Most of all their vitality is drained by having so much to repress. For this fatigue the kibbutz has little compassion. Again and again I saw groups of late adolescents lying on the grass or on their cots, totally exhausted. Universally, adult reaction to the scene was, "See how easy they have it?" Always they were comparing this mentally with how hard they had worked at that age; and always they forgot how exhilarating it was to be free at last to form their lives socially and sexually.

The founders' attitude tends to make adolescents feel guilty, while their escape into daydreams is limited. They can neither dream of getting even, nor of showing up these guilt-creating parents, as did their parents before them. Least of all can they dream the most important dream of all: to do better than their parents. How can they dream of creating a new social order when the one they live in seems juster to them than all others?

Nor can they dream of escaping to the wider world beyond. This—the fast-growing new nation around them with all its turmoil, competition, expansion—has been depicted to them as one of injustice, inequity, sometimes pure evil. True, the kibbutz is tied to Israel by great national pride, though an ambivalent one; because it is wrong for this capitalistic, exploitative state to grow so fast, when the just society of the kibbutz is stagnant by comparison.

Understandably, the ambivalence is greatest among the founding generation. Every new building, factory, hospital in Israel fills them with pride, because they feel that it was only their work in opening the land, in spearheading the immigration, that made it all possible. To them every sign of progress is new proof of their achievement. Yet every such new advance also reduces the importance of the kibbutz. In a way it puts to question the vitality of its form of society, since the advances are capitalist creations. The same progress that makes Israel herself more secure, does the opposite for the kibbutz. Their children, on the other hand, take much less pride in signs of national growth, since they do not feel it was they who gave the society birth. If anything, they feel excluded from it, and ward off the feeling by paying it little heed.

The difference between the generations shows up, for example, in their attitudes toward the Hebrew University or the Technion. To the founding generation both are a great source of pride, because where the University now stands, "there was nothing but barren land when we started our work." But to the adolescent this is a place where gifted city youth enjoy a life of learning, but which he himself dismisses with a shrug, as he says: "Our kibbutz can't afford to send me."

This contradiction met me during my first hours in Israel. Founders of Atid, and some of its educational leaders, received me at the airport. Since it was too late at night to start for Atid, they took me to the new airport hotel. As we said goodnight, some told me they would not be able to sleep in such luxury when so many essentials were still lacking in the state. All night they would lie awake, they said, wondering what happened to the Israel they fought so hard to create, feeling strongly that what they fought for was not the type of society this hotel represented. But there it was, and there they were: kibbutzniks, essentially relegated to a corner by the very state they had brought into being. (Of course, there are other kibbutzniks, who, in this situation or under other circumstances, thoroughly enjoy the comforts and achievements capitalistic Israel has to offer.)

If the adolescents follow their parents in looking askance at successes in capitalistic Israel, feelings run extraordinarily high against Europe and America, the latter being the epitome of capitalist evil. So each time an adolescent dreams of escaping to Haifa or Tel Aviv, he feels guilty. America he does not even dream about because "we could never get there!"

Essentially the kibbutz wishes to create a society of true believers, and all the ingredients are present: the deep conviction that they live the good life, the spartan frugality, the high morality and devotion to duty that set the examples, the absence of economic distinctions, the ethos of social equality. Most of all there are the strong sexual inhibitions that set off the whole process of repression.

In crucial ways, however, the second generation faces problems that the children of true believers escape. First, no father figures dominate the kibbutz, nor any god or religion to enforce parental demands with supernatural sanctions. Second, the revolt *against* tradition is glorified to near mythical proportions. Third, while sex repression in adolescence is demanded, sex itself—contrary to what obtains in most societies of true believers—is viewed as natural, and after a certain age, healthy, desirable.

Finally, and again unlike the society of true believers, the child is taught from early infancy that he must form his own opinions and go by the rules of his peer group, not those of adult authority. But always and everywhere this precept contradicts the demand that these opinions, freely arrived at, must be exactly the ones the community wants him to have.

❧ Where the Group Wind Blows

HOW THIS WORKS IN PRACTICE MAY BE ILLUSTRATED BY WHAT happened when I asked a class of eleventh graders (age about sixteen) which group discussion had been most interesting to them in the past year or two. After only a brief talk among themselves they agreed it had been a discussion that centered on what was the right way for kibbutzniks to dress. It had come about because two girls in their groups had grown long fingernails and arranged their hair in a fashion the adult group leader considered fancy and unbecoming in a kibbutz. That is, they had tried to make themselves sexually attractive as girls.

The issue debated was whether the youth society should permit such behavior or not. The group was then supposed to arrive at their own (group) decision on the matter, though it was not they but the adult leader who had raised it as a problem. From what the group and their adult leader told me, this led to a heated discussion which went on for several days with great intensity. For some time the girls "stubbornly" held to their position, and some felt for a while that the adult was railroading the decision in favor of his views. But in the end they felt they had decided on their own that such a manner of dress was unbecoming to kibbutz life and should not be allowed.

Not often does the budding desire to express sexuality get aired in group discussion. Usually it is repressed from the start. Perhaps the reason is that it takes far less repressive energy to obey the rules of the community if no inner questions are raised, than to put the question to oneself and still come up with the required answer.

A defense I saw again and again was the one used in the case of the prison song: to claim that a divergent opinion had not been seriously held. For example, when I visited a class of high school seniors, they first asked me many questions about young people in America, about our educational system, about my reactions to the kibbutz, etc., and showed a lively interest and sharpness of mind. When I asked them what they would like to see changed in the kibbutz, they said, as usual, that everything in the kibbutz was just as it ought to be, though they felt (like students anywhere) that school work was too hard, or too much. When I pressed for some specific change they would welcome, one said: "to have two movies a week instead of one."

In manner and tone his comment was matter-of-fact and straightforward. But the moment it was out, he felt the astonished, even agonized silence of the group, which until then had spoken up freely. Quite possibly they reacted this way because a kibbutz matter was being criticized to an outsider, and on so frivolous an issue as movies! But whatever the reason, he had gone against group opinion, and he sensed it immediately. Before anyone could say a word, he spoke hastily again, with what to me seemed an empty grin, saying, "I meant this only as a joke."

When I said it hadn't sounded to me as if he were joking, both he and the teacher as well as the rest of the class shouted that "he certainly was joking." So I said that, even so, there are reasons why we make jokes, and I explained. But this they refused to accept, though in my experience the point would have been granted by most American youngsters of equal intelligence. When I finally asked what would be wrong with showing two movies a week, they agreed there was nothing wrong with it, but that this was irrelevant because the boy had only spoken in jest.

Here, as in many other cases I observed, it was not so much the teacher's disapproval that brought an almost instant reversal. By adolescence, these youngsters have begun to resent individual adults and will occasionally speak their minds against them. They can and will argue with a teacher or their metapelet for some time, where he can safely be viewed as an individual. (While a metapelet still takes care of the adolescent group, by high school age she has become less important than the youth leader who advises the entire youth society, which now runs its own affairs. It is a bit harder for youngsters to go against a youth leader's opinions, though he is usually more skillful about protecting their sensitivity in matters of independence than is the typical metapelet.) But even more than adult opposition, what pulls the adolescent up short is always group pressure—first and foremost that of the peer group, and secondly the kibbutz, in the person of some adult. Their giving in starts as soon as they feel (or fear) that group opinion leans the other way.

In regard to the "prison" song, too, those who had written it and those who wanted it performed began to change their minds as soon as they felt the peer group was no longer behind them. With very rare exceptions they cannot buck the group, not for a moment; it is too threatening. This is where their emotional security resides. Without the peer group they are lost.

It is not just out of closeness to the group, but more a fear of their rejection. Fifteen or sixteen years of living not as an individual but as an integral part of a peer group has made it nearly impossible for them to conceive of standing up alone against the group. Not only have they been taught this is unpardonable, but they have no experience whatsoever that a single person could go it alone. How, then, can they believe they could do it? And indeed, no adult would support them in the effort.

Just as the parent cannot act directly on his child's desire if it goes against the group, but can only act in consensus with his own peers, so the youngster, if he turns to adults, is told to take his problem to the youth society and obey its decision. Why then, should he take it to those who will not do the deciding? Better to avoid open defeat. Better instead to switch convictions as soon as one feels where the group wind is blowing.

Usually the repression of personal desires does not stop there—witness what happened around the prison song. For a few days, debate continued while the youngsters tried to hang onto their song. But neither a denial of their real inner feelings ("it's just a joke") nor agreeing not to perform it was enough. They had to be made to internalize community standards, and the discussion went on until they themselves agreed that the song was entirely unsuitable, whether in jest or dead earnest.

After it was all over, I discussed the incident with some kibbutz educators. They felt there was nothing wrong with young people having to repress desires that go against kibbutz values, or being made to see such desires as wrong. Far from seeing this as a negative thing, they felt it was something very positive, because it helped youth to identify with kibbutz values.

Now it is true that most societies would see an identification with its values as positive. What is made hard for kibbutz youth is that they are also asked to accept, as a main kibbutz value, that one should freely express one's true feelings and convictions. (This, incidentally, is a predicament our own youth suffer from more and more. They are expected to develop critical judgment, to change and improve things, to form opinions on their own. But then society is down on them if they take these requests seriously, and wants them instead to accept things pretty much as they are.)

Kibbutz attitudes here are expressed by an educator, very familiar with psychoanalytic theory, who said: "Any repression that leads to identification with kibbutz values is good and desirable because it builds the ego." Now, a good case could be made for the fact that it builds the superego. But it reflects a strange view of what Freud meant by ego to see it as gaining strength from repression, instead of recognizing that repression depletes it.

Nevertheless, this educator had correctly transmuted Freud's concepts to fit kibbutz reality. Because, as discussed earlier, I believe that the ego of the kibbutz-born is a collective, not a personal ego. Much that with us would be a superego demand is for him indeed an ego demand. In many ways, if a highly personal ego were to oppose the group norm, it could rightly be termed a counterego. As such it would represent a split in the ego between a highly personalized set of ego attitudes and a collective set. This, Erikson describes as a negative identity, which always implies a split in the ego if not in the whole personality. So where the ego is essentially a group ego, it is true that repression (of what the individual ego opposes to the group ego) will strengthen the ego. In the kibbutz setting, then, to be group-directed is not a sign of weak ego. On the contrary, it fortifies the ego for its dealings with kibbutz reality.

Maybe Freud's concept of the ego ideal is here more to the point. There can be little doubt that kibbutz-raised youngsters share a common ego ideal. To extend Riesman's terms, they are not simply other-directed. They are to an equal extent directed *by* and *for* the other, in a process where it is impossible to see where the one ends and the other begins. Except that this other is not "someone outside of myself," as suggested by Riesman's term other-directed, but is built into himself by the kibbutz adolescent as what is most valuable within him. And this too, I believe, may be a significant aspect of the kibbutz-born personality.

❦ The Freedom to Choose

MORE SENSITIVE KIBBUTZ EDUCATORS ARE AWARE OF CONTRA-dictions in their attitudes toward freedom of thought but are at a loss how to help themselves. I asked one of them why he, personally, did not trust that young people, on their own, would eventually choose kibbutz life over life on the outside. "I guess," he said, "I'm remembering my own experience with what happens when you make up your own mind.

"I came to the kibbutz through the youth movement, which tried to make the kibbutz very attractive to us young-sters. But only about 20 percent of my group entered the kibbutz with me; the other 80 percent returned to the cities. Well, we can't be satisfied with maybe 20 percent of our children remaining in the kibbutz. We want the whole 100 percent of them to stay with us." And in another conversa-tion: "To be frank, we're not optimistic enough to believe they will choose the way of the kibbutz if we don't specifi-cally educate them to choose it."

Now this came from a top educator, deeply committed to the kibbutz way of life. But, in fact, the kibbutz really differs very little from what motivates other systems of education. Only in most other cases no contrasting society surrounds them, to which a youngster might escape. In most societies the new generation has no such option. The only major ex-ception today, outside of Israel, is that of East and West Germany; but consider the lengths both systems go to in hopes that their younger generations will not opt out. Still, whether choices exist or not, each educational system considers that its task is to instill the young with the values of the culture, to guide them toward control of the id and toward forming the ego and superego in accordance. Presently, the great concern of American education is to prevent the children of those who feel (or are) excluded from our middle-class society, or who have opted out of it, from following their parents. Our concern for them is thus essentially the same as that of the kibbutz educator who feels he cannot risk losing a sizable segment of the young. We too believe our society is better for them. But we, too, lack the optimism to believe they will choose a middle-class way of life unless we specifically educate them for it. At least we have seen that its being theoretically available to them is not enough to make them choose it.

Why are some leading kibbutz educators beset by doubts about what their children will opt for, which explains many kibbutz pressures? I believe because they recognize how much the kibbutz was, for those who chose it, an experience that removed many parental inhibitions, while for the kibbutz-born it means having to live now and for the rest of their lives with repressions bred into them by kibbutz education.

For these and similar reasons kibbutz founders worry and fret about the possibility that one of their children may leave the kibbutz. (This was a problem I was not able to discuss with the kibbutz-born parents, who simply took it for granted that their children would not leave.)

Interestingly enough they felt that if a child were to leave for ideological reasons, they could accept it, though it would hit them hard. He would still have remained true to the parents' idea that the basis of one's actions should be ideological. If, on the other hand, a child should decide to leave the kibbutz for earthly goods—a more comfortable home, greater privacy, better clothes, easier or more interesting work, longer holidays, or (in the case of girls) fancy hairdos, lipstick, etc.—this would shake the parents to the core.

They felt it would mean that all their efforts in behalf of their children had been a complete failure; would threaten their self-image. It would put in question not only the reasons for the hardships they imposed on themselves, but all those they impose on their children (though they do not think of these as hardships). That is, their belief that they provide their children with the best life there is would be threatened if the children (through what they left the kibbutz for) were to indicate this was not what they wanted or thought was good.

In a way these parents were deluded in thinking their ideology had failed when their children left the kibbutz. I met not one person who had left for truly ideological reasons; so successful is the kibbutz in transmitting its ideology to its children. But neither did they leave for greater comforts, or not in the sense their parents thought. Those who left had all left for "personal" reasons, mostly for personal aspirations, in one case because of the "selfish" wish to be a dancer. I have mentioned women who left because they wanted to keep their children with them. But even they, though they objected to communal rearing, had no quarrel with the rest of kibbutz ideology.

Others felt that without being opposed to kibbutz ideology they wanted "the little things," to be free to eat what they liked, to see a movie whenever they wanted to—though the person who gave this as one of his reasons for leaving added in the same sentence, "but since I left the kibbutz I have seen fewer movies, by and large, than when I was there." Except that they were movies that attracted his interest and not those an educational committee had selected. It is not that he did not recognize how much the kibbutz freed him from want: for example, no matter what, one always had cigarettes available. What he wanted was the freedom to choose what brand of cigarettes to smoke. (Slowly, with greater affluence has come a loosening of old rigidities. By now most kibbutzim give their members some choice of which cigarettes they want to smoke, though the choice is limited to a few of the cheapest brands. Similarly, many kibbutzim now permit their members to see a few extra movies or plays of their own choice in town, usually up to four a year.)

If the adolescent's freedom to choose is restricted, his developing ability to make choices is interfered with long before adolescence. It comes naturally for the child and young adult to avoid the risks and hard work of making personal decisions. And even these, for kibbutz children, are much fewer than with us.

In a pluralistic society such as ours, most of all in our urban centers, even the very young child is exposed to many different ways of solving life's problems. If nothing else, variations in our standards of living practically force him, from the earliest age, to question his family's way of life and to wonder for which way he will opt. In school he is exposed to the intellectually curious and the dropout, to the grind, to those who care only about social success, and to those others who care only for sports, etc. There are differences of religion, of party allegiance, of ethnic background, etc.

Things are very different in the kibbutz. There is little chance for any difference of opinion to crop up in the peer group because where would the different ideas have come from? It more or less takes an outside influence to raise issues they might differ about. Even the need for deciding which movie to see on a Saturday night does not exist. Like adult kibbutzniks, adolescents are taken to town for a few "extras" a year. For some it is a movie or a play, for others a concert, an exhibit, or a football game. But even these events they cannot choose freely. While the event is chosen in terms of their stated interests, they are taken only to those declared suitable by the group leader or the educational committee. Moreover, they go only as a group comprising those sharing like interests, though the group may be small, numbering only a few.

As one kibbutz mother told me, "Life is much easier here for children, and I speak from experience, because we lived for a couple of years in Paris, where the movement sent us. At that time my daughter was five, and choosing clothes was an ordeal. The children she went to school with wore varied types of clothing, and though she had quite definite likes and dislikes, she could never make up her mind which of her likes she should choose for herself. Her indecision in the stores exhausted her and me. But as soon as we came back to the kibbutz, there were no longer any problems for her. She saw here everybody dressing the same way. Actually she wanted here and in Paris the same: to conform. But in Paris she never knew what the other children would wear, so she couldn't choose. Here, where everybody wears more or less the same, things were incredibly easier for her."

And so indeed they are. But an important way in which a child prepares to make decisions later on, about such things as how he wants to behave, has been closed off to him by not learning earlier how he wanted to look. And the more limited the necessity for making decisions, the less the growing child learns to accept the struggle of deciding as part of his life.

Thus for the latency child in the kibbutz his entire world is one of friendliness, openness, wholly accepting and easy to grasp. He hasn't a foe in the world. He does not wish to be on his own but with his group. He wants to be one of them, not to have to make separate decisions. The closer he comes to adolescence, the more reversed is the picture. The friendly world that fostered growth at every turn changes to a limiting world that imposes narrowness and increasing demands.

While the adolescent still derives the same feeling of competence from understanding kibbutz life, he begins to want to reach out toward the bigger world, the city, the life he reads about in novels, sees in movies. This showed up clearly in the questions young people asked me about their counterparts in America. Starting with what school life is like there in general, they soon switched to detailed queries about Hollywood movies, TV programs, the Beatles, adolescent fads, etc., revealing both anxiety and fascination with all these features of an adolescent life closed to them.

From their talk it became quite clear that they did not feel they could manage such a life, that it was not for them. But how exciting they felt it to be, and how very much they itched for a good taste of it—however strong their conviction that they would find it very much wanting in the end and would return to settle down in the kibbutz. From this tempting life the adolescent feels more excluded than would a city child. Worse, he feels a bit backward compared to those sophisticates who seem to have life at their fingertips.

People in the big outer world seem an enigma to him, which makes him feel awkward, not in the know when he meets them. The popular songs they sing, the jazz, he finds suddenly attractive. But in the eyes of the community this is wrong. He longs to dress, to act, as they do in this wider world, craves to see other than the once-a-week educational movies, or the few approved ones he can see in the city. Even its alleged wickedness and dangers make it seem more attractive in a fashion. But to wish for it is wrong; makes him feel guilty. So again he has to repress such a longing.

What to the grade school child is an asset—that he need not trouble his head with the world beyond home, need not understand what he cannot—is now a liability. The child who was everywhere at home suddenly becomes an adolescent who is basically at home nowhere—always with the one big exception of his age-group.

Alienated as he is from his own community and the outside world, his sense of competence wavers. All that gave security and a feeling of well-being, up to now, turns into a symbol of oppression, and rubs the incompetence in. Where the provision of ample clothing spelled security for the child, the fact that he (or worse, *she*) cannot dress now as he pleases becomes an affront.

Shifting to the language of developmental stages may further clarify why the ages from roughly three to thirteen are such happy times for the kibbutz child, and why adolescence is so difficult for him. In the earlier period the ego is powerfully developed—in its work of mastering the environment through body control, the manipulation of external forces, and intellectual growth. Virtually no limits are set on the child's wish to be active. Little is asked that would call for repression in this area (at least little when compared to our requirements for conforming to adult standards of cleanliness, quietness, etc.). All adults are essentially supportive, and since there is little need to fight free of them at this age, they are chiefly helpful. The dominant mode for dealing with instinctual pressures is through muscular discharge, and exactly this mode is highly encouraged.

In adolescence all this changes. The ego now faces the task of forming the adult, the sexually mature personality; of deciding which instinctual desires one may satisfy and which others one is asked to repress. Developmentally, the task is to come into one's own, to become independent of the parents. And now the sexual desires are in the forefront of instinctual pressures that clamor for satisfaction. But no longer now is discharge encouraged. On the contrary, it is severely inhibited.

Even the cognitive function of the ego—to learn about a world whose horizon is widening—is no longer pushed but inhibited. The latency child is encouraged to learn all about the kibbutz, and finds it intellectually and emotionally rewarding. The learning task is made simple, and the learning highly praised. Parents and all other adults are greatly pleased by their children's growing interest and understanding of their work. But now when the adolescent's curiosity extends beyond the kibbutz, even to TV and jazz and Hollywood movies, then he has to repress part of the cognitive ego, just as he must repress the instinctual desires, now that they no longer press for motor discharge but for sexual satisfaction. An ego that was first built up by being encouraged in its task, is now suddenly depleted by having to narrow down its sphere through repression.

🌱 *Careers and the Future*

ADOLESCENCE IS A TIME OF STRUGGLE WITH THE TWO PROBlems of how to find one's place in society, and at the same time of how to find oneself. For kibbutz adolescents their place in society is assured them, and they accept this as somewhat of an asset. One great advantage of kibbutz society, they say, is that you don't have to worry about finding a job, about making a living. But while their place in society is assured, the place is designated by their elders, from whose yoke—however gentle—they wish to fight free. Most of all, though finding one's place in society is much easier, it is not much of a finding of oneself, because no personal doing won them the place.

These adolescents whose life is so strictly regulated are already working youths. From kindergarten age they have worked in their vegetable garden or at raising animals, though it was still mainly serious play. But from fifth grade on, it becomes serious work at the children's farm or some special work assignment, like cleaning and scrubbing the school building. Until recently these work assignments used to be quite heavy, though the work load has now been lightened. At Atid, for example, fifth graders now work one hour a day after class at their farm or special job. Sixth to eighth graders work about one and a half hours a day, and after ninth grade, when they used to work three hours or more, they now work at least two hours a day (and all day during school vacation) at quite demanding tasks. True, they are not exploited. The profit from their farm, or a sizable part of it, is turned back to their own youth society. But the youth society decides what the money shall be spent on. Typical is the decision to use it for an extended trip through Israel: a trip taken by the group, as planned out by the group's committee. The group may also decide to visit other kibbutzim of their movement or, more rarely, those of other movements. Or it may go to the circus, or decide to spend its funds on buying records and record players, or for sports equipment.

Even the usual dreams of finding independence in the work world are closed to the kibbutz adolescent, unless he plans to leave the kibbutz, which is extremely rare at this age. In one kibbutz only one high school age youngster thought of leaving; in two others, none. (Probably more of them will leave the kibbutz later on, as a certain percentage do. But of this they are not yet aware, since those who will leave will not do so until after the army experience has brought them closer to independence and the non-kibbutz world.)

These adolescents cannot plan what they will do someday, because that will be decided by the labor committee according to what labor may be needed at the time. Their teachers encourage them to think of their academic education, and some youngsters would like to go on to higher schooling. But, as several told me, they cannot afford to think about this, or about a field of study, because there is absolutely no assurance that the kibbutz will send anyone, or them in particular, to the Technion or the University. So, to spare themselves the heavy disappointment, they try to suppress their own plans for the future.

The kibbutz is the only place in Israel that provides free education for all up to eighteen, and they rightly pride themselves on this fact. The teaching is of such high quality that it could easily prepare the more gifted, though not all students, for matriculation; that is, for the entrance examination to the universities. This, however, it does not do. Here we see another contradiction of the system, this time partly forced on it by economic necessity. It tries to provide the best possible education for all. But in doing so it makes things extremely difficult for those who have the interest and ability to go beyond high school, by not preparing them for the university entrance exam.

Consciously this is justified by the conviction that education has to be for the many, and not for the few. But the decision not to provide for matriculation has other reasons too. The kibbutz needs for its survival the labor of the next generation. Moreover, cash is always in short supply, and they cannot afford to maintain more than a very few youngsters at a time outside the kibbutz. More important, too many of those they have sent to the University, at great economic expense, then leave the kibbutz, which dampens their impulse to send many more. The story is somewhat different for the teacher's colleges maintained by the kibbutz. These too entail great expense, but youngsters being trained there in education are neither as likely nor as able to be drawn away from the movement. Very recently some regional classes have been organized for those who wish to study for matriculation, and the various kibbutzim send some of their graduates there for six months. But even a very affluent kibbutz cannot send more than 10 percent of its high school graduates.

Most, therefore, who return from the army and wish to study for the quite demanding matriculation exam have to do so on their own. This is most difficult, since they have little time or energy for anything extra. The young adult is given a full work assignment in the kibbutz. Since it is natural for the heaviest or least desirable labor to be assigned to the newest members, he is quite tired after a day's work. Typically the kibbutz demands that they work for the first two years in the barn, or the banana plantation, or wherever else older kibbutzniks prefer not to work.

After a full day's hard work, few young adults have it in them to study several hours each night, for two or more years. The only allowance made is their being excused from work for the last week or so before exam time. But there is no assurance that if they pass, the kibbutz will let them go, or make it financially possible, or when. And even if they succeed, and the educational committee votes the funds, it does not mean they can study what they wish. The kibbutz, through its appropriate committee, decides what skills are needed and will rarely provide funds for the study of any but these subjects.

Here, too, the kibbutz is harder on the adolescent or young adult than on some of its older members. The feeling is that if a comrade has worked fifteen or more years at assigned tasks, then the kibbutz must make allowances if he now prefers one kind of work to another. And in some cases they are quite generous, even if the coveted tasks cannot easily be built into kibbutz structure.

This, incidentally, makes for some of the bad features of kibbutz education. Persons are assigned as nurses of infants, as educators, and even as therapists, whom the kibbutz rightly views as unsuited to the task. But as I was told: "We couldn't deny them their request after they've given their all to the community for fifteen or twenty years." Efforts are made to cushion the effects by providing courses that will better qualify such persons. But the result is that in every kibbutz I visited there were some very fine nurses and educators, and then there were others, some quite unsuitable, but assigned there because they had insisted. Things are not made easier by the fact that some of the younger and better qualified educators and nurses cannot assert their contrary views. These old and venerable comrades carry much more influence in the general assembly, and in electing the committee that regulates educational affairs.

I might add that for girls the prospect of what they wish to do and become in the future is even further restricted. True, it was a central kibbutz tenet that there be equality between the sexes, meaning that women should not be limited in occupation to child rearing and homemaking, but should in all respects be the equals of men. It was felt that this was possible only if they worked exactly like them, most of all in tilling the soil, since this was the work carrying highest prestige. But, interestingly enough, they were more successful in making these policies stick with regard to all women's working than to equality of the sexes at work. Women have more and more been assigned to the work tasks considered "feminine," such as child rearing, kitchen and laundry, etc.

As Weingarten notes in his *Life in a Kibbutz:*

> Kibbutzim are finding that the goal of freeing women from household tasks is becoming increasingly unworkable. In a

young community, where there are few children . . . it is possible . . . to free women for other activity. As the community grows older, a tremendous pressure develops to put more people to work in child care, to improve the dining room service, to provide more clothing. . . . The women, therefore, are pulled out one by one, often against their will, from whatever else they are doing and placed in the services.

It should be added that while men are assigned to education and some to the kitchen, too, I did not meet a single man who worked in the laundry.

This is a problem that women of the founding generation worry about a great deal. But again, to many of their kibbutz-born daughters the question of women's social disability is old hat and not very exciting. They take for granted that women work for the kibbutz, and all of them do. Since it was nothing they had to fight for, they feel less that they are losing out on something when they then work mostly in the services and in child rearing. Secure, for example, in the importance of their role as a teacher, they shrug their shoulders at all this "nonsense" of their mothers. (Which does not mean that when harvest time comes and the oranges must be picked in a hurry, they will not work as hard as any man for a few days to save the harvest.)

What girls are not spared are the same conflicts the boys feel about not being able to dream of a future career of their choosing. They are merely free of the extra burden that worries their mothers: that the restriction of occupational choice may mean they are again being confined to "women's work" and being kept from what is really "important."

Essentially what has taken place is a redefining of work. To the founders, any work that was not hard physical labor, preferably in farming, was tainted by the ghetto past and viewed as parasitic, exploitative of others. As the land was reclaimed, and as work became ever more technical to sustain a viable economy in Israel, as even the kibbutzim added small factories, even hotel operations, the notions of what work is important and what exploitative, changed.

This, plus the ever mounting concern for the future of the kibbutzim, which depended on the second generation, made the work of education increasingly "important." While the first generation remains ambivalent about the service occupations, the second generation is fully aware of how vital at least some of them are, such as those connected with child rearing.

It must again be stressed that for most of man's existence the young had no choice but to follow in their parents' footsteps, becoming a hunter or a farmer, a housewife, a mother. Things are different for the kibbutz youngster. First, he knows enough about the outside world to realize that his contemporaries abroad have a much greater chance to arrange their own lives in society in line with their own inclinations.

More important: He has heard from infancy about the founders' heroic struggle for self-realization against heaviest odds, with the implication that this is how a real man or a real woman lives. Kibbutz reality, by contrast, not only makes it easy to avoid battling society for self-realization, but disapproves of it by expecting youth to fit itself into existing society, without protest. So the adolescent is really close to an impasse: There is the inner conflict about wanting to take the easy way that adults want him to take but feeling uneasy about it because then he is not quite the person of the mythos who successfully battles society for his ideals. Most nevertheless choose the easier way—at least until such time as the army experience frees them to some degree—but their self-esteem is not helped.

Here, then, is another aspect of their rejecting their parents' "great ideas." If, in their own lives, they are presented with the culture hero and then told not to live up to that image, then the easiest solution is to debase such an image. Not of the culture hero himself—this they cannot do because the merits of the founders are too obvious—but at least of the ideas they stood for. They cannot do what seems psychologically impossible but what their parents wish them to do: venerate the great ideas that stress the revolt against custom, and also settle down to kibbutz life as it is.

They admire what their parents have done, but they cannot admire their parents' ideas. If they did, they would have to be as revolutionary as their parents were, and (like them) create a new and different society. And if the parents really admired what they said they did, they would have to give their children the same leave to defy custom that marked their own youth. The great ideas, the mythos, are thus sham to their children on both counts. But kibbutz life, stripped of its great ideas becomes less the realization of an ideal and more the normal and customary manner of life. In this respect, too, the third generation will be the true touchstone of what the kibbutzim may one day be like.

In any case, inner development, as the path to coming into one's own, is doubly indicated for kibbutz adolescents, since they cannot do it by making their own place in society. Unable to extend themselves outward because of the restrictive kibbutz outlook, being more afraid and suspicious of strangers than other adolescents, to the point where they seem downright xenophobic, they try to turn inward even more than most adolescents. But to be a person in one's own right runs not so much counter to the values of their society as it runs counter to their whole life experience. More than adolescents in any society I know of, except perhaps for the initiation societies of some preliterate peoples (though the rest of that setting is again different), they have lived almost exclusively as part of a group.

🌣 Group Values

Now, AS THE ADOLESCENT TRIES TO DRAW ON INNER RE-sources in the struggle to become a separate person, he is forced to do so without first having developed the proper tools. The most pressing problems around which a family member can and often does define himself were absent for him. Internalization of parental values, or opposition to them, has added little toward a personal superego. Instead, all values were set for him by the community, and he has made them his own. But their acceptance does not make for a very personal superego either. Lacking any values of his own that are different from the group's, he cannot set them against group values in an effort to define which are his.

As a matter of fact, kibbutz society is quite cruel in deal-ing with the occasional adolescent who dares to set his val-ues against the group's. Where a middle-class youngster might test his independence and personal value system by doing poorly in school, or even dropping out entirely, the kibbutz adolescent will as likely as not rebel by slacking off at work. This is so because the endless round of school, work, youth assembly, and other group-oriented activities gives him little time or chance to be on his own.

As one educator told me: "Their day is incredibly crowded. They have six hours of classes. Then they sup-posedly have one hour of rest, and then three hours of work. Then they have homework, then they have their hours with the parents, and then they have all kinds of social activities. There is not a single evening free for them. And things are worse when they enter high school. Every hour of their day is scheduled. They simply have no free time. I have been a teacher for twenty-five years, and I worked with young chil-dren, and I saw what happened to them. One year I was away studying in Jerusalem, and tried to correspond with my students. In every letter they complained that they were so tired. And this still goes on."

By contrast, their life as recruits in the army seems a relief. As one of them who had just finished his tour of duty told me: "The army's extremely lenient. There's no comparison between the army and the kibbutz. In the army you have your off-duty hours. You never had an after-duty time in the youth society." This last was from a person who had felt stifled by kibbutz education in his wish to become a person, so his views were no doubt somewhat jaundiced. But such was not true of the educator I have just quoted.

If the adolescent does shirk his labor assignment, the entire youth society is disgusted with him. Among their sanctions, as one of them told me, was that he was not allowed to eat with them but was sent to eat outside "like a dog," without table or chair. In some cases even meals have been withheld, except for bread and olives, because "who does not work does not earn a full meal." True, this kind of cruel practice is no longer permitted by the youth leader, but the spirit behind it is still the prevailing one toward persons who are work shy.

To be ostracized like this is most effective, because unlike ostracism in ancient Greece, the person so excluded from the community has nowhere else to go. His parents will not support him in his revolt (in childhood they say: "You must do what the metapelet tells you"; and later on: "You must be part of your group"), nor will his teachers, nor any other adults. He lacks the confidence to think of escaping to the cities, nor can he find companions who might lend him support. The metapelet is no help, because the individual metapelet was never too important to begin with.

If the group is too draconic in its sanctions, the adult youth leader steps in. For example, he objects to their withholding food and insists that the punishment not be exaggerated. After all, the adults want the group to continue, and they have no wish to drive the offender to desperation, or to quit the kibbutz. So usually the worst is prevented. But the mood of the group is quite clear. And since it is them the offender must live with and on whom he depends for almost everything that matters to him, the severe punishment they even considered is effective deterrent.

When I asked a top educator of one kibbutz movement how the work morality is otherwise enforced, he told me: "There's no one practice since each children's or youth society decides on its own how to deal with such cases, of which there are few. Some years ago, the children's society used to punish a boy or a girl who didn't want to go to work by striking him off the list of workers, and that was the most terrible thing they could do to the child, because this truly made him an outlaw. I can remember one girl who was a poor worker. The children were ready to literally tear her to pieces and throw her out, so we educators had to step in and try to calm them down. We finally got her to talk with the secretary (the highest kibbutz functionary) because no one in the children's society would talk to her anymore. He, and we educators, could show her that she would have no friends, be all alone, and this worked. Because she knew it would be true. So situations like that don't repeat themselves often."

Group sanctions are all the more effective because with no way to escape the group, there is no way to escape its rejection. The adolescent lacks a room of his own, and there is no park or public library he can withdraw to in solitude. He cannot even go to a movie and sit in the dark, because except for the visits to his parents no child can attend an activity without some others of his group.

Not only is a relative isolation completely out of reach,

but so is any intimate friendship, because the group always intrudes. It is practically impossible for two persons to form an intimate relationship; this I learned from a variety of sources and could readily observe.

As one educator told me: "If a twosome is formed, they immediately become the center of opposition. A twosome is looked on as something alien, as an effort to escape from the group. Maybe they are so unfriendly to the pair partly because of their own unsatisfied longing; because they might like to be part of a twosome themselves, but are not. If such a friendship is formed, immediately many intrigues begin against them, and the group will try everything to break it up, and succeed. I cannot think of a single instance where the group did not try to break up such a twosome, either by intrigues or in other ways. The critical ages for this are usually between thirteen and sixteen."

By then the young adolescent has given up hope and settles back into a group life that is devoid of true intimacy, though it remains intensely close. This, incidentally, worries kibbutz educators, despite their stress on group life. They realize the importance of serious friendships for the adolescent. It was the friendships they found in the youth movement that led them to create the kibbutz, but their own children seem unable to come close to each other. Though leading educators are deeply concerned about it, they do not see that their arranging for the child's life to comprise only group events so that he is never alone—has no time and no place of his own, is almost never forced back on his own resources—now prevents him from being intimate with others.

Intimacy requires a great deal of time, but also a great concentration on the other person. This too requires time, but time when one is not otherwise exhausted. For this reason intimate relations probably call for a relative leisure during the formative years, and the chance to concentrate on one meaningful relationship at a time. Neither of the two are available to kibbutz youngsters.

🌿 Sex

ADOLESCENCE IS THE AGE IN WHICH SEXUAL FEARS AND DESIRES are overriding. Much has been written about the fact that the growing up together of an age-group has led to incest taboos between members because they have always lived as brothers and sisters. And there is some truth to the matter.

Much more important, in my opinion, is the fact that unlike the sex freedom common among early kibbutzniks (or rather a semipromiscuous outward show of it, more than inner sexual freedom) the kibbutz now takes a rather puritanical stance. For example, though there is officially small concern with premarital sex, teachers are very much concerned if a youngster is tired because he is having sex relations at age seventeen or eighteen, and they warn him against it. They do not tell him that to do so is bad but express concern that he seems so tired during the day, so disinterested in his work, or so withdrawn from the group, (as the case may be), which they think is too bad. The message the boy or girl gets, though, is that to have sex relations is bad.

The true attitude to extramarital sex, as opposed to the one given lip service, shows up in the reactions to extramarital pregnancy. The severest sanctions are reserved for those whose pregnancies show that they took sex to be as "natural" and "good" as they were told. These communities which pride themselves on their nonbourgeois liberal attitudes toward sex are, by and large, very down on a girl who gets pregnant before school is over, that is before eighteen, and before she is married. (Marriage before the return from the army is extremely rare, and I learned of none before the age of eighteen, except in the very rare case of a girl getting pregnant before then.)

Such a girl has to quit school and may not return, even if the boy marries her, as he usually does. While she is not automatically expelled from the kibbutz, her exclusion from school amounts to exclusion from the peer group. And to risk that is virtually impossible, psychologically, as I have described. Interestingly enough, the kibbutz here displays a double moral standard, despite their avowed belief in equality of the sexes: the boy who got the girl pregnant is criticized, but that is all. He is not excluded from school, nor are there any other sanctions against him.

Though the grave concern with early and illegitimate pregnancies has much to do with the puritanical attitude, it has also to do with a concern for cohesion in the kibbutz. Sanctions are meant less as punishment than as deterrent, out of a fear of contagion. But it was puritanism that led to decreeing that two boys and two girls must sleep in the same room, shower together, etc., till the age of eighteen.

Of course, kibbutzniks did not see this as puritanism; just the reverse. They were convinced that old ghetto attitudes toward sex and the body were all wrong, as many of them certainly were. (If sexual mores in the ghetto differed from those on the outside, they were more repressive.) The body was considered something shameful that decency required one to keep hidden; menstruation was explicitly viewed as making the woman "unclean," etc. These were "unnatural" attitudes that crippled one's life.

The new Jew, in the new society, would not be bound by these age-old sexual anxieties; all such taboos would be done away with. It was a liberating experience the founders meant to provide for their children: From infancy on everything would be open about sex and the body. Nothing would be hidden as shameful.

Actually such arrangements lead to sexual stimulation. This forces one either to act upon it—as occurs typically among children who share life together very "openly" under slum conditions—or leads to early and far-reaching sex repression, and thence to the development of a deeply puritanical attitude toward sex. But kibbutz children have little option. Because they are not only asked to be "natural and open" about their bodies, it is expected that this will make them "pure" about it. That is, they should not only not have sex, but should not even desire it.

In fact, it is precisely because these boys and girls have always shared a bedroom with each other and have showered together, that they have been sexually stirred by each other, felt ashamed, and been forced to suppress what they felt. Not just (as the literature suggests) because these others are their "siblings": Repression does not work all that neatly. Nor is it because of the reason they give when asked why they do not fall in love with or marry any of those they grew up with. They say, and kibbutz theory holds, that one does not fall in love with the person one sat next to on the toilet, as a child; an explanation that has also entered the literature.

It is not because of the sitting on the toilet together, but because of the sexual feelings thus aroused, of which the youngsters are made to feel guilty (and hence ashamed). It is because of the feelings one had to suppress about oneself as others watched one sitting on the toilet, or masturbating (or wanting to), or having an erection, or menstruating. It is because of those other feelings one had to suppress too— feelings one had about the other as one watched him or her eliminating, or masturbating (or wishing to), or having an erection, or menstruating—not to mention those other instinctual behaviors that characterize children's "polymorphous" sex play.

These (in theory) are practiced in our middle-class families only in secret, while in the kibbutz (in theory) they are openly observed by the children in each other. Actually kibbutz theory holds they are just not engaged in because of how "naturally" the children are raised. Thus I was told again and again by educators that "our children and adolescents are entirely natural about sex," meaning always that they do not masturbate or practice any other sexual behavior. "They don't have to," I was told, "because we've taught them it's all natural." Instead, they repress and sublimate into the "purity" that kibbutzniks view as resulting from their "natural" rearing, and as proving its merits.[1]

In this way the children protect themselves not only from shame and embarrassment, but from their own sexual desires and the guilt these engender. Because to feel sexual desires for each other runs counter to the value of the youth society "to keep things pure," which is the highest value taught to youth. It comes right after the value of being a good comrade, to which, in their minds, it is closely connected. This is something on which parents, metapelets, kibbutz, and age-group agree. It is wrong for the children to have sexual feelings for each other, period.

Such a far-reaching repression of feelings about having one's body observed and about observing others leads to alienation from the erotic feelings roused in one's body. Most of all, one cannot afford to recognize them. Because, if

[1] One might speculate that the very effort to create a just society leads to puritanism, if only because the new and better society is expected to have erased all the problems of the old one. Given man's sexual problems, no society yet has solved them perfectly, but this fact the creators of a utopian society cannot accept. Thus the earliest period of the kibbutz saw a widespread promiscuity, which was supposed to rid man of his sexual difficulties. When this did not happen, then "purity" under the guise (or in consequence) of being "natural and open" about sex was expected to do it.

one did, one simply could not go on showering together, sleeping together, etc., without acting on the feelings thus aroused.

It is the totality of all these sublimations and repressions that prevents intimacy with these others—because of whom, and about whom, one had so many feelings to deny or repress. Neither can there be intimacy with others when none is possible with oneself, because so much of one's feelings have been repressed. And while the exogamous love relations or marriage outside the peer group (that is with youngsters outside one's own age-group) lifts some repression of feelings about others, it cannot undo the repressions about one's intimate, innermost self, including one's body and its functions.

These functions are with reason called intimate functions. One can perform them with (or in the presence of) others, only if one feels free to be intimate with them. If not, then one feels ashamed, which is painful and must be repressed. But if the repression of one's feelings about the bodily functions has been radical, then one cannot engage in them freely, with another. Worse, no true intimacy is possible with oneself or with anyone else.

That is why, in adolescence and later on, there seems so much physical (and emotional) distance between kibbutz-born persons, even when they love each other. They seem hesitant to touch and be touched. They cannot freely enjoy it because there has been too much repression about their own bodies.

True, boys and girls in the right-wing movement now sleep in separate rooms, from anywhere between twelve and fourteen. This, however, is not timed by the child's sexual maturation but by the availability of rooms. Thus a girl who begins to menstruate at eleven or twelve may have to go on sleeping in the same room with boys for a few years before a room is freed in the adolescent building through someone's having left for the army. (In the left-wing movement it is still typical that two boys and two girls of high school age share a room until induction into the army at eighteen.) So even in the right-wing kibbutz the sexes separate only as rooms become available, and not when sexual maturity is reached. There, as in the left-wing, boys have to blind themselves to the menstruating girl, since they are not supposed to see, just as the girls must not see the boys' erections.

When I asked a group of boys in a left-wing kibbutz how it was, for example, when the girls had their menses, I was told, "That's no problem. They simply tell us to turn around." And turn around they do, both boys and girls, making themselves unseeing, and to a large degree unfeeling, about sex.

Now there is some truth to the kibbutznik's conviction that their way of rearing makes the children feel "natural" about sex, depending on what one views as being "natural." For example, living as closely and openly as they do, they have been stimulated in the "anal" stage by observing others defecating or at "anal" play, and in the "phallic" stage by observing boys and girls in those instinctual behaviors and seeking those instinctual satisfactions belonging to this phase of development. They were also forced, during these stages to suppress a lot of the stimulation thus aroused. But then, when they reach adolescence and more "genital" desires, the controls they must now develop for dealing with new pressures build on all the previous defenses (inhibitions, repressions, reaction formations, denials, etc.) they have long since developed to manage living so "openly" together. And I include here the defense of sublimating their sexual desires into a desire for "purity."

It may be that a repression of genital sexuality which builds on the repression of instinctual desires belonging to earlier stages of development is indeed more "natural" than how things are in many of our middle-class families. Because with us the body of the other sex has to be newly discovered, as it were, in adolescence. And the anxieties and defenses this evokes cannot build on defenses developed all along the way for dealing with stimulations that come of observing both sexes daily in all their "intimate" bodily activities. Except that this is not the being "natural" about sex that kibbutz theory has in mind.

Certainly in those preliterate societies, where sex inhibitions are few, adult sexual freedom builds very much on the instinctual freedom that infants and children enjoy through all stages of their psychosexual development. Actually I know of no society where sexual freedom is unlimited; what seems so is only by comparison with ourselves. Nevertheless, in societies that enjoy a relative sexual freedom, those sublimations and inhibitions never developed that alone permit higher social and intellectual achievements. And since these the kibbutz very much wants for its children, it can hardly afford them such a "naturalness" in their instinctual and sexual development.

Here, though, as elsewhere, there are counterbalancing experiences, and that is why sex repression in the kibbutz is not more constricting than it is. Because if sex repression is massive, it is balanced by the bodily freedom enjoyed during toilet training, for example, but also around eating, in the use of the body during infancy and the toddler age, etc. Thus they use the body freely, though they are not truly at home with it, in intimacy. Here, too, what makes for the final personality, is the sum total of what is experienced during infancy, childhood, adolescence, and later. Kibbutz children experience much more freedom in some areas, compared to our middle-class settings, and much more repression in regard to other kinds of experiences with their own bodies and that of others.

In the left-wing kibbutzim there is a very important ceremony that takes place at the end of high school, before en-
tering the army. The group that has lived together for the
whole eighteen years of their lives gets together and each
member evaluates himself and the others for their worthiness
to full kibbutz standing. They question each other, and particularly their behavior in the high school years: Have they
been good comrades, good workers, and "kept themselves
pure"?

This mutual and self-examination is quite an ordeal.
Much anxiety precedes it, and it is terrible for those whom
the group decides are not ready for membership because of
one failing or another. Anticipating how one's peers will
evaluate one's innermost self and one's failings, or what this
may bring to light, are just further reason to repress thoroughly one's wrongful desires.

At Atid, educators questioned the youngsters after a few
years of the new regime by which boys and girls of high
school age were given separate sleeping quarters, toilets, and
shower rooms. Asked whether they wanted to keep the new
arrangement or return to the old one, all the youngsters
clearly favored the separation. As one of the boys put it:
"When we want to be with our girls together [meaning not
their 'girl friends' but the girls of their age-group], we have
enough occasion for that. But when we sleep, we want to be
by ourselves."

This conversation came about because a group of left-
wing adolescents were visiting Atid at the time, giving both
groups a chance to learn about and react to their different
sleeping and living arrangements. The educator then asked
some of the visitors how they felt about the two kinds of
arrangements. At first the visiting youngsters talked at length
of how it makes for more socialism and equality if the boys

and girls sleep together; they avoided all personal expression of feelings.

So the educator said, "Look, do you really want to tell me that when the girl sleeps only one half meter from your bed, and you are aware of it, don't you have sometimes a desire to be with her, stretch out your hand and touch her?" After some evasion, and more pressing questions, one of the boys admitted this was so. So the educator continued: "Doesn't it put you on a spot where you, so to say, by just reaching out your hand, can have her, be with her? Doesn't it create tension in you?" To this both the boys and girls refused to answer and broke off the conversation.

Interestingly enough, the educator who reported this exchange to me then mentioned with satisfaction that adolescent girls in the kibbutz are much more modest, show none of the "sex craziness" that is typical of American and also Israeli (non-kibbutz) girls of this age. But later he wondered uneasily why "at a time when the American girls preen themselves, and try to show off as much as possible sexually, our girls cover themselves up and refuse to wear clothing that might show their breasts or in any other fashion be revealing." It was difficult for him to recognize that this came from the same sex repression in the girls that made them show "none of the sex craziness" he and the community so thoroughly disapproved of.

Nor is it only his sexual feelings the adolescent must repress. Their very repression builds on those repressions of infancy and childhood discussed earlier (but also on the steady sublimation into high work morality and "purity"). Resentment, too, must be swallowed, except for what he permits himself to show about the founding generation's "big ideas." If he wants to get along with his parents, he must repress his resentment of the metapelets. If he wants to get along with community and peer group, he must repress his resentment of everything the group disapproves of, such as resenting that he cannot have or want the excitement or comforts of city life.[2]

Here, his position is much harder than for an American child growing up in a small rural community, or a child who has no more amenities than kibbutz youngsters enjoy—which is true for our children of the poor. The difference is that with us the disadvantaged child is expected and encouraged to want for himself what more fortunate youngsters enjoy; his resentment and jealousy are taken for granted. In the kibbutz the opposite is true. To wish for these advantages is a dreadful offense. Since the adolescent is nevertheless fascinated, he must suppress both the jealousy and resentment.

The very reason for the taboo on private property is to keep jealousy from interfering with group life. But there are deeper jealousies than the jealousy of material possessions. So all jealousy must be repressed. Even the small child must repress his jealousy and accept that kibbutz affairs count more to his parents than spending their evenings with him. Our children, too, are jealous at being excluded from grown-up activities, and this again is taken for granted, considered natural. But to object in the kibbutz is to violate the basic kibbutz law: that the peer group comes first.

Repression of jealousy (but always also its sublimation) is the only way out and also what all adults expect. It is what the children observe in the relations between parents and metapelets, sometimes metapelets and teachers, or even parents and teachers. Parents, as discussed, are often jealous

---

[2] It must again be borne in mind that in many other respects the kibbutz youngster has less to repress than the middle-class child. He has no cause to resent parental power (whether at the oedipal or adolescent age), nor economic dependence, nor social and academic pressure, etc.

of the role of metapelets in the lives of their children, though the relation is not very intense. Perhaps for that very reason the metapelets are much readier to criticize the parents, though they do not recognize the jealousy behind it. But with this one exception, their jealousy too is repressed.

With so much repression of their negative feelings toward each other, many of the positive feelings get repressed along with them. But positive feelings get repressed on other grounds too. Every day parents and children have to repress their attachment to each other, as for example on saying good-bye at the end of the daily visit. (By adolescence, visiting with parents has become very casual; often youngsters do not see their parents for days, except for chance meetings that occur daily as kibbutzniks go about their business.) But while the children are still little, and particularly at difficult moments, they cling to their parents, not wanting to let go. For this they are severely criticized by the group (the other children do not want to be reminded of their own pain in the same situation).

Some parents rebuff the efforts too, but all parents insist that the right thing to do is let go. If the right thing is to let go of personal attachments, then better not to form them, or not too deeply, because it hurts too much to let go. This accounts for their bedtime behavior in childhood: the relative ease with which children learn to let go of their parents, and how easily they then go to bed.

But while all this dates back to childhood, it is in adolescence that the casual attitude to each other, to teachers, to parents, has finally become so habitual as to dominate their life, and so ingrained that it deflects the adolescent's longing to be intimate with himself and with others.

❦ *The Hedgehog's Dilemma*

I HAVE DISCUSSED INTIMACY BEFORE AS A PROBLEM THE KIB-butz seems to struggle with unsuccessfully. Somehow the kibbutz has not fought free of the youth societies in which the movement began. This is not the place to discuss the nature of youth movements. But to a considerable degree they remain stuck in an adolescent stance where intimacy is highly praised in theory but fearfully avoided in practice; where peer relations are desperately sought and overvalued, because they have to stand for an intimacy longed for but unattainable; where the underlying fear is that by giving too much of oneself, one may lose one's emerging self before it is firmly established. Thus all youth societies are deeply con-cerned with the problem of personal identity and that of intimacy, while the attachment to and high valuation of the peer group keeps them from both.

The impression given is that this ambiguity, this conflict, marks relations between all kibbutz comrades. It is why they cherish their comradeship so much, and why it is also a burden to them. The inner tensions of kibbutz life are those that stem from exactly this conflict. They need and seek comradeship, but find it wanting. They seek intimacy in their marital relations, and with their children, but since they themselves are wary of being intimate, they do not find it there easily. Most of all, while the kibbutz was designed to enable one to be intimate with others, it disregards the fact that this is not possible without knowing how to be intimate with oneself.

It is not so much the age old "know thyself" that is meant here, but more an intimate acquaintance with one's feelings. To then be intimate with a chosen few is to be free to show these, our true feelings, to another, feeling sure he will meet them with empathy and not with dislike or indifference. Obviously, we can hardly show to somebody else what we ourselves do not recognize as existing within ourselves. Yet this lack of self-awareness is fostered in the kibbutz, first by the lack of solitude and privacy, and second by the need to repress so much of one's feelings.

Kibbutz founders hoped that by removing all external impediments to human relations they would flower most fully. What they did not recognize was that it was the shared worries about those impediments, and all the fighting in the ghetto family, that revealed its members to each other and eventually to themselves.

Intimacy thrived because people depended on each other, not only for security, but also for being the only ones on whom they could safely discharge their aggressions and frustrations. They provided for each other the chance to have a good fight, and a good cry. Outside the family all negative feelings had to be totally repressed. Against the outside no one could rail, because the world would destroy them if they approached it with anything but submission. Neither could they cry in it—because it would only make fun of their misery. Only inside the family—both the immediate, and the larger ghetto family—did their crying meet with empathy and compassion. Only there could one safely get rid of one's negative feelings without risking steadfast relations.

But even this is not enough for true intimacy. To it must be added the freedom to be truly oneself. And there were some in the ghetto for whom full selfhood required throwing off its constraints. So, in their case, ghetto life asked for too much repression. Though they could laugh and cry in it, they could not be fully themselves.

To find a likelier world, a true community of like-minded peers, this was the promise the kibbutz held out. What was overlooked was that one cannot really cry with some thirty people. One cannot fight with them and avoid getting badly bruised, because it is hard to make up with so many when the fighting is over, however close one's relationships with them. Two or three dozen people can sing and dance together, can laugh together, and this they did in early kibbutz days. But to satisfy the good feelings is not enough to bring about true intimacy. For that one must also feel free to vent one's anger and fear and disappointment without its having bad effects.

The good comrade can and does have good times with his comrades. Their support is also strong in bad times—and many kibbutzniks stress how important it is that when things go wrong, one's comrades are both compassionate and helpful—so long as the source of the injury is not the kibbutz; so long as the fight is not against it. That is the serious limitation on how much, and about what, one can really let go. This is why true intimacy fails to develop.

Kibbutz children, like adults, need others too, for emotional comfort. But there are no adults around at whom it would be absolutely safe for the child to scream, nor does the parents' behavior invite it. The kibbutz parent whose child screams at him is so hurt and desperate about it that the child cannot afford to "let go." He is so much more hurt because deep down he cannot tell himself what the ghetto parents could: "Let him scream as much as he wants, he fools neither me nor himself: We both know he needs me." The outburst was nothing but a passing interruption of relations that were soon reestablished, if on no other basis than necessity.

And if the ghetto child screamed out his anguish about the hurt he suffered out in the world, he did so to a parent who was just as acquainted with the grief. The kibbutz child, if he cries out his distress at what he suffers outside the home, does so to a parent who will defend with sweet reason the behavior of those on the outside, since those outsiders are his comrades.

In our setting, the middle-class child can sometimes discharge against his parents. And he can discharge a lot of aggression against his age-mates. The kibbutz child depends far too much on the peer group. He cannot afford to scream at them, to fight with them, knowing that if things get too rough he can always retire to the womb of his family, to the safety of his home. And even there, if his parents don't side with him, the middle-class child can at least go to his room, shut the door, and be by himself. The kibbutz child has no such room.

The result is that the child concludes it is useless to look to his parents, and dares not turn to his peers. Since there is no other place to take his hurt, he soon learns he is alone with his anguish and will either repress his deepest feelings, or be convinced there is no one with whom he can share them.

Another reason why there is very little fighting among peers in the kibbutz, just as there is very little fighting between parents and children. But there is also no (or very little) crying of youngsters on each others' shoulders. The present day adolescent conflict between the generations is not openly enacted between parent and youth. The young merely withdraw from the parents ever more, spend less and less of their free time with them. This avoids the open conflicts, but also reduces considerably their intimate exchanges.

Here, the kibbutz itself interferes, where it means only to make intimacy secure. For example, the communality of living requires that one should at all times be available to the comrades. But how can intimacy develop if others are at all times free to intrude? Or how can one be intimate with children, when the timing for the intimate exchange is beyond one's control?

How it can, instead, result in withdrawing from contacts,

I learned within the short weeks I spent in the kibbutz. My photographer-companion could not accustom himself to how kibbutzniks felt free to walk in on him at any hour of the day or night, no matter what he was occupied with. Eventually both of us, who had initially liked the idea of living in a true community, felt a recurrent need to escape for a few hours to the anonymity of city life, where we could for moments be ourselves; where we were not expected to want to be always with others.

What made it so hard was that this longing for a bit of privacy, which to us seemed so natural, was felt by others to be a deliberate shunning of their company. It was not so much that others were so intrusive—this was true only for a small minority; most kibbutzniks we found very considerate. Our dilemma was that they so obviously meant well but were truly offended if we wanted some time to ourselves. And this was true for most kibbutz members. But who wants to be rude to those who mean to be friendly? Since we did not want that, we had no choice but to escape what (within kibbutz confines) was their inescapable presence. We either left the kibbutz physically, or withdrew psychologically to an inner, unshared privacy. At such times we met them only on a superficial level, to retain some privacy within us. Since the kibbutz member cannot escape to the outside if he needs privacy, only the second way is open to him.

Here the anarchists have a point: True personal freedom cannot be assured through any societal arrangements. Any regulation designed to assure it, infringes on it, and the more it tries to assure freedom, the more it infringes. The same is true for intimacy. The logic of this dialectic process—which turns intimacy into its opposite—is by no means as obvious, but is just as effective.

It is thus an extension of what pessimistic Schopenhauer described as the predicament of all human relations. Comparing men to hedgehogs in freezing winter, he said that their problem is to find a position of closeness to each other so that they can enjoy the warmth given off by their bodies and not freeze to death, while at the same time keeping enough distance from each other so that their quills do not prick. Unfortunately, it seems that the distance that protects us from being pricked does not offer much warmth or creature comfort.

All these problems are only too familiar in our own society to consider them specific to the kibbutz. The difference is that kibbutz society is built and organized around the conscious desire for intimacy. Hence the conflict around it is more pervasive.

Our society has gone far in seeking privacy and avoiding the pains of closeness. It therefore suffers from too much distance, shall we say, or alienation. The kibbutz, in its striving to undo social alienation on the one hand, and too much family closeness on the other, has gone way out in seeking a solidarity of equals. But having enjoyed collective closeness for a while now, they seem to find it hard to bear at times.

Precisely because they share so much of daily life with each other, they have a great need, like turtles, to withdraw into their shells. Though they greet each other with a "*Shalom!*" or "How's things?" twenty times or more every day, they really have little to talk about, since everyone knows everything about everyone else—good reason to withhold the really important things for oneself and to share them with no one.

It could be argued that for the kibbutz-born adolescent nothing in his previous life can have evoked in him any longing for intimacy. If the longing is not innate, but is born of one's experience in growing up, why should the kibbutz-raised adolescent feel a need to be intimate? How can he miss what was never available to him? And there is considerable truth to the argument, in the sense that little in his previous experience with others has prepared him for such a craving. I very much doubt, for example, that there is anything like what we mean by intimacy in preliterate societies. Nor do I know what its equivalent might be among people who grow up, for example, in a society where the compound family prevails.

But for us in the West, I believe that we all wish to be terribly important to someone. This alone gives us a feeling of security, since those who find us so important will take care of us. Only with them can we drop our defenses—as we must, for example, if our sexual relations are really to be satisfying, emotionally. But this is very different from being important to some hundred persons as a member of their community. In modern Western society, this not being very important to the whole community is our loss; being extremely important to a very few (if we are) is our gain. The Western adolescent who dreams of having a family of his own thinks that his wife and children will need him uniquely and hence make him feel he is extraordinarily important, if only to them. The kibbutz adolescent knows that the kibbutz, as such, needs him, and that he is important to his parents in a sense. But since his parents were not too important to him, he may wonder to whom *he* will be very important.

Now it should be remembered that, while the kibbutz youngster had little chance to get close to others in a fully intimate relation, the community he grew up in is full of the stated importance of close relations with one's comrades. Moreover, the kibbutz is not a backward, inarticulate society, and its culture is mostly West European-American. The adolescent is deliberately exposed to this Western tradition with its love stories, poems, and ballads of longing. In the absence of psychoanalytic investigation in depth, I cannot be sure whether the kibbutz-born represses a craving for intimacy, sexual and otherwise, or simply does not develop such a craving.

For example, that such desires seem to be absent in him does not prove they are repressed, or that their derivatives may not be present—namely the feeling that something is lacking. But, if present, this may make him feel vaguely dissatisfied, uneasy. To the observer he seems not aware of such a feeling, and even less of what may be missing from his life. Hence, to speak of a longing for intimacy would indeed be a misstatement. He may long for something he feels to be lacking, but without knowing what. And to escape the discomfort of the longing, he may eventually repress it.

Here and throughout, when I discuss intimacy, it must be realized that both the desire and the experience depend on the presence of a rich and personal fantasy life, which one can then share. Sex alone does not make for intimacy; otherwise all who cohabit would also be intimate. But as we know, the quality of the sexual experience varies from person to person, and from culture to culture (or subculture). Thus it may be mainly a physiological relief, or a very unshared experience. It becomes something intimate only to the degree that the closeness is at once physical and emotional. Only then is the private fantasy life also shared, and one's loneliness ended.

Yael Dayan, the Israeli novelist, knows from personal experience what life in the Jewish agricultural settlements is like. In her *Envy the Frightened* (1961) she tells of a family and community who live closely together, share many desires and convictions, but who nevertheless destroy in their members the capacity for intimacy by destroying the rich inner fantasy life. Yet it does not follow from one story, real or invented, that each of us, at one time, has a desire for a private fantasy life. It may well be that the conditions of one's growing up simply do not create such a craving or desire.

In our society it is quite commonplace, in late adolescence, for a boy and a girl who belong to a group, like their college class, to find each other through the group and what initially attracted them to it. But as they turn more and more to each other, they loosen their group ties to the very degree that their mutual intimacy deepens.

If this does not happen, then other reality factors take them out of the group; they have to move away, or other members do. Even if this does not lead to true intimacy, it forces them toward each other and they form a twosome. But in the kibbutz, husband and wife remain first and foremost part of the group. So even in the marital relationship this makes for a more outward relatedness to the kibbutz than toward each other. There is less of the feeling (as in our best and most intimate marital relations) that "you and I belong to each other body and soul, and together we two meet the world"; and much more the feeling that "each of us belongs to this common world we share, and also to each other within it."

Here in the West, too, the world becomes much less exclusive. No longer is the world outside the home peopled by the enemy, against whom one must carefully defend oneself by making one's home one's castle. There is more of a spirit of cooperation, of taking in the outsider even when he comes from another class or ethnic background. There is even a marked interest in the person whose family background is different, rather than a shunning of every oddness as spelling danger. While this other-directedness, to use Riesman's concepts, makes for a lonely crowd, it is nevertheless a significant modern phenomenon, which reduces intimacy and the craving for it. Because as one grows up, more and more of one's interests and attachments come to be located outside of the family circle.

In the middle-class family this later openness to strangers, which starts very early with the children on the block and in the nursery school, is nevertheless preceded by the still earlier intimate relationship to the mother. That is why it brings a sense of loneliness in the crowd. But in the kibbutz there is much less of an intimate mother-child relationship, and a much earlier concentration on the group. Hence, while I believe there are rudiments of intimacy in the kibbutz too, and a desire for it, they are weaker than in the middle-class family. Even where the relationship of the parents to each other and to their child has a deeper emotional content, the child will respond first to his awareness that the parent's deepest allegiance is to the kibbutz and only secondly to his sense of their belonging to each other and their child.

The same primacy of allegiance to the group becomes more and more typical of the children's relations with other persons as they near the end of the latency period. Their development away from strong feelings for a particular partner becomes much more marked in adolescence, when to show emotions for only that person is so shunned that it seems anathema to them. The kibbutz is well aware of all this and explains it in part as a reaction to ghetto ways, particularly those of Eastern Jewry, for whom the open show of feeling was so central.

To quote one psychoanalyst, much of whose professional life is devoted to the kibbutz: "The result of all this repression is that our children are ashamed to be ashamed, are afraid to be afraid. They are afraid to love, are afraid to give of themselves. And part of the reason is that their mothers are terribly afraid of being Jewish mamas. I still am not sure whether it's a deficiency in emotions, or a being afraid of feeling. One gets the impression that even the small child, the infant, has to defend himself against his own feelings." (These thoughts, taken verbatim from the interview tapes, echo a passage in Dayan's *Envy the Frightened*. Speaking of the damage wrought on her hero's emotional life by how much the Israelis stress, even in childhood, the need to be fearless and brave, she writes: "Do you know what he's afraid of? To be afraid—this is the fear that masters him, until all other fears, human, normal, healthy ones, are pushed aside and stop existing.")

❧ Private Property, Private Emotions

THERE IS ONE CLASS OF FEELINGS THE ENTIRE GROUP STRONGLY approves of: This is their feelings for the kibbutz and its struggles, and for the Jewish homeland. Like most Israelis they are ready to die for Israel if necessary. But among the second and third generations this does not compare with their willingness to give their lives for their peer group, the boys and girls they grew up with. This is their deepest most abiding attachment, and the focus of powerful feelings about emotional events they have shared with their group.

I have described how all kibbutz founders are full of stories about their laboring together by day and then singing and dancing through the night. For adolescents some of this is still happening, though less intensely.

For example, it is true even for recently formed kibbutzim, or at least those organized by fresh immigrant groups trained abroad for the task. (The story is very different for young kibbutzniks who have served their time in the army and are sent out to form a new kibbutz.) But it is also true for kibbutz-born adolescents, as when they go on a group trip through Israel or on the yearly hike to Jerusalem. These are important emotional experiences that bind the group together—as with the children who set the doll house on fire. But each is an experience "we all had together," not "an experience *I* had." Nor are they the kind of happenings that invite intimacy, an opening to each other of one's innermost personal feelings.

The group, and each of its members, gets a lift out of such an event. Because of it everyone feels more alive—but chiefly because "we're all in it together," and not because now, thanks to this event, "I am more myself." It is almost as if the high value placed on the collective emotional experience makes the deeply private one—the experience that belongs to oneself or a twosome—seem kind of indecent.

Exceptions do occur when there is radical upheaval. One such was the six-day war, which shook many a kibbutznik to his very foundations. Because in the heat of battle he found himself facing death and himself, all alone, not as a member of a group. (After the fighting was over, kibbutz-born soldiers were interviewed by the movement about their reactions during combat. At the present writing, these very moving interviews had only been circulated privately.)

Many of them spoke of the horror they felt when they realized they had to kill. All their upbringing had taught them to regard the human beings in front of them not as "the enemy" but as essentially poor devils whom they had to kill if they did not want to be killed. This is not an experience unique to the kibbutz-born soldier. What was unique for him was to be all alone when it happened. It was not an experience he could share at the moment of decision, as he had shared all other experiences, even those of building a new settlement on the dangerous border, or of going on missions in the dead of night. Facing his own death and his killing of another human being brought a sudden aloneness, a being up against himself, for which his group life had not prepared him. Because dying is never a collective experience. Nor is killing. As one of them put it: "It forced us to think. Types like us don't really know how to ruminate about problems of good and bad, justice and injustice, about what is permissible and what is forbidden. Within the framework of our way of life, we are generally not the type of people who go into depth in matters of soul-searching. For a person who doesn't have an inner world of his own, who cannot work things through with himself, the group of us now have some contact with our feelings, are asking whether things are right or wrong, all as a result of the battles. It's a pity we achieved this only through the war experience, but it's good that it motivates us to do a bit of soul-searching."

Nevertheless, while it was a solitary experience that forced this soldier to question the essence of his existence, the same had also happened to his comrades, though each of them, too, was alone at the moment it happened. And because the members of the group had now had "some contact with their feelings about it," they could also share with each other an intensely personal experience: They would "do a bit of soul-searching" together. Even the greater selfhood they found in battle became another link that forged them together.

Here, in their revulsion against killing, and their nevertheless having the grit to get on with the dirty business of war, they could afford to show deep personal feelings. It indicated that their upbringing had not robbed them of the capacity, but that it took an extreme experience to make their feelings accessible to them. For the rest (and returning to my peace-time observations) they shun any show of emotions.

Many informants explain this as a defensive reaction to the extravagant show of feelings in the ghetto. Others, like Talmon, explain it by still another factor I have mentioned:

that kibbutzniks live in such constant proximity that they have an inordinate craving for some privacy, a great need not to share. But this cannot be the whole story, because if it were, they would arrange their lives differently.

By this time, for example, if one were to show strong private emotions, it would be an imposition on those one lives with so closely, because they would be forced to react. One simply cannot remain indifferent in the presence of strong emotions. If the reaction were negative, it would mean a rift in the community. Or one might envy the other his strong feelings, his ability to be so much himself, which would again be disruptive for the group.

So one might equally well say that because kibbutzniks have a great need not to share their deepest emotions (in my opinion because of their unhappy conviction that their most private feelings would be welcomed by no one), they have created a setting in which showing them is well nigh impossible; which fortifies the repression.

Actually things are much simpler. The kibbutzniks have, of course, strong emotions. They have strong and deep feelings about the kibbutz and about Israel. They have difficulty only with emotions not shared by the group or running counter to it. Now some of what I have called here our deepest emotions, particularly those making for intimacy, are emotions that imply something shared by "the two of us (or at most the three or four of us) as against all the rest." This is what creates the early basis for intimacy: the small child's convictions that "mother is all for me, and the two of us are just for each other and stand against the rest of the world," which at this age is represented by the father, the siblings, etc.

Later, it will be the adolescent and one or a few friends who will feel so different from (and superior to) those hopeless squares, their parents, and from the world of their parents. Intimacy is thus very much based on "we select few" as opposed to "those impossible others." What binds an intimate group together is as much the feeling of being different from those others as of sharing deepest accord among themselves.

On the basis of this analysis it becomes clear why true intimacy finds no fertile soil to grow on in the kibbutz. It is not the exclusiveness as such that runs counter to all kibbutz values (though it adds) but the feeling that "we are right, and superior to them." No such attitude can prevail, and the kibbutz still exist. What makes a kibbutz is the feeling that "we share so many important things." Any hint of the feeling that "we share so much that is different from and better than theirs" would of necessity destroy it.

This is why the kibbutz-born generations grow up in a society that neither shows, nor approves, nor provides opportunities for strong private emotions, as powered by a sense of the two or three of us against all the rest. In addition, the community has provided them with such a puritanical background in their formative years (as far as private emotions are concerned) that by adulthood their strong emotions do not press toward intimacy as a means to satisfaction.

The only sign I noted of what may have been a longing for emotional involvement once wished for was their rejection of the parents' "big ideas." As children they could never compete with the place held by kibbutz ideology in their parents' emotional life. And this focus of their parents' deepest feelings the children reject and disown.

If a kibbutznik has strong emotions, the kibbutz allows only that they be kept to himself. Comrades can be kind or playful with each other, or devoted to the death, but they cannot show deep personal feeling. They cannot commit themselves emotionally to each other. When emotions do break through, they are understated and quickly suppressed.

Whatever one can share, one must share with the kibbutz or be a bad comrade. Emotion shared with only one other person is a sign of selfishness no less than other private possessions. Nowhere more than in the kibbutz did I realize the degree to which private property, in the deep layers of the mind, relates to private emotions. If one is absent, the other tends to be absent as well.

Among numerous consequences here is a complaint by kibbutz educators that the children have trouble expressing themselves. A teacher who had been a kibbutznik and now taught both in kibbutz and city schools told me: "I tried all kinds of methods of teaching them to be spontaneous, to be creative in their writings. The methods that worked in the city schools did not work in the kibbutz. When I encouraged them, the children in the kibbutz wrote eagerly, but they would never read out what they wrote in front of the class, nor would they show it to the other youngsters." When I asked if the children felt that some personal information was involved, he said: "It wasn't at all a question of personal or not personal statements. Wherever they felt there might be something that would give them away, even if it wasn't personal at all, they couldn't bring it out."

On the other hand, they can be very outspoken when they feel certain the group is behind them, even if it goes against cherished kibbutz values. This happens, for example, in their rejection of Zionism and the "big ideas" of the kibbutz, but also in many smaller matters. They only dare not cling to an opinion if they find it opposed (or fear it will be) by the group.

Here again I would posit something like a group ego at work, where certain ego functions, such as that of evaluating situations, seem to be carried out largely by the group ego instead of by the personal ego.

By the same token I found that the statement "to show

any emotion is anathema to kibbutzniks" was untrue in this extreme form. To show group emotions is quite acceptable. Only the personal emotions seem impossible to have.

I believe this is not simply a case of repressing all feelings, because if that were so, then neither could they feel strongly as a group. Yet this is where their strongest feelings find expression; incredibly more so, for example, than would be true of an American group who had gone through high school or college together. I believe they find it nearly impossible to have a deeply personal opinion that differs from the group's, or to express themselves in a piece of creative writing—not because of the repression of feelings alone, but because it would shatter the ego. If one's ego is essentially a group ego, then to set one's private ego against the group ego is a shattering experience. And the personal ego feels too weak to survive when its strongest aspect, the group ego, gets lost.

At the close of this book I shall speak of how the highest ego achievement in the kibbutz is the ability "to work well with others," which indeed is the highest moral precept of the community. Here I might add that, as far as the world of emotions is concerned, the height of emotional experience for the kibbutznik is to "feel with others what they feel" or, more correctly, "as we all feel together." This is different from a repression of all emotions, though it looks so to us who are so committed to the idea that one's deepest emotions must be private, or at least personal.

This may also be the source of shyness among the kibbutz-born, which is another great concern to their elders, and on which most observers remark. It is again the shyness of the person, not the group. As a group they are anything but shy. On the contrary they are often rudely self-assertive. Only as individuals are they most difficult to reach, by themselves or by others. The kibbutz (and many outsiders) explain this seeming shyness as being like the warding-off exterior of the prickly cactus, one that shelters a deep inner sweetness.

In the words of the teacher quoted above: "Contrary to what is claimed, I am convinced from my teaching experience and from living with them that there is no such thing as an inner soul if it doesn't have any connection with the outer world. I mean, if this were so, then when they are alone with themselves, they would live by this inner soul, but they don't. Part of it, of course, is that they are not with themselves. To be with oneself is not something they value or know." While I too believe there is no hidden core to the kibbutz-raised person, I am convinced there is a very high degree of group strength within them. Together they can all feel, act, be; alone by themselves, they seem to have very little capacity for any of these.

Maybe what I learned from the armed forces about their experience with kibbutz-born and educated soldiers may illustrate both sides of the story. (These remarks are based on observations made of the army during peacetime, before the six-day war, when combat was restricted to fighting Arab raiders, or an occasional punitive expedition. Things are probably very different in actual combat, when defending Israel and fighting together made for a different situation.) There is a legend in Israel that kibbutz-educated youngsters make the best soldiers, a legend given equal credence in the kibbutz and outside of it. Also that a large segment of the officer corps is drawn from among them, far larger than the percentage they form in the army; and on both these scores their outstanding performance during the 1967 war, gives credence to the legend. But from what I was told it seems the reality is more complex.

From the moment they join the army until the end of their service, they tend to stick together, feeling superior to the others, whom they accuse (and probably rightly) of being selfish, of not subordinating personal interest to the group.

But their inner conviction of being superior does not make for good feelings among the rest of the peacetime army. They, themselves, have a remarkable *esprit de corps*, are excellent comrades to their own group, but their comradely feelings for the rest of the army are on a different level.

Though they dislike army life, they are courageous soldiers, even to a fault. In emergencies they will act with bravery beyond the call of duty, particularly if they are fighting as a group, but also when alone in combat.

Here again the war of 1967 has not changed my opinion. From my peacetime findings, I did not doubt that they would fight with utmost bravery and devotion, which they did. But several high-ranking officers in the military, some of them particularly concerned with soldier selection and evaluation, had some reservations, which were best expressed by one of them who told me: "They make wonderful soldiers in the sense of the Roman sentry at Pompei who would rather die than desert his post until ordered to. But modern war needs soldiers who try to survive the battle in order to fight in the next one." And the inordinately high number of casualties among them in the six-day war seems to bear out his contentions.

Despite great courage and devotion, he went on to imply, they are lacking in that immediate and flexible evaluation, a spontaneous adjustment to ever-changing situations that make for the most useful soldier today. Not for them "every man for himself and the devil take the hindmost," but neither for them "the lonely deed," when it requires not heroism but unusually complex decisions. For that they are somehow not flexible enough. They are at their very best in the direct attack, in making direct decisions and in sticking with them. They have little taste for the back and forth vagaries of complex developments.

(The highly individualistic stance of a soldier like Moshe

Dayan, who is so often referred to as kibbutz-born, seems a direct contradiction. I should therefore note that while Dayan was born in a kibbutz, his parents left it to join the more individualistic moshav movement, and it is there he grew up.)

I have watched the kibbutz-born take part in the general assembly many times. How starkly it contrasted with the gusto for widely ranging discussion shown by the founding generation, and by those who joined the kibbutz as young adults. How freely and volubly the latter argued, who in their previous lives had grown accustomed to making decisions all by themselves. How obvious their enjoyment of the chance for personal expression in the argument, over and above fighting for a stand shared with others. And how self-assured and definite, but also impassive, was the kibbutz-born generation. They seemed to have arrived at a group consensus on the issue, and were ready to stand behind it with definite conviction; it was not that they would give in. But the argument they did not enjoy. For them the issue was *this* and not *that*; what else was there to talk about, and why all the fuss?

❦ A Private Piece of Ground

NEVERTHELESS, BEING ADOLESCENTS, THESE YOUNGSTERS SEEM not entirely free of the desire to be (or have) something uniquely their own. I have mentioned before how the children become attached to their infants' and children's houses because these do not rebuff their emotional attachment, do not disappoint them. These at least stay put, and were at one time truly "theirs." I cannot claim that my chance sampling now permits me to speak about the whole group. But it seemed to me that in adolescence, all or most of those who will stay in the kibbutz, and many who will later leave it, develop an incredibly deep attachment to nature.

Usually it was not nature in general a kibbutznik would speak of, but a particular feature of his kibbutz that he alone had embraced (or so he thought): a place by the lake; the view from (or at) a hill; a glen; or some other small place which, by loving, he had made his own. The romantic attachment of their parents to Israel-as-idea has been translated by their children into a fierce love for a particular landscape, which will keep many at the kibbutz, despite strong pulls to leave.

To mention only two examples: One young man spent fourteen and more hours a day, often seven days a week tending sheep, because it allowed him to be out in his beloved landscape all by himself. Another had a wife who wanted desperately to leave the kibbutz so that their children could live with them at home. But though a good father and husband (by the wife's account), he could not bear to leave behind him the small lake where he spent nearly all his time as a fisherman—not for the fishing, but because of the beauty of the lake.

A counterpart to these young men is an old man I observed who spent every free minute of his time tending the lawns and flowers of the kibbutz, paying no attention whatsoever to anyone. This was explained to me as a sign of his devotion to the kibbutz, but also of his utter weariness at seeing the same faces year after year. Though he obviously related to no one and felt only for his lawns and their perfection, he was universally held up as an example of an ideal kibbutznik, since he had never once left the confines in sixteen years. There seemed no doubt that he carried on a love relationship with what for him, in the kibbutz, was nature.

The difference between him and the younger men I describe is that he was not born in the kibbutz; that he may have longed for intimacy and only sought it in nature because he was disappointed in his search for it among men. The opposite seems true for the kibbutz-born: They seem not to expect to be intimate with others; only with nature can they commune in the deepest sense. (Those who feel otherwise will form part of the group who will leave.)

Theirs is not a farmer's love for his land; it is a true love relation with nature. Since nature does not disappoint them, in relation to it they can let themselves feel deeply. Since nature makes no demands, there is no risk in letting oneself go; one will not be made vulnerable thereby. Virtually every person I interviewed who had grown up in the kibbutz and then left it spoke with deepest longing for the natural beauty of his kibbutz, though none wanted to return.

But something else belongs to this feeling that only in nature can they be most themselves. There alone do they feel it is truly all right to be solitary. There they do not feel that something is lacking because they are not with their comrades. And there they are scrutinized by no one, are unobserved.

Many times, when I asked a person who had joined the kibbutz from the outside if he had got what he hoped for and expected, he told me he thought it the best society for most people; certainly much better for him than the conditions he had left. But when asked if kibbutz life had any shortcomings, his doubts often centered around feelings like those of an informant who told me, "It's a little too heavy for me. Maybe things would be easier if I didn't live in an environment where twenty-four hours a day I have to be all right. You see, you're watched as a parent, you're watched as a worker, as a comrade, a kibbutznik." And it is true: if you don't feel "all right," if you are tired or disgruntled, or want to be by yourself, it is taken that you are critical of the community. But not so with nature; to be there all by your-self, this is accepted.

Unfortunately, I could not penetrate any further into this deep attachment. But I could not help thinking of "Mother Earth"—as if the kibbutz-born was trying to find in nature an undemanding acceptance that was absent from his child-hood where there were always those demands that come with living forever with others. Yet if this was so, and it seemed so for both sexes, I wondered why it seemed much more marked in the male.

Since there was one story I got identically from several different women—that they wanted to leave the kibbutz to have their children with them, but their husbands were bound to it by a love of nature that could not be satisfied anywhere else—it may be that these women looked to their children, instead of to nature, to satisfy their longing for intimacy.

From a very small sample (three) who did persuade their reluctant husbands to leave, it seemed that much as these women sought for intimacy with their children, it did not work out very well. Again the story is very different if, as a child, the woman has lived with her parents for as much as the first three years of her life. If not, then something seems to have happened to her ability to be intimate, even with her own child. Be this as it may, I found again and again, in the kibbutz-born of both sexes that their deepest love was con-centrated on Israel (the mother land) in general, and for males on a select part of nature in particular.

Things were quite different for those not born in the kib-butz, but who had joined it in adolescence or later. Their strongest love belonged to the kibbutz-as-idea. Thus one might speculate that those who joined it from the outside were moved by a deep longing for closeness to people, though a closeness that would not impinge on their free-dom.

It is as if their children (the second generation) realize that by living only for these cherished ideas, their parents cheated themselves and their children out of the closeness they hoped it would bring. Having lost faith in this hope of their parents, the second generation turns for satisfaction to nature, if they are men, or to children if they are women. But since they cannot come close to each other, their reaching out, even to substitutes, seems to end in disappointment.

The story seems very different for the third generation, though again, most of those I could interview or observe were much too young to permit any valid conclusions. But all this seems by no means such a problem for them. Their parents (the second generation) seem never to have sought among people for any genuine closeness, and they themselves (the third generation) seem less aware of any need for it at all.

As for the great ideas, they couldn't care less. They neither hate them, nor make fun of them. Since these ideas never preoccupied their parents to the point where it came between them and their children, they feel nothing special about them, one way or the other. Kibbutz life, for this third generation, is not supposed to make this a better world, nor to prove anything. It is just the life they were born to and continue.

❧ Those Who Leave

Much as his own group supports the kibbutznik—both psychologically and in everyday life—so it rejects him, as deeply and radically, for the ultimate crime: that of leaving the kibbutz. However deep the pain, for those who leave, of living far from the nature they love so intensely, much deeper is their hurt at being rejected by the group. Because of it they can barely manage to visit the kibbutz, much as

they would like to see their parents, for example. It is unbearable that their own age-group, the people for whom they
feel the strongest attachment, not only won't talk to them,
but turn their faces away so as not to see them.

It is not, of course, any conscious decision that makes the
kibbutznik who stayed be so utterly rejecting. On the contrary, his conscious desire is that the ex-kibbutznik should
return, or at least that their ties be preserved. In some kibbutzim, committees have repeatedly been formed to seek out
ex-comrades, to keep up the ties, to possibly induce them to
rejoin the kibbutz. But while the idea was always taken up
with enthusiasm, it always petered out quickly. It all seemed
too difficult, and nothing ever came of it. The inner resistance among those who stayed, based on their deep disappointment at being deserted and rejected, was just too great
to be bridged.

When I discussed this problem in the kibbutz, I was told
that some of those who leave do come back to visit. By way
of example I was told of how one of them, on the eve of a
holiday, was found by chance, hiding in the dark behind the
kitchen (that is, at the rear of the dining hall where he knew
the entire community would be gathered). He had come
from the city, drawn back by the holiday spirit, but lacked
the courage to reveal himself once he got there. Even now he
was reluctant to come forward, though his old teacher would
not hear of his not joining the others in the hall. And while
everyone tried to make a go of things, it did not really work.
The ex-comrade knew he had stopped belonging. Though his
old teacher could accept him back, his own age-group could
not. His teacher was glad to see him again, but his peer
group, though overtly accepting, was not. The net experience was not something he would likely repeat often or even
soon.

That those for whom the ex-kibbutznik still feels deepest

attachment should turn away from him is too painful to be
borne. But he also feels greatest guilt about deserting the
group, and this guilt is part of what makes him hide. Not
toward the kibbutz does he feel guilty, though he knows it
has cared for him well; not toward his parents, though he
regrets having hurt them by leaving; nor toward his old
teacher, though he knows what a disappointment his leaving
has been; but toward the others of his age-group.

All the guilt and remorse felt by a middle-class American
who sets himself against his parents, the kibbutz-born feels
toward his age-group. This is just as true for those who remain as for those who leave, only the guilt felt by the latter is
infinitely stronger. Without exceptions, all those I spoke with
who were born in the kibbutz and had left it as grown-ups
felt deeply guilty about deserting their age-group. And this
though most felt there had been very good reasons for leaving, were certain they had done the right thing.

The story was entirely different for those who had entered
the kibbutz as older children (in my sample, at or after
puberty). They felt guilt about leaving the kibbutz because
of what it had offered them, and because of how well they
had been taken in and cared for. By comparison they felt
little or no remorse about deserting their age-group.

On the positive side, the approval of his age-group comes
first with the kibbutz-born, while that of his parents seems
unimportant by comparison. But by the same token I have
nowhere encountered such violent, all-consuming hatred of
a group as in the very few I met who felt that their group
had never really taken them in. There was a quality of desperation and unreasonableness to their emotional outbursts
which again I have nowhere encountered so typically in our
society, save in those who felt their parents did not want
them.

For all these reasons people who leave the kibbutz find

the high point of their lives in those occasions when they meet with others of their old peer group who have also broken away. These are their happiest times, as I was told by every one I spoke to. Reminiscing about their childhood and youth, about the beloved landscape at their kibbutz, they feel once again, for a moment, that they belong to the group, have come home.

A few who had left the kibbutz described for me what it felt like to gain personal maturity after long inner struggle (as opposed to maturing as part of a unit). They used a term for it that seemed standard among them: to be *Bar Mitzvahed* (confirmed). It signified arrival at manhood.

One of them, a kibbutz-born social worker who was employed both in Tel Aviv and in her old kibbutz, told me: "Whenever I'm in the city, I feel grown up, but as soon as I return to the kibbutz, I feel again as if I were a child. So much is decided for me, so few decisions do I have to make on my own, so guilty do I feel if I do differently from what in kibbutz terms I am supposed to think, do, and feel." As might be inferred here, this young woman was not sure if she would remain a kibbutz member all her life, or would eventually leave it. Both had their attractions for her—having adult independence and a personal ego, and enjoying the kind of dependence that comes of having a group ego. But on balance she was not sure what she was going to prefer in the end.

Leaving was differently experienced by a man I spoke with who was born and raised in the free world and had joined the youth movement in late adolescence, as did the girl he married. Not having spent his childhood and youth as part of a group, the wrench of leaving, even after many years, came easier for him. Nor did it feel to him like being *Bar Mitzvahed*. Yet his reasons for leaving were not too different in kind.

He felt that the pervasive, though benevolent control of the kibbutz had muted his personality; that it kept him from experiencing not only his own passions but also his own weaknesses, because the kibbutz always protected him from their consequences. It had denied him the right to experience his own grief and his own joys. Since the community decided what his actions should be in most matters that count, often acted for him in fact, he could never feel it was he who had done the right thing. He wanted the privilege of feeling all this, even of doing wrong if he had to.

What he meant was that all his comrades want (and expect) to be very much part of his life, including his joys and his griefs. As many told me repeatedly, kibbutz life is far more meaningful than life in the cities because there are so many who feel *with* you. Once, for example, a couple of years after my visit to Atid, I received a letter from a kibbutznik who was completing a year's study abroad, in which he told me of his deep grief because a child in his kibbutz was killed in the service, and another kibbutznik had died of old age. Part of his grief was that he was away and could not help those who had been closest to the two at such trying times. Though he himself had not been specially close to either one of those who had died, or to their families, he not only felt deeply and personally for those who suffered the loss, but the loss suffered by the kibbutz.

To so participate in the personal grief of others means that it has to be truly and unfailingly felt. If not, it would not bind one but estrange one from the community. This is what my informant meant when he spoke of the kibbutz having denied him the chance to experience his personal emotions. The kibbutz expected to share in them whether he wished it or not, though the sharing modified them—or forced him to modify them on his own—to make possible the sharing.

I might add here what he thought it meant for his children, when he left the kibbutz to live in Israel's largest city. (They, the children, were born in the kibbutz and had never left it till then.) He felt that kibbutz life was much easier for them, for somewhat the same reasons I have adduced for the latency child's enjoying this setting.

"But now," he said, "living outside the kibbutz as parents too, my wife and I are confronted with richer complexities of living. This is much more burdensome, for my wife, for myself, and for our children. But I also feel it is somehow more human. I feel these difficulties we now face are important experiences of learning, and I don't want anybody to take that away from me and my children."

Results of Kibbutz Education

ANY SYSTEM OF EDUCATION CAN BE JUDGED IN A NUMBER of ways but at least two of them seem specially important. The first is: How well does the system achieve what it was designed for? The second: How viable are its results for the individual, for his society, and for mankind in general?

The first question is much easier to answer because one need only compare results with expressed goals. The second is impossible to answer while we lack for a universal consensus on what is the ultimate good for individual or society.

Either way, there is one count on which kibbutz education is an unqualified success, though I doubt that its founders gave it a thought: It has disproved the critics. Much as some economists were convinced, a few decades ago, that the soviet system would have to break down because of inner contradictions, so did psychologists and psychiatrists predict that a system that removed the infant from his family, particularly from his mother, and raised him in institutions would have to result in total failure. Kibbutz education has conformed as little to these predictions as did communism. More important, it has clearly reached its own goal: to create a radically new personality in a single generation.

❧ A New Kind of Jew

BOTH AS IDEA AND ETHIC, THE KIBBUTZ ORIGINATED WITH MEN and women who were born to a way of life as different from kibbutz ways as one can imagine. Among its founders—mainly Jews of Eastern Europe—the two highest aspirations were intellectual achievement and the acquisition of property. Ghetto life was utterly remote from any livelihood wrested from the earth. Its redeeming virtues were extremely close kinship ties; deep feelings openly shown, often histrionically displayed; strong emotional attachments between parents and children; and a deep commitment to religious custom. The founders' defensive rejection of these parental mores shows up in almost every aspect of their life and behavior.

A total absence of such defensiveness—or indeed of any interest in ghetto values and attitudes, pro or con—is the clearest sign of how different is the kibbutz-born generation from their parents.

It could be argued that this is because they were not born in a ghetto but in a country that wanted them for its own; that it therefore has little to do with kibbutz education. But my impression is that children who were born and raised in Israel outside the kibbutz, while they differ from their parents, still show clearly many of those features that marked Eastern Jewry. They show the same desire for intellectual achievement and the acquisition of property, for close family ties and more open emotionality, though the show of feeling is more subdued.

While I have known many children whose personalities differed radically from their parents', partly because of an entirely different education, I have never seen an entire generation so unlike their own parents. Not only do their personalities differ from their parents, but their ideas and the nature of their commitment. (Because there are puritanical parents whose radical children are as puritanical in devotion to their radical ideas as their parents ever were about religion.) In fact, this very difference from their parents welds the second generation together and makes for a relative disinterest in their parents. In many ways they embrace the ideas their parents hoped to instill in them much more ardently than their parents, but in wholly different ways. At least this is so for the ones who remain in the kibbutz.

The founding generation (like the non-puritanical children of puritans) were and still are as emotional about their new kibbutz values as their parents were about old ghetto values. While the two creeds differ radically, the emotional stance is the same. Kibbutz life, to its founders, is as much holy scripture as the religious life was to their parents. To them, as the other was to their parents, it is the only good life, permitting no deviation, and invested with deepest emotions.

The kibbutz-born generation is committed to an entirely different *Sachlichkeit*, a literalness, a matter-of-fact objectivity which has no place for emotions. On the contrary, those emotions their parents show seem a bit ridiculous to them, unbefitting the new kibbutz generation. As an educator of the founding generation put it: "It's not only the minute we get romantic about our values that they say in disgust, 'Oh, come on! That's Zionism!' It's also in other matters. For example in my own field, biology, they approach it with dispassion. We had real feeling for our animals because of our humanism. They are only interested in the usefulness of the animal. We've had heated discussions, for example, about the artificial insemination of cows— whether we should do that to our animals. But the reactions of our youngsters are quite realistic, and they have no feeling for our qualms. Their attitude is 'that's how things are!' "

And this rationality, this unemotional attitude is not restricted to animals. It extends to human beings, even their own children. For example, I was told that the kibbutz-born generation felt that nurses, metapelets, and teachers used to be much too involved in their work with the children; that theirs should have been a work assignment like any other.

As another of the founding generation told me: "We brought up our children with such careful consideration for them as human beings, but when they grow up and work as nurses, even those who have children of their own, they are much less concerned. Let's say they're more realistic, mechanistic, objective, than we are; less humanistic, less involved. They are much quicker to do things, even those things that might hurt the children, because they see it in a framework of necessities and reasons, of rational work. They've lost some of the consideration we had all the time."

Georges Friedmann, the French sociologist (*The End of the Jewish People?* 1967), writes that though he was told (of this new generation of kibbutzniks) that "they have lost the defects of their parents and also their qualities," it took him "weeks or months to explore the implications of those few words." Eventually Friedmann came to accept J. Ben David's conclusions (1964) that "in fact . . . there was nothing idealistic for them in living and working in the settlements where they were born; it was just part of their inherited way of life." Friedmann also comments on the changing image of the kibbutz in Israel. During the thirties, he writes, the kibbutz-born generation

> became an ideal image, closely linked with the older ideal image of the Halutz, the altruistic pioneer. . . . Thanks to their real qualities, but also aided by the image that floated around them, [they] had meteoric careers in Israeli society. . . . After the [1948] war of independence this splendid image deteriorated and rapidly gave place to another. J. Ben David gives an ingenious explanation of the process. This ideal image, of the Israeli-born generation as a rejuvenated version of the Halutz image . . . was based on a mistake. Altruism and devotion to duty are always displayed in wars of national or social liberation. During the period of the heroic fraternity of wartime they had shared the collectivist ideals of the first generation only in appearance. The return to settled conditions brought to the surface the moral discontinuity between the generations that had been temporarily papered over. . . . Parallel with this, the collective principles of Israeli society propagated in the schools and by the youth movements, the press, the radio and the army implied a critical image of the Sabra that is a revised version of that of the thirties. According to this image, the Israeli [non-kibbutz born and raised] Sabra thinks only of himself; Halutz ideals are alien to him, indeed in his "egoism" all ideals are alien to him. In short, he is a materialist. His manners are not just offhand, they are positively discourteous and rude.

To which I would like to add that the kibbutz-born and raised Sabra has retained many of the Halutz ideals, but he, too, is otherwise a materialist, kibbutz-egocentric, offhand, and often discourteous.

At the same time I was deeply impressed by the lengths the kibbutzniks go to in taking care of the few children who are mentally retarded, brain damaged, etc. The whole kibbutz makes these children its concern. Metapelets and teachers make all necessary allowances and go out of their way to help them adjust to kibbutz life. I saw some of these children as grown-ups, and although one or the other of them was most difficult to live with and work with—obstinate, cantankerous, etc.—the kibbutz felt they had to be accepted and special allowances made, not only because they were children of the kibbutz, but because one must make their parents (who are also kibbutzniks) feel their children are being well taken care of. I state this very forcefully, because it was most moving to see how wonderful they were about keeping such defectives within their society.

I have spoken of the kibbutznik's love for the land. In the founding generation this was and remains very much a romantic idea, a love intellectually cherished, but by no means strongly felt. Though many love their flowers, they love them as many a suburbanite does. The opposite is true for their children. Their love is deep, unquestioning, unromantic, not for the flowers in their little gardens, but for the very terrain. The same is true for their attitude toward private possessions. The founding generation has slowly acquired some private property, usually just a handful of things, some of them presents from relatives outside the kibbutz. But owning them makes quite a difference. And though they try to restrict and regulate such gifts, the wish for possessions seems so strong that there are many infractions of the principle of common property. The reason, I believe, is that the abolition of property was an idea defensively embraced in revolt against the old ways of parents and society; hence the ambivalence about it continues to seethe.

Things are very different for the second generation, those raised in the kibbutz. Rarely do they leave because of any wish for property. To be with their children, yes; or to have greater freedom to develop emotionally or otherwise. But to own things, hardly ever, or for only a very few. Even those who leave are much less ambivalent about property than their parents, while those who stay are universally critical of their elders for the concessions they make. For them, communal property is not an idea defensively or consciously embraced, but the only normal way to live.

The same goes for having their children raised by the community. I have said that mothers of the first generation were conflicted about their femininity—feared they would not make good as mothers, showed strong tendencies toward "masculine protest," etc.—and that all this was reflected in how their infants reacted to them and to communal rearing. I found little of all this among mothers who were born in the kibbutz. Many of them are quite secure in their femininity. True, they hold on to all the gains their mothers have won toward equality of the sexes; but these, too, they take for granted and hence are very casual about.

For the same reason they are much more casual about having their children live in the children's houses. It does not disturb them to have their children as emotionally distant from them as they are from their children. To them it is not a deliberate means of creating a better society, not even so much the right or the natural way, but the most convenient order of things. Since they are much less ambivalent about it than their parents were, their own children, the third generation, accept it more easily in turn.

The founding generation complains that their pre-teen or adolescent children are cool or indifferent to them, even rude; that they are too engrossed in their peer group. Behind it is the old ambivalence: "I expected you to love me, as I loved (or wanted to love) my parents. But I wanted you to love me, and not also hate me as I hated my parents (and hated hating them). That's why I gave you up to the children's house. It is wrong of you to repay me for this sacrifice with indifference." And behind it lies the greater fear:

"Maybe I gave you up to the children's house for selfish reasons: because I wanted to live my own life with my comrades, without the burden of taking care of you all day long. Love me, to prove that my reasons were not selfish; to prove that I sacrificed much to make a better world for you than the one I grew up in."

None of these involuted fears and desires can bedevil the second generation. They are indeed a new generation in a new land. The founding generation tore the messianic idea from its religious matrix and turned hope into fact. They did not wait for the Messiah, as did all the generations before them. But in bringing a lofty vision to earth, they brought forth an earthy generation—the price of transforming ideals into everyday life. This second generation expects nothing more of its children than that they live out this everyday reality, and is well content with things as they are.

Hence I feel there is good reason to accept that kibbutz education has achieved its major purpose: to create a personality type that is not only different from, but more suited to kibbutz life than that of the parents who devised it.

❦ World of Kibbutzim?

THIS BRINGS ME TO MY SECOND SET OF CRITERIA ABOUT KIBbutz education; one that is much harder, if not impossible to answer: the question of how successful a system it is, for the individual and for his society? But this will depend on whether or not we believe that kibbutz life makes for a more successful individual, and whether a society composed of kibbutzim would make for a better world. That the vast majority of Israelis opt against this idea, and quite a few kibbutz-born also opt against it, by leaving, hardly settles the question.

Does Israel, even in kibbutz eyes, need an entire population that is satisfied with living in small, self-contained agricultural communities, even with small industries attached? If the kibbutz answer were yes, it could only be yes with many reservations, since they realize that Israel is not self-sufficient in providing the modern war machinery she feels she must have for her security. But even if the kibbutz answer were yes, I could not accept it. Because even the most cursory inspection convinces one that kibbutz society could not survive economically without drawing on the highly developed technology of surrounding Israel.

The kibbutz could never provide itself with the farm machinery it needs, nor with enough of experimental science and its findings. Yet these alone permit its farms to survive, even to flourish, as do the low interest loans and special tax advantages they enjoy. Nor could a society based on small groups create the complex machinery they need for even the small industries they have.

All efforts to create kibbutzim among urban groups who work in large-scale production have failed. Kibbutzim can exist only (it seems) if the group life is not interfered with by meeting non-group members at every step. They may even need the emotional replenishment that comes of a love for and contact with nature.

Kibbutzniks, or at least nearly all those I talked with, are quite aware that, while they wish the kibbutz were the universal image of the good life, as it is for them and many others, it is not so for all. They are also very concerned about the number of persons who leave the kibbutz. They are well aware that the kibbutz movement has so far survived, has even grown in population, not so much by keeping or increasing its own, but by attracting new blood from the outside. And a great deal of effort goes into recruiting through the youth movement, both in Israel and abroad.

Thus the kibbutz, somewhat like our farming communities, represents a process of self-selection. Kibbutzniks of the second generation are those who remained behind on the farm or, depending on how one looks at it, those who stayed in the forefront of the struggle for a juster society. It is impossible to say what the kibbutz would be like today if no one had ever left. What divisive, even disruptive influence might its leavers have exerted, had they stayed? Or what reforms might they have pressed for and gotten through? This question is important because kibbutz educators wish very much to feed Israeli society with future leaders for the good life.

Now it is nothing unusual in history for yesterday's radicals, once the new religion or society is safely rooted, to become its staunchest defenders against further change. The question is: Does kibbutz education *of necessity* lead to a status quo society? And related to this: What are the educational goals of this system as to the individual's role in society?

Here I found the system strangely contradictory, in which it resembles our own. Its goal is to have the next generation carry on kibbutz life exactly like their parents, and also wield moral leadership in Israel (if not the world), preferably as political leaders. I have mentioned the feeling of many thoughtful Israelis: that were it not for the kibbutz, the creation of a new state simply to harbor a persecuted religious minority would by now be of limited appeal. The more so, since the persecution of Jews—at least in the free world—is no longer imminent, and religion not too vital anymore in the life of the people.

There can be no doubt that the kibbutz provides a new secular religion for its members, along with a moral and emotional focus for Israel. It represents the new Jewish covenant—no longer now between a stern God and his children, but between equals; a covenant resting not on obedience to a supernatural power, but on individual freedom and a rational ordering of things. In a fashion it replaces the old religion as the link binding Jewry together. The kibbutz—international in its basic tenets, though also nationalistic—tries to weld the Jewish people into a nation by becoming its new collective conscience. (Of course, the Arab threat too, ties Israeli Jews together, and world Jewry to Israel. But this has little to do with the role of the kibbutz within Israel.)

Here too, we see a strange difference between the founding generation and its children. The first generation provided political and moral leadership for Israel, and to some degree still does, both through an active role in politics, and through the living example of the kibbutz. Things have shifted radically for the second generation, which is still looked to for moral leadership, but no longer in actual politics. For that they are far too estranged from the world of ideas, including political ideas; are too unused to extending themselves in a world at large, where they feel out of place. Theirs is a kind of monasticism that provides spiritual leadership by its sheer existence, not by any actual inducement to change.

Thus to the question of whether kibbutz education can and does provide leadership in Israel one can tentatively answer that indeed it can, but of a very unique kind: by setting an example rather than by actual doings for the nation; by a modern monasticism rather than the kind of intellectual, scientific, and social advances we associate with leadership and change.

Once again we find the second generation extremely different from the first. In the founding generation was an inordinately high percentage of imaginative persons given to innovation, deep thought, and strong convictions, at the heart of whose commitments stood social problems. Given these and related characteristics in such high degree, one cannot help expecting to find them in the children, to whose rearing they devoted so much planning and thought. But this one does not.

Somehow these dynamic people managed to create a static society. This does not mean that the kibbutz is not changing. But it resists change, worries about innovations rather than rising to the challenge of the new with alacrity. Behind this is no lack of concern or sensitivity, but a fear of what it may do to the integrity of the kibbutz idea. For example, while they are very much concerned about a social problem that has long been central for Israel—namely the assimilation of North African Jews and groups like them— they do almost nothing about it. Kibbutzniks make token efforts, halfhearted at best, because they are convinced that these Jews cannot fit themselves into kibbutz life. They feel that an influx of people so variant in background, holding values so radically different, would seriously hinder their comradely life. Therefore, and much as they would like to help, kibbutzniks feel they cannot afford to. They act in self-protection. And the self-protection, by drawing them inward, has become more alluring than to meet crisis with daring new solutions. This is why I feel that despite inner change, as in the sleeping arrangements of children, the kibbutz has become a static society.

As for these African newcomers, the kibbutz relies on the state of Israel to do the job. Not just economically now, but morally too, though they recognize and accept the Jewish obligation to take them in. At the same time they continue with active efforts to recruit members elsewhere: from Europe, our own continent, South America, South Africa.

But modern science and technology, along with poetry and the arts, require a dynamic, an open society. If Israel is to survive, even to keep and improve a living standard that is already far superior to that of neighboring countries, she will have to stay in the forefront of scientific and cultural development. To these it is doubtful that kibbutzniks will contribute importantly. Here, of course, one might ask: But how many great scientists or artists are apt to be born to a group numbering less than 100,000 who live in small, scattered, farming communities? In short, is my question valid?

The answer is probably both: yes and no. It is valid insofar as this small group does indeed produce men and women who make significant contributions to Israeli life. It is invalid because to make their contributions, nearly all such persons feel they must leave the kibbutz either officially or *de facto*. Some of them remain members out of sentiment, or for the high prestige that membership still confers. But in fact they live in the cities and only visit their kibbutz for a few days a year on the High Holidays.

As one of them told me, "I'm a good kibbutznik by virtue of my wife," meaning that his wife took part in all kibbutz affairs while he was busy outside the kibbutz. And another who holds a high government position confided, "Most of this is foolishness in modern Israel. But they're the ones who made Israel possible; they built it; they did such wonderful things in the past; they are the friends of my youth. So as long as I don't have to spend more than the holidays with them, I stay a member and thoroughly enjoy it."

Even more significant is what seemed like an emotional flatness in the second generation. To this question, when I raised it with kibbutz educators, I was told again and again —so much so, that one got the feeling it had become a pat answer—that these young people are very shy of strangers. That they turn inward so very much that they cannot reveal themselves to any but those persons most intimate with them, but they are possessed of great depth. Which brings us back to their own age group, the only ones who respond to them instantly with deep understanding based on a common life experience. But a depth that cannot reveal itself in varied intercourse is a solipsistic virtue, at best. I failed to evoke any such depth in the younger generation, though I found it often enough in the founding generation and in those who were kibbutz-born but had left.

Or is this again posing an unfair question? Because how many "deep feeling" persons are we apt to find among 100,000 farmers? And who, in this day and age, are the ones who stay on the farm? A relative emotional flatness may be just the selective factor that determines who stays on, in this relatively simple, undemanding environment.

Still another strange factor is involved here. What the world has labeled typically Jewish has fallen away from the second generation, and in many ways they are like those others who peopled the non-Jewish world their parents once had to contend with. So another question is: What, of all this, is the consequence of this second generation's having been born and raised in a farming community, out in the country, in rather small settlements? And what is the consequence of their having been born, not as members of a small and discriminated-against minority, but as those of the dominant in-group?

But why have I felt compelled at all to ask questions that seem unanswerable, or ones that I then call unfair because of the small numbers involved and the fact that these people live a rather remote life?

My reason has to do with a final and fundamental difficulty in evaluating this system of education: that one's estimate of the kibbutz population depends on who and what one is mentally comparing them with.

The Middle Reaches

THE RESULTS OF A NATIONWIDE STUDY OF SCHOLASTIC ACHIEVEMENT in Israel highlight this problem. It is a study in which five groups of Israeli youngsters were compared; those attending (1) urban schools with high academic standards, serving mainly upper-middle-class families; (2) urban schools of middle standards, used mainly by the middle-class population; (3) urban schools of relatively low standards, used mainly by lower class families; (4) rural schools serving rural families and including the cooperative settlements called moshavim; and finally (5) kibbutz schools.

Without detailing all findings, but looking at how the five groups scored percentage-wise on the tests, the kibbutz appears to rank second in achievement, whether one looks at those who scored highest or lowest. For example, looking at those who scored in the upper quarter of the test (scores of 75 and above), the distribution was 42.8 percent for the high-standard urban schools, 29.9 percent for the kibbutz, 24.5 percent for the rural and moshav, 18.2 percent for the middle-urban group, and 10.2 percent for the low-urban group. Thus the kibbutz students did considerably less well than the highest urban group, but otherwise better than all the rest, and considerably so.

If we look at the low performers on these tests (scores of 64 or lower) we find parallel results. The smallest number falls in the upper urban group (27.6 percent) and the next smallest number in the kibbutz (38.2 percent). The rural and moshav again take a position between the kibbutz and the middle-urban group with 52.7 percent, compared to 56.4 percent in the middle-urban, and 75.7 percent in the lower urban group.

A very interesting subfinding was the distribution of top

290 · *The Children of the Dream*

achievers (scores of 85 and above) among the five groups.[1] In the urban high-level schools 5.2 percent of the group were top achievers. This percentage drops to 2.3 percent for the rural and moshav group; 1.6 percent for the middle-urban group; and 0.7 percent for the lower urban group. For the kibbutz the figure for these top achievers is only 2.1 percent, which is slightly below the rural and moshav groups.

The leveling impact of kibbutz education is quite apparent from these scores. In over-all achievement, the spread is narrower than one might expect, because both ends of the distribution are smaller while the middle is larger. If, on the other hand, we look at top performers alone, the story differs. Then the leveling influence seems to have reduced to a respectable middle level those students who (we must assume from their high over-all performance) had the potential to be top performers. At the same time, it also leveled up (if one may use the term), the low performers. Again the educational system shows up as favoring the middle reaches, or the group. In statistical terms, kibbutz educational achievement shows that both ends of the distribution curve are radically reduced, while the middle is expanded.

That is why—if one views the kibbutz as populated by children who would otherwise be living in a good middle-class home, one of education and culture—it is doubtful if kibbutz education is superior to other systems we know of, in helping students toward intellectual, aesthetic, and scientific achievements. The question is: Are such achievements more important than setting an example of moral leadership? And even this consideration holds only if such

---

[1] These data were taken from a tabulation showing educational level according to national origin of the parent: e.g., Israeli-born, European or Middle-Eastern. Of these, the Middle-Eastern subdivision was omitted here, since that population is nearly absent in most kibbutzim.

a cultivated, middle-class home is the kind that many (though by no means all) of the first generation would have provided for their children. If, on the other hand, one looks at them as children who would otherwise have grown up in a lower working-class environment, then the picture is entirely different—and a few of the first generation would probably have belonged to this group.

Also, while a sizable segment of the founding generation can be considered well educated and essentially middle-class in origin, the story is entirely different if we go by the work they perform. By kibbutz claims, most of its members would have been factory workers or done other lower class work, had they not joined the kibbutz. Therefore (they claim) the comparison should be with lower class families, whose children, unless very gifted, would have enjoyed only limited schooling. But my observation of the founding generation does not bear out this claim.

Most of them, I believe, though not all, would have risen in any society, educationally and socially. As a matter of fact, there are many for whom it was only their having joined the kibbutz at an early age that pegged them to a limited educational level, while their brothers or sisters who bypassed the kibbutz movement typically advanced to higher social and educational levels. Had the founding generation striven as hard in society at large as they strove in and for the kibbutz, they could not have failed, in their majority, to rise to professional or upper-middle-class levels. And if some few had not made it that far for themselves, they would certainly have secured it for their children.

I believe it is myth to claim—as do kibbutzniks—that most of them would have lived a lower class life. But they wish to believe it because, if true, kibbutz achievements for its members would be even greater. If I could agree with them, my task would be easy and the findings clear.

That is, were this an average population of small agricultural communities, the results of kibbutz child rearing would be close to miraculous—so well educated, for such an assumed background, are most of its younger generation. That they would be a static, conservative, provincial group, one would take for granted, because what else could one expect of the children of such a community? And if they were not, who would stay and tend the farm? Certainly they are puritanical in their way of life and outlook. But what else would one expect of people, born and raised in a small rural community, who have chosen to remain there for the rest of their lives?

Much more important is the question of whether kibbutz education does not produce exactly the personality type the kibbutz needs—though a type not too acceptable to American middle-class parents, nor to those who (like the first kibbutz generation) put a high value on leadership.

Here it should be added that the test results, noted earlier, reflect an essentially non-kibbutz outlook on life and on what constitutes academic achievement. Results might have been radically different had these tests been constructed by kibbutz educators. That is, they were designed to measure the kind of achievement the test constructors valued: an intellectual development that prepares well for ever higher (competitive) academic achievement, without regard for what effect it has on the student's personality and social relations. But the kibbutz youngster spends a vast amount of his emotional energy on becoming a highly socialized person, in terms of kibbutz standards. And this achievement none of the tests measure.

In many ways the second generation of kibbutzniks are farmers in a true and real sense, though not peasants in the style of Eastern Europe. They are very modern farmers, but farmers nonetheless, concerned chiefly with kibbutz goings on, uninvolved in the broader society, save for Israel, and even then only with aspects that concern them.

Political life, for example, is highly diversified and active in Israel, and the literature of politics abounds. But the second generation in their vast majority are well satisfied with arrangements that provide them with only the party newspaper. There is little desire to read the press of other parties, even if the kibbutz did not frown on its distribution. Most are satisfied to read what their own party organ has to say about the politics of others.

While they probably read more (and more widely) than the average farmer, they shy away from material that differs in viewpoint from theirs. Partly this is for lack of interest, but largely because it might inspire disagreement with their peers. They do read those professional publications that advance knowledge in their own field of work. That is, they try to educate themselves in ways that will help them do better at work they are already doing.

Quite a few kibbutzniks follow serious intellectual pursuits. Several kibbutzim have archeological museums, others have folklore collections and so forth. Interest is particularly avid for anything pertaining to Israel, for her archeology and history, biblical and otherwise. But more often than not these come about through individual efforts—and in all cases I could observe, that of non-kibbutz born persons—which then carry others along. For the most part kibbutzniks try very hard to keep from growing boorish. Though dead tired, they read "serious" literature, listen to "good" music. But the way they do it I found moving, even pathetic, given the heavy odds against them. Because their efforts spring from a defensive need not to slip into boorishness, rather than a spontaneous delight in the pleasures of literature and the arts. For too many their enjoyment of the "finer" things in life is very hard labor indeed: something they owe to themselves, or feel they owe the kibbutz movement, to show it is not incompatible with the higher things in life. But with rare exceptions what else can it be, given the long hours and hard work they put into the kibbutz economy, the hours spent on kibbutz affairs, and the relative lack of privacy. In their vast majority, they read little out of intellectual curiosity, and their aesthetic interest in art, music, and letters is standard rather than original. So far as I could observe, they read nothing controversial or experimental, see no movies or theater that would throw their values in question.

In this respect, too, the personality of the kibbutz-born generation seems depleted, compared to a complexity and richness in some of the first generation. On the other hand, compared with the often severe neuroses of that first generation, these young people seem much less neurotic than their parents, secure within their limitations, though these are often marked.

Perhaps the assets and liabilities of kibbutz education may best be summarized by the deep peer attachments felt by the second generation. On the one hand, their reluctance to contemplate a life apart from each other, the way each one, alone, seems to feel things only half as acutely as when all function together as a unit—all these seem to speak more of bondage than attachment. (Though what is bondage in one society may be experienced very differently in another.) On the other hand, if intense group ties discourage individuation, neither do they breed human isolation, asocial behavior or other forms of social disorganizations that plague modern man in competitive society.

What I have said here about the results of kibbutz rearing may sound quite critical. But let us consider for a moment how many people in our society, or anywhere, grow up to be full individuals? How many, if they had a choice, would prefer to live with their own mistakes? How many would wish to suffer their own personal grief sooner than be supported by the group, when distressed, even if that means casting their feelings into a mold the community provides? We have no idea how many, among us, reach the individuation that some hoped to reach when they left the kibbutz. But until we know that, we are in no position to judge how many are denied it by kibbutz education.

Much, too, has been said here about the reluctance of kibbutz-reared persons to have opinions of their own in the face of group disapproval. This, too, may have sounded quite critical. But how large a percentage in our society are very different? Or I speak of the inability to form truly intimate relations. But how many in our society can?

On the other hand, and in favor of kibbutz education, how many in our society form ties as meaningful and rewarding as those between the kibbutz-born and his group? Or how many in our society are able, as grown-ups, to break away from all values instilled by home and society in order to strike out on their own against greatest odds? How many can as radically shed a viewpoint and way of life that no longer tally with inner convictions. Because this, a percentage of kibbutz-reared persons do when they leave the kibbutz.

Perhaps to leave takes less strength because of the lesser attachments to parents. Estimates vary incredibly, and some claim that up to half or more of all kibbutz-raised children leave the kibbutz. Others, like Professor Talmon, put the percentage at less than 15 percent. Friedmann (1967) reports that "only 5 percent of young people leave the kibbutzim of the left wing movement annually, according to Darin-Drabkin." He adds that according to Shlomo Rosen, joint secretary of the seventy-two kibbutzim of this movement, their population includes 2,080 who were kibbutz-born, of whom 93 percent have remained. Clearly the kibbutz offers to some of those it educates the freedom to follow their convictions, however radical.

The exceptions here would be those very few who are so stunted by communal rearing that they cannot use the opportunity. My impression is that while a few are thus penalized, percentage-wise their number is considerably smaller than in most social systems.

❦ A Fine Way for Some

SINCE IN PSYCHOLOGY, UNLIKE ETHICS OR RELIGION, WE ARE not dealing with absolute values, I think it would be very wrong to pass judgment on kibbutz education on grounds of individuation. Any educational system has to be judged not by what it attains for a very few, but for the vast majority—and without preventing the very few from going far beyond it. In regard to the latter, kibbutzniks are specially fortunate. If all Israel were composed of kibbutzim this would not be so, and then I might worry more, and so might they. But Israel is an open society, unusually so for such a very new nation. Hence nothing worse than economic and psychological barriers keep anyone from leaving the closed kibbutz society for the open society of Israel.

No doubt the system prevents some from developing as fully as they might, witness the data I have quoted on scholastic achievement. But in sheer number they are more than offset by those who (based again on these data) would have achieved much lower were it not for ample support from the group and the educational system. Moreover, there are no children in the kibbutz who, because of economic and social deprivation, never attain even that minimum of human development the kibbutz assures to all whom it educates.

There are, for example, no neglected children in the kibbutz, none whose physical needs in sickness and health are not well taken care of, none who could not learn in school because they had no decent place to sleep, or enough to eat. There is no child there who fails because of too much pressure to compete and perform. There are no drunken parents in the kibbutz, nor any who beat their children. I could go on but I think my point is clear. These protections the kibbutz can offer precisely because, in return for protection, its members grant it so much control of their lives.

To sum up with a truism: The more egalitarian a society, the more all are equal. Given the personal variations of history and endowment, there will always be differences from person to person, but they will always be the smaller, the more egalitarian the system. An egalitarian system of education will both lift up the bottom group and lower the top group toward the middle. And it will do so the more, the more egalitarian the system.

What this leveling could mean for the future of society, if it became universal, is an open question. How one evaluates it will again depend on whether one cares more about raising up the lower groups, or about lifting the top toward still higher achievement. I personally believe that at this stage of our knowledge the issue can be argued either way: that society benefits most if the lowest group is raised to the middle level and there is not too much difference between groups; but also that the top group should be given every chance to lift itself higher, and grow in number, because only this group through its intellectual achievement can best improve the welfare of all.

At least kibbutz education seems free of the contradiction that presently bedevils much of the American educational scene: the wish, at one and the same time, to lift our lowest achievers to considerably higher levels, and to speed and push upward our highest achievers. That this contradiction has not torn apart our educational system is thanks only to the fact that we operate two separate and different educational systems: the public one, where the avowed concentration is on the first task, and a widespread private and suburban educational system where we concentrate on the second. Only this division into two (or, considering the parochial schools, three or more) different educational systems has so far prevented our running head on into stresses that would otherwise tear education to pieces, with disastrous results for what it can do for all students.

Certainly kibbutz education turns out a majority of persons well content with themselves and their lives. For others it is stifling. But as long as they can escape, leave and join, with some effort, a world beyond the kibbutz, I personally would not worry about them. On the other hand, I am confronted daily in my life's work with children whose anguish is the tragic result of their parents' alienation, but for whom no community stands ready to shield them. I am not sure that it wouldn't be nice to have a few kibbutzim around for those who long to escape the anonymity, selfishness, competitiveness, social disorganization and widespread feeling of purposelessness which are so often found in modern mass society. The more so since fate has denied them individuation anyway, whether because of low native ability or the conditions they were born to.

Such a suggestion bespeaks my preference for an open society which, by its very pluralism, invites kibbutz and non-kibbutz alike to exist. Unhappily, pluralism and the open society are anathema to the kibbutz; which leaves my problem and theirs insoluble, as are many key problems of human existence.

Fortunately my task is not to judge the kibbutz, nor even kibbutz education, but to try to understand it. Moreover, with only the second generation to go by, so far as results in maturity are concerned, final answers will have to wait till their children are grown. Only this third generation will have been raised without the pressures of parental ambivalence, without desires strongly felt and just as strongly controlled or repressed. Since this third generation has not yet matured, everything further I might say, or have said, about kibbutz education, is tentative, very open to question, beset by uncertainties.

I have tried to suggest why I believe this system of education came into being, what some of its roots may have been, and some of its results as I saw them. My visit convinced me that, as a system of rearing, the kibbutz way is as viable as any other and could become more so in time, if the kibbutz should survive. It is a fine system for some and not for others. Like all educational systems it shapes the human personality in ways that differ importantly from those our own system produces. I conclude, therefore, with an effort to see how well fact and speculation fit into a theoretical system. This, it is hoped, may shed further light on the question: What is essentially different about personality formation between the kibbutz system of rearing and ours?

6

Their Mold and Ours

THE MOST IMPORTANT MODEL WE HAVE FOR PERSONALITY
development is the psychoanalytic, with those modifica-
tions suggested by Erikson (*Childhood and Society* 1950,
and "Identity and the Life Cycle," 1959). To help the reader
follow my discussion, Erikson's model is reprinted on the
following page.

It took Freud a lifetime to make the discoveries Erikson
built on. It took Erikson a lifetime of studying childhood
and society in interaction, to develop such a model. Having
studied kibbutz rearing no more than a matter of weeks I am
unable to suggest how his categories would need to be modified, or new ones created, to correctly apply them to our
problem.

A futher caveat: Erikson's scheme is a theoretical model
derived from middle-class rearing, and not a description of
things as they are. Because things are very different for
many of our families, and I do not mean just lower class

	A PSYCHOSOCIAL CRISES	B RADIUS OF SIGNIFICANT RELATIONS	C RELATED ELEMENTS OF SOCIAL ORDER	D PSYCHOSOCIAL MODALITIES	E PSYCHOSEXUAL STAGES
I Infancy	Trust vs. Mistrust	Maternal Person	Cosmic Order	To Get To give in return	Oral-Respiratory, Sensory-Kinesthetic (Incorporative Modes)
II Early Childhood	Autonomy vs. Shame, Doubt	Parental Persons	"Law and Order"	To hold (on) To let (go)	Anal-Urethral, Muscular (Retentive- Eliminative)
III Play Age	Initiative vs. Guilt	Basic Family	Ideal Prototypes	To make (= going after) To "make like" (= playing)	Infantile-Genital, Locomotor (Intrusive, Inclusive)
IV School Age	Industry vs. Inferiority	"Neighborhood," School	Technological Elements	To make things (= completing) To make things together	"Latency"
V Adolescence	Identity and Repudiation vs. Identity Diffusion	Peer Groups and Outgroups; Models of Leadership	Ideological Perspectives	To be oneself (or not to be) To share being oneself	Puberty
VI Young Adult	Intimacy and Solidarity vs. Isolation	Partners in friend- ship, sex, competition, cooperation	Patterns of Cooperation and Competition	To lose and find oneself in another	Genitality
VII Adulthood	Generativity vs. Self-Absorption	Divided labor and shared household	Currents of Education and Tradition	To make be To take care of	
VIII Mature Age	Integrity vs. Despair	"Mankind" "My Kind"	Wisdom	To be, through having been To face not being	

This table combines the two to be found on pp. 120 and 166 of E. Erikson's "Identity and the Life Cycle," Monograph 1, Psychological Issues, International Universities Press, New York, 1959.

families. Still a deeper reservation: most of what we believe to be true about earliest personality development is conjecture, including Erikson's notions about the origin of basic trust. It is derived from what we observe the infant getting and doing, and what we believe this may mean to the infant. I am most reluctant to add here, from very small indices, to the welter of speculations which is taken for fact in the absence of solid knowledge. Thus what follows are tentative suggestions, nothing more.

❧ *Trust Versus Mistrust*

WITH THIS CAVEAT, AND STARTING WITH THE *first* psychosocial crisis, that of trust versus mistrust, there seems little doubt of how different is the kibbutz infant's radius of significant relations. Because trust, in the kibbutz, derives not so much from *the* maternal person as from a number of maternal persons. From the very beginning, things are hence very different in the kibbutz than Erikson's model would suggest.

One might say here that what counts for the basic personality in infancy, and for the fundamental outlook on life later on, is not any absolute quantity, either of trust or mistrust, but the balance between them. To state it crudely: deep experiences prompting trust, and deep experiences leading to mistrust, may inspire an outlook on life essentially similar to one caused by a moderate taste of both trust and mistrust. Because when the negative is deducted from the positive, the remainders may be equal. This is so, even if the absolute size of what is deducted from what, differs vastly.

Thus a small basis for trust may produce the same basic security—if little interfered with by cause for basic mistrust —as would a vast experience creating trust when eroded by considerable cause for mistrust. My crude example may also suggest that the absolute size of what is deducted from what, may affect how deep the experience, but not its nature. Because the nature of the outlook, in this crude approximation, depends on what remains after subtraction.

Now, basic trust, from a very early age, is born of how the mothering task is performed. When the child's needs are well and responsively met, he develops, we think, a sense of trust. But in the kibbutz these tasks are performed by several mothering persons. One might assume then that the need to adjust to a variety of caretakers interferes with the feeling that this world and its ministrations are most reliable.

On the other hand, because there are several persons to take care of the nurseling, and this is the metapelet's central task, the infant has less cause for waiting and worrying, which may breed less mistrust. So here we might assume there is less interference with mothering than where a child depends on a mother's ministrations but this mother belongs also to many other tasks (housekeeping, siblings, husband).

Or again: With other infants eternally present, there will be less distrust and fear of desertion. But with no adult immediately available at night there will be less security. Multiple mothering, then, and the particular situation in kibbutz nurseries, may create less of both: less basic trust and also less basic mistrust.

According to Erikson's model, the "related element of social order" which flows from this earliest encounter with trust and mistrust, he calls "Cosmic Order." For the typical middle-class family this sense of order derives from one central person. As such, it lends credence to a world order created by one Supreme Being, with all its consequent feelings of bondage. Since cosmic order, for the kibbutz infant, is from the very first derived not from one person only, but from several, this too may create far-reaching differences in what will give order to his world.[1]

Initial learning, in the kibbutz, may be more difficult for the infant, given the need to adjust to different ways of how things are done. At least Rabin (*Growing Up in the Kibbutz*, 1965) suggests possible retardation of certain social and motor responses, when compared with adaptation in the infant who faces the much simpler task of adjusting his responses mainly to one person.

My own observation of infants was not extensive enough to permit me to agree or disagree with Rabin's findings on early behavior. But after presenting them, he goes on to say that the "relative developmental retardation noted in kibbutz infants is not maintained in later years." My foregoing comment may suggest why such retardation, if it occurs (Rabin's findings are not conclusive) would, by the toddler age, be made up for. Perhaps it is not that retardation ever took place—because if it had, and the child could so easily catch up, if there were no lasting effects, then we would have to change our entire model of how human development takes place. Perhaps what occurs is not retardation but simply that it takes longer to master a more complex bit of learning. It is fairly easy to adjust one's movements and social responses to one person alone. Hence the response is learned sooner. If the task is to adjust one's motor and social responses to several persons at once, then the learning task is more complex and takes longer to achieve.

Eventually, of course, all infants have to learn to adjust to several persons; certainly in the oedipal phase. But perhaps those who have learned it from the beginning come out

[1] One might even wonder if the compound family system (or any arrangements wherein many different persons look after the infant) does not create fertile ground for a cosmic order based not on the rule of one God but of many—and of a group of deities where none is very superior to the rest.

ahead in the long run, compared to those who learned first to respond to one person and later had to transfer the learning to many. Multiple mothering may also explain the absence in the kibbutz of what is technically called symbiotic psychosis of childhood. This is a disturbance marked by the child's utter dependence on his mother, which prevents him from having any life of his own. In the kibbutz there is no chance for symbiosis to develop in the first place.

Just as important, even at the very start of life, is how different are the social and psychological procedures that mark this first stage of human development. Here the essential experience for the kibbutz infant is to get, while to give in return is emphasized much less. No doubt, if the infant reaches out to his caretakers, he will get more from them. But since there are several caretakers, how they give to him will be less uniform in manner, and it will make much less difference how he gives in return.

Which means that from the beginning of life the extremes of development will be absent. In the kibbutz, with its multiple mothering, the infant has neither the utter security that may come of feeling himself at the core of his mother's existence, nor will he know the bondage it can bring. The heights of intimate mutuality (or later, of individuation) will not be reached that are possible in some mother-infant relationships. But neither will he know the extremes of nonmutuality (and hence of isolation and alienation) that result from bad mother-infant relations. And these occur in quite a few of our families where the mother, in the way she handles her infant, fails to adjust to his cues because of her own emotional problems, or because of the pressures of time or other interests.

One result is that grounds may be laid even at this early stage for the so-called "flatness" so often remarked upon in the kibbutz-born personality. It may be the consequence of a shallowness in the experience of mutuality—or of both trust and mistrust. Perhaps in these terms, most persons in the middle reaches of our society have equally flat personalities, or worse. Where we seem to differ from the kibbutz is in the presence of extremes, both of intensity and withdrawal.

One last comment before leaving this earliest of all developmental stages. Many of the concerns that led Erikson to formulate his model had to do with the severe identity crisis he observed in American middle-class youth (but which also afflicts our Negro and lower-class youth), and which is rooted in this earliest period of life. Perhaps relative absence of an identity crisis in kibbutz youth indicates that their experience, at the very beginning, is more benign by comparison.

✿ Autonomy, Shame, and Doubt

THE DIFFERENCE BETWEEN ERIKSON'S MODEL AND KIBBUTZ reality is as marked in the *second* psychosocial crisis, that of autonomy versus shame and doubt. The importance of the peer group, in Erikson's model, does not make itself felt until the fifth of these crises, at puberty. In the kibbutz the peer group is already greatly important during this second psychosocial crisis, or stage of development, not only through its presence, but through its actual help, as with toilet training and other forms of early socialization. Indeed, the peer group is significant even in the first stage, given the intense watching of other infants in adjacent cribs, as it reduces feelings of loneliness and abandonment.

Since it is the other children who set examples and influence the education to cleanliness, there is much less shaming than is typical when adults toilet train the child. Also the "radius of significant relations" is much larger, because to the "parental persons" must be added the peer group, if not almost the entire kibbutz.

"To hold (on)" and "to (let go)" are much less important in the kibbutz, since there is so much less emphasis on toilet training, table manners, cleanliness, the care of clothing, etc. (Which may be why private property and the holding on to it become less important.) We find a reduction in the kind of autonomy that is based on a stubborn insistence on having one's way as it may develop around these activities, and with it a radical decrease in doubt. But in other spheres a much greater autonomy develops because the kibbutz child is left so much to his own devices.

With far fewer dos and don'ts and a much more lenient toilet training, the internalized feeling for "law and order" is less stringent. Law and order derive less from toilet training and much more from the "laws" of the kibbutz. Even at this early age it is less the voice of conscience, and much more the peer group that utters the dos and don'ts. And these are enforced by group influence, through shaming.

But the shaming is much gentler and less severe than when it comes from adults, not because the other children may be less forceful, but because the child observes how much the children who shame him transgress themselves. Because of it, their injunctions carry less weight and lead to much less self-doubt. Which makes the experience of shame very different from what is typical for the middle-class child. It comes not from any vast difference between "my behavior" and that of the shaming adult, but from a rather small difference between two comparative equals. Which, again, engenders less doubt.

Let me use this period for a few brief comparisons. Erikson lists some items discussed by Spock to suggest the problems now besetting parent and child, such as "Feeling his oats" and "The passion to explore." In consequence of these come the parent's problems of "Arranging the house for a wandering baby. Putting poison out of reach. Making him leave certain things alone. Making him stay in bed."

Each is a problematic issue in the middle-class home at this period of development. Around them, battles are fought that often scar the infant for life, and sometimes the parent. But these issues hardly exist for the kibbutz child. The infant house is arranged specially for him, there is no poison, nor anything he must not touch. Since there are no parents to turn to after bedtime and nothing going on around him in the evening, keeping children in bed is as little a problem for the parent as is staying in bed for the child.

🌻 *Initiative Versus Guilt*

DURING THE PERIOD OF THE *third* PSYCHOSOCIAL CRISIS, THAT of initiative versus guilt, the basic family, according to Erikson, becomes important in addition to parental persons. But in the kibbutz there is no basic family in our sense. What replaces it are the two parents on one hand, and the metapelets and peer group on the other. Much more important, the radius of significant relations has by this time expanded far more than the model suggests. It extends to the kibbutz as a whole, because the kibbutz performs so many functions that parents do in our setting, such as offering physical protection, being the main provider, etc.

Speaking of this third period Erikson writes: "the child must now find out *what kind* of person he is going to be . . . he wants to be like his parents, who to him appear very powerful and very beautiful, although quite unreasonably dangerous. He 'identifies with them,' he plays with the idea of how it would be to be them." These are the ideal prototypes of the period in our middle-class family.

How different things are for the kibbutz child. He, too, in this period must find out what kind of person he is going to be. But while his parents are very important to him, they certainly do not appear to him as very powerful, and even less so as unreasonably dangerous.

The most powerful persons, to the kibbutz child of this age, are the metapelets. And typically if the children play the role of adults, as they do at this age just as often as do children in our society, the girls play at being metapelets, and both boys and girls play at being persons carrying high prestige in the kibbutz, such as truck drivers.

Thus at a much earlier age the identification is with the society's "culture carrier," not the parent. And in the kibbutz the culture carrier embodies the culture much more closely than does the parent (or the cowboy or Indian or athlete) in our society. So again the identification with what the kibbutz stands for takes precedence over the identification with parents. Children also identify less with a particular individual, and more with some role the group admires. The child wishes less to become like a particular, unique person—a wish also largely suppressed in his parents and metapelets—than to become a good comrade. Such an ideal accords with both his parents' ego ideal and the moral valuation of the entire society.

In the kibbutz, however, far more than is true of many middle-class families, the ego ideals of father and mother are very much akin to each other, and to those of the metapelets. Even if the child wished to be different from them, he has hardly any images that differ enough to serve him as variant ideals. Life is much simpler at this age, a boon for which a price will be exacted of those adolescents who may yearn for a highly personal identity that eludes them.

Social crisis in this third period centers around the issue of initiative versus guilt. But guilt in the kibbutz derives from transgressing the rules of the children's community and not from violating the basic values of a nuclear family. Hence the nature of guilt is very different. The essential experience creating guilt in the kibbutz is based on the anxiety: "*They* will think I'm no good" rather than "*I* will think I'm no good"; while in the middle-class conscience the relative importance of the two personal elements is exactly reversed.

Grounds for this difference are laid in the second phase of development, where from the much gentler shaming comes the fear that "they'll think I'm no good," versus the middle-class child's feeling of "I'm no good compared to my parents." The first permits ready relief. One has only to catch up with peers who are only one step ahead. The latter makes the child feel hopeless about himself because the gap between his own self-control and that of the shaming parent is just too great—or seems so to him. In the nuclear family the heir of the personal voices of the parents is thus a highly personalized superego. In the kibbutz the outer voices internalized are those of the entire community, and lead to a collective superego.

But if internalization is weaker, along with inner initiative, locomotor initiative in trying to master the physical world is much more encouraged. This is because the children must so largely fend for themselves, and because the whole life of their community is an open book to them (the exception here is the private life of adults, including the sexual life; but in the kibbutz the adult's life is much less private than with us). There is continual challenge to do things, and hardly any to sit and think and feel. I am tempted to exaggerate and say this starts at the beginning of life, for it is not much of an exaggeration.

Any budding inner experience the child has with himself is interfered with or extinguished before it can go very far by some group experience directing him outward. The children are always busy doing things. And if they don't seduce or even push each other in that direction, the metapelet will. There is no time, no opportunity and no challenge for them to think their own thoughts or to yield themselves up to their own feelings.

Neither are there introjects to converse with in fantasy. And when, later on in adolescence, the desire for all this is much stronger, there is no prior experience on which it can build. To have to build it from scratch at so late a developmental stage seems impossible for most. One consequence is that these adolescents who use their bodies so skillfully to do things, are not "at home" with the body itself, their own or another's. Having looked inward so little they are not very intimate with feelings generated by the body, though they can use it with competence; they are more familiar with what it does than what it feels.

Kibbutz living arrangements have far-reaching consequences for the nature of the children's fantasies about sex. Living apart from their parents prevents the children from watching primal scenes and from having it forcefully brought home to them each night that now their parents are in bed together, just the two of them, a fact at once known to and hidden from the middle-class child. For example, since they do not observe human intercourse, neither might they get the notion that this is an aggressive, sadistic act performed by the male on the female. Since there was so much less of anal or urethral inhibitions in the preceding period, initiative is much less impeded by guilt than it is in our middle-class families. Muscular development, too, except for the sphincter, is far more encouraged and facilitated in both the second and third periods, because kibbutz children can roam so freely through the landscape (perhaps an origin of their deep seated love for it).

❧ *Industry Versus Inferiority*

SPEAKING OF THE LATENCY PERIOD AND OF THE *fourth* PSYCHO-social crisis, that of industry versus inferiority, Erikson remarks: "While all children at times need to be left alone in solitary play (or later in the company of books . . .) and while all children need their hours and days of make believe in games, they all, sooner or later, become dissatisfied and disgruntled without a sense of being useful, without a sense of being able to make things and make them well and even perfectly: this is what I call the sense of industry."

His statement illustrates once more how different matters are in American society compared to the kibbutz. Our mid-dle-class children used to get more than their fill of being left alone in solitary play. But their lives, in many cases, were deficient in the experience of being useful. Lately, it must be said, their days have become so crowded that their chances for solitary activity have severely contracted. As a result they neither get enough of solitary play nor of useful activity.

By comparison the kibbutz child is much advantaged by the chance to do useful things and do them well. But his life, and again only by comparison, is deficient in the chances for being alone with himself or in the company of books. The kibbutz child is never alone. Even if he engages for moments in solitary play, he is quickly interrupted by some other child or adult, since nonprivacy in the kibbutz does not stop short at the child. And this he accepts as part of the everyday fabric of his life.

On the other hand, his devotion to, and high valuation of, industry appears even before the start of the latency period. As early as the play age he contributes to kibbutz economy, be it by growing things or raising animals. And from school age on, he will work on the children's farm, and work there industriously.

How different the timetables are by which human development unfolds in kibbutz society compared to our own. Solitude will not be available to the kibbutz youngster, if at all, before the end of adolescence, and then only rarely, for short time periods, and against heavy odds. But by then it is too late for the internalization that creative solitude forces on the young child.

The middle-class parent's often desperate plea, "Can't you find something to do?" is replaced in the kibbutz by the tacit (but often open) command: "Don't go off by yourself; be a good comrade, be part of your group." The middle-class child has a powerful but largely frustrated desire to be useful, to make things that count. For the kibbutz child this is replaced by an easy access to and demand for exactly such constructive doing. And this means not just what will count toward his later development, but what will bring him rewards here and now, just as it does for his parents and all other adults.

With so much more chance for early industry in ways that matter importantly to his society, less feeling of inferiority develops. From now on, the youngster will feel little or no sense of inferiority within his society.

True, the limited nature of his industry, and the absence of solitude will develop him mostly for life in this society, and he will feel himself unsuited to any other. But he will respond to this less with a feeling of personal inferiority than of superiority. "Those others are bad societies, not fit to be lived in. So if I don't fit in, why should I feel inferior?" He will feel uncomfortable there, out of place, awkward, insecure, even lost, but not inferior. He will shun other types of living conditions (his xenophobia). But despite the sense of awkwardness, he feels inwardly superior. Hence the so-called arrogance of the kibbutz-born adult which, to outsiders, contrasts strangely with what we look upon as his very limited and limiting outlook. In fact, both reflect his self-sufficiency when at home with his group, and his sense of being robbed of it when apart from his group, in an alien world.

Since he is not made to feel inferior by the society around him, but on the contrary feels very secure, and since he can satisfy his desire for industry to the full, this fourth psychosocial crisis is much reduced in its stresses. Once again the kibbutz child is much happier than a child of his age in our society. But not having to resolve a crisis of great depth as regards industry versus inferiority, he again has no need to develop great inner resources to weather it. Nor will his personality deepen for having resolved such a conflict successfully.

During this same period, according to Erikson's scheme, the neighborhood and school stand in the center of significant relations. But the kibbutz child has long since made the entire kibbutz the focus of his relations. More important for his later development, the radius of significant relations will not expand any further. Thus in the growth of significant relations (Erikson's problem area B) we see in the kibbutz a tremendous speeding up of the developmental process.

Possibly by as early as the second period of crisis, and certainly during the third, the entire world of significant relations will have been mastered, which is very different from the slow and steady development of our middle-class children. But contrary to what happens in our setting, this radius will not significantly widen for the kibbutz child during the following periods of development. In this area of significant relations we see that a much greater mastery is expected (and usually achieved) rather early in life, and not much more later on. It is just one indication of how any educational system, compared to another, pushes certain developments and retards others, with far-reaching consequences for the type of personality it will finally produce.

Two other problem areas show the same pattern of early mastery and later stasis, namely in problem area C (related elements of social order) and particularly in area D (psychosocial modalities). In the latter case, development seems essentially to stop at the fourth stage, which is only natural: no higher stage seems possible for a kibbutznik than "to make things together." There is no superego or ego demand, no ego ideal and no social or group pressure to strive for anything beyond a concentration on work morality. No other examples are accepted as valid that could even serve as incentives.

Indeed, no further psychosocial crises are necessary beyond Erikson's fourth, that of industry versus inferiority. Since the *fifth* struggle, the one for a personal identity, would almost have to take the adolescent caught up in it away from the kibbutz, it is not pertinent for those who will stay. Nor can this crisis really develop. Those who fit into kibbutz life have no need to struggle for identity of a personal nature, since the community so largely defines it for them. In this way the kibbutz adolescent escapes the identity diffusion that afflicts so many of our middle-class adolescents, and which Erikson has discussed for us at length.

Since the kibbutz child does not experience solitude, the typical adolescent crisis does not occur either—that of whether to be essentially oneself, or to mesh one's being with that of others. Because this crisis presupposes the childhood experience of being left to one's very own devices, with only oneself and one's introjects for company. The adolescent's deep desire to be himself is based on this childhood experience of loneliness, and of the need to now integrate various introjects with the rest of his own personality—which of them to keep, and which not, how to modify them all until they are part of one integrated personality. But without the previous experience of playing and being by oneself, and without the introjects, there is no essential conflict between wishing to be most oneself, and also wishing to be deeply with others. The kibbutz-born is essentially himself when among others.

Since this struggle, in Erikson's scheme, leads up to the *sixth* psychosocial crisis, that of intimacy versus isolation, it may now be apparent for theoretical reasons, too, why intimacy is essentially not available to many kibbutz-born. Each of these crises is marked by struggle between two opposites. But the struggle between isolation and intimacy cannot be a problem to someone raised in a kibbutz, since he has never lived in isolation. I could go on, but I meant only to suggest how kibbutz education can be understood in terms of a developmental psychology based on psychoanalytic insight.

❧ Integrity Versus Despair

ONE LAST THOUGHT BASED ON ERIKSON'S SCHEME: IN APPLYING his model to my observations I was struck by how—for those who were born in the kibbutz and felt no need to leave it—psychosocial development seems for the most part to conclude with the fourth in the sequence of crises. This means that they never reach that *eighth* psychosocial crisis of integrity versus despair.

The existential despair that seems to haunt Western society, the kibbutznik escapes: despair about oneself or the world, about the fact that one's life is to end, and that it had little meaning or purpose. But in terms of all I have said, the kibbutznik escapes at a price. By now it should be clear what that consists of. In terms of Erikson's model, despair is escaped at some cost to personal identity, emotional intimacy, and individual achievement. On the other hand, this may seem a very small price to many of our aging and aged who suffer a feeling of uselessness, a sharp sense of isolation, because there is nothing meaningful for them to do any more, nor any place of importance in society. Those who grow old in the kibbutz are never alone. They remain as before in the middle of things, feeling needed. To the end of their natural days there is as much for them, or as little, of importance to be done as they wish.

Just as latency is a happier time for kibbutz children, so too is old age, which in the kibbutz is infinitely richer than is typical in our setting.

Though the founding generation is pleased with the results of its unique educational system, this does not mean that misgivings are absent. Essentially they wanted both for their children: utter egalitarianism, and highest individuation. It comes hard to them to realize that these are contradictory values. But despite some hesitation, their actions show that for the present they have opted for egalitarianism. It is just possible that their children of the second (and particularly the third) generation, brought up in this spirit, will no longer be able to opt otherwise.

Ordinarily the sense of personal uniqueness and utter immersion in the group are contradictory. But there are rare occasions when this contradiction is temporarily canceled out. In the interviews referred to earlier, those of kibbutz-born soldiers after the six-day war, one of them said: "The very fact of going to war gave you a greater feeling of belonging. This prods you to give more of yourself to the kibbutz. And also you feel that it belongs to you. There is a saying among us that the kibbutz belongs to you, but in reality this is lost because the real meaning of it is that you belong to everyone more than to yourself." It was again the intensely personal encounter with naked death in battle that led this young man—and probably many like him—to new awareness. Up to that time he had felt mainly how much he belonged to the kibbutz. Only now did he recognize how much it also belonged to him. All his life he had been told "the kibbutz needs you," but to him this had meant that he belonged to the kibbutz. Only now, in his readiness to die before his time in order to save himself and the kibbutz did he affirm the central meaning of his life: that he belonged to them and they to him by virtue of their needing him. He had made his own the central conviction on which the kibbutz is built: that the more you belong to your comrades, the more deeply they belong to you, and hence the more you are deeply and truly yourself.

It was the high degree of individuation among the founding generation that rendered them so sensitive to the sense of isolation in their lives. To overcome it for themselves and their children, they set out to build a society of great personal freedom that would also be a true folk society of comrades. As with all dreams, they realized it only in part. The more closely knit they became as a group, the more truly a kibbutz, the more it cost them in individuation. Those who set personal realization higher than the value of consensus excluded themselves from the kibbutz and left.

Having achieved great individuation, great enough to suffer from the loneliness it breeds, the founding generation could only glance into the Promised Land of communal life. They could never really shake off the individuation; hence the painful ambivalence between them and their children.

Things are simpler for those of the second generation who remain. Knowing nothing of apartness, they are content with satisfactions not destroyed for them by having to fight for a sense of belonging. Neither must they strive for an individuation that might compensate, through a rich inner life, for what is absent from their group life. They feel no need to push ahead, but neither do they have the impulse to push anyone down. While such people do not create science or art, are neither leaders nor great philosophers nor innovators, maybe it is they who are the salt of the earth without whom no society can endure.

The dreams parents dream for their children never come true—though neither are they wholly in vain. One cannot dream up a life for the other, one can only fashion a life of one's own. This the founders of the kibbutz have done, and it left its mark on their children. Perhaps it says something of kibbutz education that in some ways its children turned out as their parents expected and hoped, but in other respects very differently. These children of theirs are not the stuff dreams are made of, but real people, at home since their birth, on native ground.

APPENDICES

❦ A. *Choosing a Field*

HAVING CHOSEN TO STUDY MAINLY ONE KIBBUTZ, IN DEPTH, the next decision was which of the three kibbutz movements to select from: the left wing, center, or right? Here the real issue was whether to select from a movement where the kibbutz spirit was at its most rigorous, in pure culture as it were—which would be from the left wing—or from one that had relaxed in some of the more extreme features. Since the focus of this study was not the kibbutz per se, but its child rearing methods and whether they have something of importance to teach us, it seemed best to select a kibbutz more akin to our democratic aspirations than one leaning more toward a centralized, authoritarian, communistic philosophy.

In part, too, I was motivated by the fact that some of the most extensive studies on kibbutz child rearing published in this country (Spiro's and Rabin's) seem to have concentrated on kibbutzim of the left wing so that this group was by now somewhat covered in the literature. More important were my conversations with kibbutzniks. These suggested to me that the left-wing kibbutzim (those most radical in their child rearing methods) were moving more and more in the direction of those methods now in use by the least radical movement of the three.

For example, while I was in Israel the left-wing movement changed its official policy on dormitory arrangements for late adolescents. Prior to that, as discussed in the chapter on adolescence, youngsters up to eighteen (when they join the army and become full-fledged kibbutz members) had to sleep four to a room: two girls and two boys together. The new policy allowed each kibbutz to decide if they wished to keep the old policy, or adopt one that allowed the sexes to sleep apart after reaching fourteen. This change had been decided on by the right-wing kibbutz movement several years earlier. It is one of many examples suggesting that in response to past experience and to the surrounding mores of Israel, the right-wing movement was merely the first to move in directions that all three movements seem headed toward at this moment.

Another decision was which particular kibbutz of the one movement to select as a base of operations. Here personal reasons were also at work. Some members of a particular right-wing kibbutz, which I have here called Atid, had studied with me in Chicago, a few of them quite intensively so. I had gotten to know them personally enough to hope it would speed my access to deeper material (a hope not entirely born out by experience). Also, one of the top educators of the entire right-wing movement had been a student of mine in Chicago, and I had found him a particularly sensitive and intelligent person who could be of great help in interpreting the child rearing methods of his movement. Finally, one of

the earliest and best-known educators of all kibbutz movements (since the death of Shmuel Golan) was still alive,
though by now an old man, and he too lived at Atid. This
meant the opportunity to have as my informants there two of
the foremost educators of this movement, one from its past
and the other from its present leadership. The decision was
therefore made to spend as much time as possible at Atid, a
choice I did not come to regret.

I did in fact spend the bulk of my time there. But since
Atid adjoins two other kibbutzim, all three of which share a
single school system, my living and observing at Atid extended somewhat to these other two kibbutzim.

Though I visited several others, there were only three kibbutzim where I spent enough time to collect significant data.
One belonged to the same right-wing movement as Atid but
was settled mainly by West European Jews. The other two
belonged to the left-wing movement, one of them founded
by German and East European Jews, the second an "American" kibbutz settled mainly by persons brought up in the
United States.

Both in observing and assessing, I have concentrated on
features that for one reason or another were of particular
interest to me. And not even all of those were discussed
here, because some were extraneous to this report, though of
relevance, for example, to my work at the Orthogenic
School.

❦ B. The Data

THE MOST IMPORTANT OF THE DATA ON WHICH THIS REPORT IS
based were the informal observations I made, both while
gathering "objective" information, and while just trying to
take in and understand.

Obviously it would have been preferable for a study such as this one to be conducted by someone who speaks Hebrew or at least understands it, which I do not. It was fortunate therefore that most of the kibbutz intelligentsia, including all educators, speak English, since they were important informants because of their deeper understanding of the problems that concerned me, and because it is they who shape kibbutz educational policy.

Hebrew is the native tongue only of the younger age groups. Among the older groups, the native language is most often German, French, Yiddish, or Russian. I am fluent in the first two and understand the third. Thus I could speak easily and directly with most older kibbutzniks in their own native tongues. Only with the younger generations was my lack of Hebrew a serious handicap, except again for the intelligentsia among them who speak English very well. All adolescents and young adults speak and understand simple English, since it is taught to all kibbutz children in school; but they are often unresponsive to the more subtle nuances of language, and many speak it only haltingly.

My biggest problem was the children who were too young to have learned English in school. In speaking with them, I almost always used their metapelets as interpreters when in the children's houses, and their teachers when I spoke with them in school. In addition to these interpreters, the kibbutz of Atid assigned one of its members to me as interpreter for my entire stay in Israel. This person too, some years earlier, had spent time with me in Chicago, studying at the Orthogenic School, and I would like to thank her here for her generous help to Charles Sharp and me.

I hope that what I lost out on by my ignorance of Hebrew was compensated for by an intimate knowledge of the rearing of children away from their parents. As a matter of fact, one of my many initial reasons for wanting to study kibbutz rearing was the reports on how destructive it is for children to be reared away from their mothers. These reports I could not accept, having for some twenty years directed a center where children are brought up not by their parents, but by professional educators, and to the children's advantage. Thus I felt I was in a better position than most to evaluate the assets and liabilities of group rearing and that this, in the long run, might be as important for understanding such a method of education as it would be to command the language of the children.

The objective data consisted of interviews with several hundred persons, as recorded on tape, and other materials such as projective tests (three wishes, draw-a-person). These tests were given to 191 children drawn from four different kibbutzim, and at all grade levels from the second to the highest. I do not report here on the results of these tests for the same reason that I was critical of the results of the academic tests discussed in the preceding chapter. Because these tests, too, are standardized for a culture that values different traits from the kibbutz. This qualification apart, the test findings strongly support the views presented in this book on the results of kibbutz education and the personality it produces.

I talked informally to more than one hundred children of all ages, sometimes in English but mostly through interpreters. I also spoke with a wide variety of kibbutz educators: metapelets, teachers, child therapists, youth leaders, and those we would call educational administrators, i.e., the directors of schools and teachers' colleges.

I held several conferences, each of many hours duration, with all the teachers of a school system serving a group of three kibbutzim (some thirty teachers); with all the metapelets of the same three kibbutzim (again about thirty persons); and with many individual metapelets and teachers of two other kibbutzim. That is, I held group discussions with about a hundred educators, and interviewed some thirty others separately and in depth.

I interviewed separately, for one hour or longer, some fifty kibbutz members who either felt they had something of importance to tell me, or because for one reason or another they seemed worthwhile subjects to be interviewed. I interviewed all the kibbutz-born married couples of one kibbutz (some twelve couples). I spoke to all those youngsters of one kibbutz who had just finished high school and were about to enter the army (some twelve persons). I interviewed a group of parents of young kibbutz children (some ten parents). I interviewed in depth all those persons I could get hold of who were kibbutz-born and had left it as young adults (some ten people).

I spent many hours of discussion (in some cases twenty or more hours) with the following: the director of a school where I visited nearly all classes; two teachers of this school; the two persons in charge of education at two different kibbutzim; the person in charge of all higher education for one of the three kibbutz movements; and the director of a teachers' college for one of the kibbutz movements.

To gauge the success of kibbutz rearing it was also important to ask: since their youngsters do not show delinquent tendencies, homosexuality, etc., are there psychological disturbances particular to *them?* So I had preplanned for a seminar with all child therapists, psychologists, etc., of all the three movements, to discuss with them what pathology they encountered among their child patients. Since they wished to learn from me, too, this was easily arranged, and for four days we met at the right-wing teachers' college at Beth Beril. The meeting gave fascinating sidelights, not only on the nature of disturbances among kibbutz children but on how the kibbutz setting affects therapy in turn.

These meetings further enabled me to acquaint myself

with the kind of attitudes and knowledge imparted by the teachers' college to those who were going to be the future metapelets and teachers of the movement I intended to study. Meeting both these educators of teachers and their students helped to round out my observations and interviews at a single right-wing kibbutz. Then, to be able to compare the experience, a similar one-day institute was conducted at the quite different teachers' college of the left-wing movement at Oranim.

Again, not wanting to have to rely on what I was told or could only casually observe, I made special efforts to track down emotional disturbances in children and youth, as well as in adults who were kibbutz-born and educated.

There is only one residential treatment institution for children of all kibbutz movements, Neve Zeelim at Ramat Hashavim, and a visit there proved most instructive.

Along the same line of investigation I met with the Israeli psychoanalysts at one of their monthly meetings and thus had a chance to talk with some of them informally about their experience with patients who were (or still are) kibbutz members. In addition, several analysts gave me repeated chances to talk with them separately, and at length. The same was true of some psychiatrists who are not analysts but who, in their professional capacity, are closely related to various kibbutzim or have treated many persons who were or still are kibbutz members. (I might mention, incidentally, that not a single psychiatrist or psychoanalyst is a kibbutz member. But this is hardly remarkable, given the size of the kibbutz population and the rarity of specialists in our own agricultural communities.)

In addition, many interviews with Israeli educators, psychologists, and sociologists who were not kibbutz members but who had studied it or been close to it for years were most helpful.

But however valuable the information so gained, it was

peripheral to my goal: to study kibbutz child rearing where it took place, first and foremost by direct observation, secondly by talking with youngsters willing and able to communicate, and by doing the same with their metapelets, teachers, and parents.

As mentioned at the start of this book, Charles Sharp joined me in Israel for about three weeks, during which time more than ten thousand feet of motion pictures were filmed, mainly of interactions between children of various ages, and between children and their parents, metapelets, and teachers. It is hoped that a documentary film on kibbutz child rearing will help to tell about this unique educational venture.

From what I was told in Israel, people there are as anxious to learn about the findings reported here as are interested educators and psychologists in the United States. This is so because of widely divergent opinions in Israel at large about kibbutz education. Even on the most basic issues there is little consensus between kibbutz leaders and those most critical of the system. Perhaps most astonishing to me, as an outsider, was the lack of factual information within a given kibbutz movement as to what child rearing practices prevailed in the other movements, and with what outcome. I found blatantly erroneous notions about some aspects of kibbutz education being held by prominent non-kibbutz educators, psychologists, and psychiatrists in Israel, as well as by psychoanalysts who were treating kibbutz-educated persons. This was even true of psychiatrists who had made special studies of kibbutz education.

Let me give two examples, one from the report of a United States psychiatrist who has published on the kibbutz and been widely quoted; the other to show how misleading it can be to accept the statements even of leading kibbutz educators, unless they are carefully examined.

Gerald Caplan, an American psychiatrist who has studied kibbutzim in Israel firsthand (1954), states that he found "a tremendous amount of thumb-sucking, temper tantrums, and general lack of control over aggression. . . . The toddlers look like deprived children in institutions. Up to the age of five or six, the children look puny and small."

I do not know if this description was valid at some previous time, but when I visited the various kibbutzim, a most striking observation was the physical and emotional well-being of exactly this toddler group. Thumb-sucking was certainly not more widespread than in the United States, with the possible exception of children in particularly puritanical American homes, and temper tantrums far less common than here. It was to confute statements like these that the decision was made to produce a documentary film. Because the health and well-being of the toddler group, for example, would be strikingly evident to the viewer.

On the other hand, the literature abounds with statements that there is no (or very little) delinquency among kibbutz-reared adolescents. Yet in my interviews with kibbutz educators and psychologists they seemed deeply concerned with a "widespread" occurrence of delinquent behavior. By contrast they seemed little perturbed (in my opinion, rightly so) about the development of infants and toddlers, which is so persistent an issue in non-Israeli publications.

I therefore made it a point to ask about delinquency, without naming any particular kind. What then appeared was the following: In regard to car stealing, which they mentioned spontaneously, and which is a major form of delinquency in America, they told me that "this has become quite a problem here." When I asked how frequently it happens, the answer was "All the time." I asked, "In this kibbutz here?" and again the answer was "yes." I asked how recently a car had been stolen, and it appeared that this had happened more than a year ago. Why, then, did they talk as if it happens all the time? "Because it also happened a few months ago in a neighboring kibbutz." Thus the stated urgency and frequency of a phenomenon had clearly to do with the intensity of alarm felt by educators, and not with the facts.

When I asked for a detailed description of the last incident of car theft, it turned out to involve a group of adolescent boys who had used a kibbutz truck after hours. They drove to the nearest city (fifteen miles) to see a movie, after which they put the truck back in place. The truck, of course, was kibbutz property, and since the boys were children of the kibbutz, they viewed it as their property too, a fact that nobody questioned. What constituted the delinquency was their staying out after hours. Under these circumstances their use of the car, in the eyes of the educators, made it stealing.

Sex delinquency, too, I was told by kibbutz educators and psychologists, is a serious problem to them. I asked, "When was the last case of it in your kibbutz?" and the answer was "six years ago." When I asked what happened to the girl, I was told that the boy who got her pregnant "of course" married her. So I asked why they then called it widespread, and again the answer was that they had heard of a case less than a year ago in another kibbutz of their movement. This case I tried to track down but was unsuccessful. The kibbutz they named was not the one where it happened, and when I inquired again, they said it was hard to remember, and they could no longer recall exactly which one it had been.

These examples of how things look from inside the kibbutz and how they look to an investigator tracing facts, may indicate the difficulties of arriving at an unbiased evaluation of kibbutz education. They suggest again that what I have presented here is an impressionistic account.

❧ C. Kibbutz Settlements

OPERATIONALLY A KIBBUTZ IS A RELATIVELY SMALL AGRICUL-
tural settlement, though in recent years most of them have
added small industries. Their size varies from less than one
hundred to a maximum of two thousand inhabitants. What
is unique about them is that each community forms a single
unit: economic, political, and social. All property belongs to
the community except for some small personal belongings,
and even the latter is a recent development. Originally, not
even the clothes he wore belonged to the person, but came
and went from a common supply, and this is still true for the
children. Again: Only recently was it decided to give each
member a very small yearly allowance (about thirty dollars)
to spend as he wished.

On becoming a member of the kibbutz, the person turns
over to the community all his private possessions, though on
leaving he is not entitled to receive them back, nor any share
of the communal property.

Everything is provided by the community. And the community, through its general assembly, decides what should
thus be provided: for example, whether each member should
be given a radio, or how many trips a year to a cultural
event in a neighboring city may be paid for out of community funds.

Not only is the community run as a single economic unit,
but as a single big household. It provides food, clothing,
shelter, and all necessities of life, plus small luxuries when
feasible. Food, for example, is provided by a communal
kitchen, and is eaten in a common dining hall, though here
again an important relaxation has lately set in. Members are
now given some food items and a hot plate so that they can
fix tea and snacks in their rooms.

All services, including all schooling and medical care, are provided by the community. Big decisions are made by a general assembly of all members. (There are always a number of nonmembers living in a kibbutz: parents of members who did not themselves become members; persons who want to become members but are in their trial year; visitors, whom I shall refer to again; and of course all the children of the kibbutz.) The assembly meets weekly and is headed by a secretariat elected by the assembly. The secretariat usually consists of a secretary and treasurer, plus the farm manager, the manager of the factory, etc.

It is the secretariat that prepares the agenda for the weekly assembly and carries out its decisions through committees. One committee, for example, assigns to each member his daily work. Another committee is in charge of all education. Still another one decides who may take a trip that extends beyond the weekly day off, or the two-weeks yearly vacation. In practice the chairman of these committees carries a great deal of weight in the committee's decisions.

❧ D. Atid

THIS KIBBUTZ WAS FOUNDED IN 1932, MAINLY BY EAST EUROpean Jews. It ranks as an old, well-established kibbutz, with as high a standard of living as one may find among kibbutzim.

All members live in permanent quarters, which makes quite a difference. During the first years of a kibbutz, members live in rather primitive tents, huts, or other temporary structures, often with quite a few persons to a room. As the kibbutz prospers, the older members are allotted one-and-a-half rooms per bachelor member, or per married couple, each with its small shower room, toilet, and kitchenette. But even in so well-established a kibbutz as Atid there was still quite a range in housing standards. Even there, married couples may have held membership for fifteen years or more before the one-and-a-half rooms became available to them.

I go into some detail about housing because it affects children. Thus housing space poses problems when a family has several children of different ages, and they all arrive at the same time for their late afternoon "visit." Things do become crowded then, in the rather small living-sleeping room of the parents. It also poses problems in those few kibbutzim where the children sleep with their parents. While such families usually have two small rooms, perhaps even three if the children are many, their rooms are even smaller and quarters become even more crowded.

The main income of Atid comes from agriculture. In 1964 it was about three million Israeli pounds (one million dollars). Of this sum £700,000 was the value of what the kibbutz produced to keep itself going, such as food, clothing, etc. The rest was sold on the market by an all-kibbutz organization (individual kibbutzim do not trade with the outside), and the money so earned went for buying things on the market, for building new houses, improving the farm, etc. Again, these purchases are not made directly by Atid but are purchased for it by the kibbutz organizations.

By 1964 Atid had about three hundred members. Practically all three hundred worked, though some old people worked only four or five hours a day. There were 170 children living in the kibbutz at the time, of whom quite a few were not the children of members. In addition there are at any one time some forty or fifty visitors. Mostly these are young people who stay from six months to a year to learn about life in a kibbutz, and who may then go on to found a new kibbutz elsewhere.

Of the three hundred members, 120 worked in agriculture

and fifty to sixty in education. The remaining 130 worked to keep these 170 going. When we assume that somewhat less than half of our own adult population stays home to permit the other half to keep going at work, the percentages are not much different in the kibbutz. Again: as in most kibbutzim, about a fifth of the entire working force is devoted to education, or more precisely to all aspects of the care and rearing of children. This may seem exorbitant, but it must be remembered that much of what the kibbutz working force provides (through cooking, cleaning, laundry, sewing, child care) is provided in our society by women who stay at home or who only work part time.

Fifteen kibbutzniks work outside the kibbutz, and the salaries they earn are turned over to the kibbutz, forming part of its income. In addition Atid, like all other kibbutzim, lends some persons to work for the movement of which it is part. These persons earn no salary and hence are maintained by the kibbutz. There were twelve of them at Atid.

From the fifteen who work outside and are paid, the kibbutz receives 300,000 Israeli pounds in salaries, or about £20,000 per worker. If all three hundred in the working force earned as these do, kibbutz income would be exactly twice as high as it is, namely six million pounds. Thus, despite the large capital investments in the kibbutz (loans from the National Fund, the government, etc.), that it earns only half of what it might suggests that something is economically not very sound from our capitalistic point of view. But then it must be remembered that as likely as not it is mostly the highly skilled who are requested to work outside, and that the kibbutz was created to maximize not income but the quality of life for its members.

❧ E. The Children's House

KIBBUTZ CHILDREN LIVE FROM BIRTH ON (USUALLY FROM THE fourth day after delivery) with their age group, not at home with their families. That is, they are raised as a group, in separate children's houses, by members of the community assigned to the task. Usually the children's houses are built in a cluster, set off from other kibbutz structures.

In what I describe here there will be some variation from kibbutz to kibbutz. Things are naturally different in a young and small kibbutz where there are too few children to allow for the more general pattern. But usually the newborn who enters the infants' house is placed in a room with four to six cribs. The house has four or five such rooms and contains some twenty or more infants.

Each group of infants has one metapelet who is essentially in charge of that room, or else in charge of two rooms, but with a helper. In most kibbutzim for the first six months of his life the infant does not leave the infants' house, though his mother nurses him there, and his father may visit. After that he will visit daily with his parents in their room—at first for half an hour and by the end of the first year for as much as two hours. If an infant, or later an older child, is sick and does not require hospitalization, he does not go to school but remains in his crib or bed in the children's house and is nursed there by the metapelet. Thus sickness does not alter the child care arrangements. I do not know from first hand knowledge what happens when a child is hospitalized, but my guess is that the parents would be excused from work to visit their child.

When the infant is anywhere between one and two years old, he leaves the infants' house and moves to the toddlers' house. There a group of about six children are cared for by one metapelet. Each toddlers' house contains two or more such groups who share a common playroom and dining room.

When the children are somewhere between three-and-a-half and four, they move to the kindergarten house. Ideally the group consists of some eighteen children—that is, three toddler groups are combined. (Sometimes not enough babies are born in one year, and then the group may be smaller. At Atid, during my visit, two groups of five infants each were combined into one group of toddlers.) Now, one metapelet plus a kindergarten teacher are responsible for the group of eighteen, and the children will remain there until about seven years of age. These kindergarten children share in common one large room that serves as class and playroom combined, and a small dining room.

Children aged seven to twelve live in a children's house and number up to twenty. There they form a children's society with some self-regulation, under the direction of a teacher and one metapelet. The only common room in the children's house is the dining room, though I speak here of kibbutzim like Atid that have a separate classroom building. In many kibbutzim the grade school children's classroom is part of the children's house, just as it is for the kindergartners. The rest of the children's house consists of rather small bedrooms, with usually four beds to a room.

Youngsters of thirteen to eighteen live in youth houses and form a much more autonomous youth society. Life there is regulated chiefly by the group, though under the direction or supervision of a youth leader. But all youngsters of this age-group, however many youth houses there are, form a single youth society. Usually a few kibbutzim combine to build and operate one high school for their children. In such cases the youth houses may be close to the school but quite a distance from the youngsters' own kibbutz.

It is this method of child rearing that I consider remarkable about the kibbutz and its most unique contribution. Without this it would still be an institution that mattered greatly in the creation of Israel, but beyond that something of a historical oddity by now; a social organism made necessary by the need to establish rural outposts in a barren, hostile world, just as parallel needs and ideals led to many utopian settlements when America was first opened up.

BIBLIOGRAPHY

Aries, Philippe. *Centuries of Childhood,* Translated from the French by Robert Baldick. New York: Alfred A. Knopf, Inc., 1962.

Baratz, G. A *Village by the Jordan,* London: Harville Press, 1954.

Bar-Yoseph, R. "Patterns of Early Socialization in the Collective Settlements in Israel," *Human Relations,* XII (1959), 345-360.

Bettelheim, B. *Love Is Not Enough,* Glencoe, Illinois: The Free Press, 1950.

————. *Symbolic Wounds: Puberty Rites and the Envious Male,* Glencoe, Illinois: The Free Press, 1954.

————. "Nakhes Fun Kinder," *Reconstructionist,* XXV, 4 (1959), No. 4, 20-24.

————. *The Informed Heart,* Glencoe, Illinois: The Free Press, 1960.

————. "Does Communal Education Work? The Case of the Kibbutz," *Commentary,* XXXIII (1962), 117-126.

————. Book Review of Peter B. Neubauer (ed.) *Children in Collectives: Childrearing Aims and Practices in the Kibbutz* (Springfield, Ill.: Charles C. Thomas, Publisher, 1965), in *The New York Review of Books,* VII, 3 (1966).

————. *The Empty Fortress*, New York: The Free Press, 1967.

Bowlby, J. *Maternal Care and Mental Health*, Geneva: World Health Organization Monograph, 1951.

————. "Critical Phases in the Development of Social Responses in Man," *New Biology*, XIV (London: Penguin), 1953.

————. "An Ethological Approach to Research in Child Development," *British Journal of Medical Psychology*, XXXIII, 1957.

————. "The Nature of the Child's Tie to His Mother," *International Journal of Psycho-Analysis*, XXXIX (1958), 350-373.

————. "Ethology and the Development of Object Relations," *International Journal of Psycho-Analysis*, XLI (1960), 313-317.

————. "Separation Anxiety," *International Journal of Psycho-Analysis*, XLI (1960), 89-111.

————. "Grief and Mourning in Infancy and Early Childhood." in *The Psychoanalytic Study of the Child*, New York: International Universities Press, XV (1960), 9-52.

Caplan, Gerald. "Clinical Observations on the Emotional Life of Children in the Communal Settlements in Israel," in M.S.E. Senn (ed.) *Problems of Infancy and Early Childhood: Transactions of the Seventh Conference*, New York: Josiah Macy, Jr. Foundation, 1954, 91-120.

Chassell, Joseph O. "Old Wine in New Bottles: Superego as a Structuring of Roles," *Crosscurrents*, 1967, 203-218.

Darin-Drabkin, H. *The Other Society*, London: Victor Gollancz, Ltd., 1962.

David, J. Ben. "Conforming and Deviant Images of Youth in a New Society," in *Actes du Ve Congres Mondial de Sociologie*, Louvain: Association Internationale de Sociologie, IV (1964), 405-414.

Dayan, Yael. *Envy the Frightened*, New York: The World Publishing Company, 1961.

Diamond, S. "The Kibbutz: Utopia in Crisis," *Dissent*, IV (1957), 132-140.

————. "Introduction," *Social Problems*, V, 2 (1957), 68-70.

————. "Kibbutz and Shtetl: The History of an Idea," *Social Problems*, V, 2 (1957), 71-99.

Eisenberg, Leon and Peter B. Neubauer. "Mental Health Issues in Israeli Collectives: Kibbutzim," *Journal of the American Academy of Child Psychiatry*, IV, 3 (1965), 426-442.

Eisenstadt, S.N. *Age Groups and Social Structure*, Jerusalem: Hebrew University, 1950.

———. Book Review of M. Spiro, *Kibbutz: Venture in Utopia* (Cambridge: Harvard University Press, 1958), in *American Anthropologist*, LVIII, 5 (1956).

Erikson, Erik H. *Childhood and Society*, New York: W. W. Norton & Company, Inc., 1950.

———. "Identity and the Life Cycle—Selected Papers," *Psychological Issues*, I, 1 (1959).

Etzioni, A. "The Organizational Structure of Closed Educational Institutions in Israel," *Harvard Educational Review*, XXVII (1957), 107-125.

Faigin, Helen. "Social Behavior of Young Children in the Kibbutz," *Journal of Abnormal and Social Psychology*, LVI (1958), 117-129.

Flavell, J.H. *The Developmental Psychology of Jean Piaget*, Princeton, N.J.: D. Van Nostrand Company, Inc., 1963.

Freud, S. "An Outline of Psychoanalysis," in *The Standard Edition of the Complete Psychological Works of Sigmund Freud*, London: Hogarth Press, Ltd., 1940, XXIII.

Friedmann, Georges. *The End of the Jewish People?* Translated from the French by Eric Mosbacher, New York: Doubleday and Company, Inc., 1967.

Golan, Shmuel. *The Theory of Collective Education*, Johannesburg: Hashomer Hazair, 1952.

———. "Behavior Research in Collective Settlements in Israel: Collective Education in the Kibbutz," *American Journal of Orthopsychiatry*, XXVIII (1958), 549-556.

———. "Collective Education in the Kibbutz," *Psychiatry*, XXII, 2 (1959), 167-177.

——— and Zvi Lavi. "Communal Education." in S. Golan (ed.), *Collective Education in the Kibbutz*, Merchavia: Education Department of the Kibbutz Artzi Hashomer Hazair, 1961, 23-45.

Gruneberg, R. "Education in the Kibbutz," in N. Bentwich (ed.), *A New Way of Life: The Collective Settlements of Israel*, London: Shindler and Golomb, 1949.

Halpern, B. "The Israeli Commune, Privacy and the Collective Life," *Modern Review*, III, 1 (1949).

Harlow, Harry F. "The Nature of Love," *American Psychologist*, XII (1958), 673-685.

——— and M. K. Harlow. "Social Deprivation in Monkeys," *Scientific American*, CCVII, 5 (1962), 136-146.

Heiman, L. "The Changing Kibbutz," *The Reconstructionist*, XXIX, 16 (1963), 6-11.

Henry, Jules. "Child Rearing, Culture and the Natural World," *Psychiatry*, XV (1952), 261-271.

Hinsie, L.E. and J. Shatzky. *Psychiatric Dictionary*, New York: Oxford University Press, 1940.

Infield, Henrik F. *Cooperative Living in Palestine*, New York: The Dryden Press, Inc., 1944.

———. *Cooperative Communities at Work*, New York: The Dryden Press, Inc., 1945.

———. "Present Day Problems of Cooperative Living in Israel," *Cooperative Living*, I (1949), 1-8.

———. *Utopia and Experiment—Essays in the Sociology of Cooperation*, New York: Frederic A. Praeger, Inc., 1955.

Irvine, Elizabeth E. "Observations on the Aims and Methods of Child Rearing in Communal Settlements in Israel," *Human Relations*, V (1952), 247-276.

———. "Children in Kibbutzim: Thirteen Years After," *Journal of Child Psychology and Psychiatry*, VII (1966), 167-178.

Kaffman, M. "Another Look at 'Children of the Kibbutz,'" *Israel Horizons*, VII, 5 (1959), 15-20.

———. "Evaluation of Emotional Disturbance in 403 Israeli Kibbutz Children," *American Journal of Psychiatry*, CXVII (1961), 732-738.

Karpe, Richard. "Behavior Research in Collective Settlements in Israel: Editorial Statement," *American Journal of Orthopsychiatry*, XXVIII (1958), 547-548.

Laqueur, W. *Young Germany: History of the Youth Movement*, London: Routledge and Kegan Paul Ltd., 1962.

Luft, Gerda. "The Kibbutz in Crisis," Commentary, XXXII (1961), 334-340.

Mahler, Margaret. "On the Significance of the Normal Separation-Individuation Phase: with Reference to Research in Symbiotic Child Psychosis, in M. Schur (ed.), Drives, Affects, Behavior, New York: International Universities Press, II (1965), 161-169.

Mohr, George J. "Behavior Research in Collective Settlements in Israel: Discussion," American Journal of Orthopsychiatry, XXVIII (1958), 584-586.

Nagler, Shmuel. "Clinical Observations on Kibbutz Children," The Israeli Annals of Psychiatry and Related Disciplines, I, 2 (1963), 201-216.

Neubauer, Peter B. (ed.) Children in Collectives: Childrearing Aims and Practices in the Kibbutz, Springfield, Ill.: Charles G. Thomas, Publisher, 1965.

Nevins, Allan. "The Limits of Individualism," Saturday Review, November, 1967.

Parsons, E.I. "Children of Kfar Blum," Midstream: A Quarterly Jewish Review, V, 3, 1959.

Piaget, Jean. The Development of Moral Judgment in the Child, London: Kegan Paul, 1932.

Rabin, A.I. "Personality Maturity of Kibbutz and Non-Kibbutz Israeli Boys," Journal of Projective Techniques, XXI (1957), 148-153.

———. "The Israeli Kibbutz as a 'Laboratory' for Testing Psychodynamic Hypotheses," Psychological Records, VII (1957), 111-115.

———. "Kibbutz Children: Research Findings to Date," Children, V (1958), 179-185.

———. "Infants and Children Under Conditions of 'Intermittent' Mothering in the Kibbutz," American Journal of Orthopsychiatry, XXVIII (1958), 577-584.

———. Some Psychosexual Differences Between Kibbutz and Non-Kibbutz Israeli Boys," Journal of Projective Techniques, XXII (1958), 328-332.

———. "Attitudes of Kibbutz Children to Family and Parents," American Journal of Orthopsychiatry, XXIX (1959), 172-179.

―――. "Kibbutz Adolescents," *American Journal of Orthopsychiatry*, XXXI (1961), 493-504.

―――. *Growing Up in the Kibbutz*. New York: Springer Publishing Company, Inc., 1965.

Rapaport, David. "The Study of Kibbutz Education and its Bearing on the Theory of Development," *American Journal of Orthopsychiatry*, XXVIII (1958), 587-597.

―――. "Die Kibbutz-Erziehung und ihre Bedeutung für die Entwicklungspsychologie," *Psyche*, XII (1959), 353-366.

Riesman, David. *The Lonely Crowd*, New Haven: Yale University Press, 1950.

Rosenfeld, Eva. "Social Stratification in a 'Classless' Society." *American Sociological Review*, XVI (1951), 766-774.

―――. "Institutional Change in the Kibbutz," *Social Problems*, V (1957), 110-136.

Schwartz, Richard. "Democracy and Collectivism in the Kibbutz," *Social Problems*, V (1957), 137-146.

Spiro, M.E. "Is the Family Universal?" *American Anthropologist*, LVI (1954), 839-846.

―――. "Education in a Communal Village in Israel," *American Journal of Orthopsychiatry*, XXV (1955), 283-292.

―――. *Kibbutz: Venture in Utopia*, Cambridge: Harvard University Press, 1956.

―――. "The Sabras and Zionism: A Study in Personality and Ideology," *Social Problems*, V (1957), 100-109.

―――. *Children of the Kibbutz*, Cambridge: Harvard University Press, 1958.

―――. "Is the Family Universal?—Addendum," in N.W. Bell and E.F. Vogel (eds.), *A Modern Introduction to the Family*, Glencoe, Ill.: The Free Press, 1960, 64-75.

Spitz, Rene. "Hospitalism: An Inquiry into the Genesis of Psychiatric Conditions in Early Childhood," in *The Psychoanalytic Study of the Child*, New York: International Universities Press, I (1945), 53-74.

―――. "Hospitalism: A Follow-up Report," in *The Psychoanalytic Study of the Child*, New York: International Universities Press, II (1946), 113-117.

———. "The Psychogenic Diseases in Infancy: An Attempt at Their Etiologic Classification," in *The Psychoanalytic Study of the Child*, New York: International Universities Press, VI (1951), 255-275.

———. "Autoerotism Re-examined: The Role of Early Sexual Behavior Patterns in Personality Formation," in *The Psychoanalytic Study of the Child*, New York: International Universities Press, XVII (1962), 283-315.

———. *The First Year of Life*, New York: International Universities Press, 1965.

——— and K. M. Wolf. "Anaclitic Depression: An Inquiry into the Genesis of Psychiatric Conditions in Early Childhood, II," in *The Psychoanalytic Study of the Child*, New York: International Universities Press, II (1946), 313-342.

Talmon-Garber, Y. "Social Differentiation in Cooperative Communities," *British Journal of Sociology*, III (1952), 339-357.

———. "The Family in Israel," *Marriage and Family Living*, XVI, 1954.

———. "The Family in Collective Settlements," in *The Third World Congress of Sociology*, IV, 1956.

———. "Social Structure and Family Size," *Human Relations*, XII, 1959.

———. "Social Change and Family Structure," *International Social Science Journal*, XIV, 3 (1963), 468-487.

———. "Mate Selection in Collective Settlements," *American Sociological Review*, XXIX, 4 (1964), 491-508.

———. "Sex-Role Differentiation in an Equalitarian Society," in T. G. Lasswell, J. Burma, and S. Aronson (eds.), *Life in Society*, Chicago: Scott, Foresman and Company, 1965.

Weingarten, M. *Life in a Kibbutz*, New York: Reconstructionist Press, 1955.

Winograd, Merilyn. "The Development of the Young Child in a Collective Settlement," *American Journal of Orthopsychiatry*, XXVIII (1958), 557-562.

INDEX

INDEX

A

Academic achievement, 289-90
Academic training, 225-26
ADC mothers, 43, 47-49
Adolescence
  alienation, 54-56
  dependence, 207-208
  developmental tasks, 222-23
  ego development, 222-23
  emotional flatness, 51
  fads, 221
  founders vs. kibbutz-born,
    203-204
  friendships, 234
  revolt, 205-208
Adolescent crisis, 316-17
Adolescents, vanishing, 54-56
Adult leadership, 58, 60
Adult world, child's grasp of,
  163-64
Adults
  disappointment in, 106-107
  impermanence of, 97 ff.

Affluence
  and adolescent revolt, 207-208
  and alienation, 55
  and childrearing, 61-64, 200
Aged, the, 318
Age grading, 103
  in children's houses, 335-36
Age group, see Peer group
Aggression, 249
  control of, 63, 329
  physical, 175
  premium on, 78
Agricultural life, 22
Agriculture, 163, 333
Airport, 209-10
Alienation, 53 ff., 251, 306
  absence of, 123
  body, 63, 238 ff.
  in childhood, 54
Allowance, annual cash, 331
Ambivalence, 36, 132, 158-59
Amish, the, 109
Anal inhibitions, 312
Anal play, 240

Private property, 10, 101, 265, 280, 308, 331
  and private emotions, 261
  critics on, 81
  taboo on, 156-58, 166
  See also Belonging; Possession
Private rooms, 332-33
  children's corner in, 157-58
  functions of, 153
  snacks in, 27, 331
Private schools, 298
Profit, monetary, 224
Promiscuity, 63
Property, *see* Possession; Private property
Provider
  and basic necessities, 198
  continuity and sameness of, 66 ff., 108
Psychoanalysis, 148-50, 189-91, 327
Psychologist, consultant, 40, 93-94
Psychologists, 326
Psychosis, 306
Psychosocial crises, 303-17
Psychotherapeutic services, 52
Psychotherapy, 191, 326-27
Public school system, 298
Puritanism, 51, 76, 198-200, 235 ff.
Puritans, 15

R

Rabin, A. I., 7, 305, 321
Radios, 331
Ramat Hashavim, 327
Rapaport, D., 1-3, 34
Reality principle, 61 ff.
Recruitment, kibbutz, 283
Reformation, 130
Relations, radius of significant, 303 ff.
Religion, 23-24, 284
  See also Atheism; Orthodox kibbutzim

Repression
  and ego formation, 215
  at bedtime, 113-14
  cumulative, 243-45
  in kindergartners, 107
  instinctual, 62
  of negative emotions, 114, 182-84
  sexual, 204, 237 ff.
Responsibility, personal vs. collective, 176-77
Retardation, 279-80
  infant, 305
Revolt, adolescent, 205-208
Riesman, D., 61, 104, 129 n., 215-16, 254
Right wing movement, 10
Rinot, H., xiii
Rosen, S., 295
Rudeness, 279
"Rules of the game," 128-29

S

Sabra, 279
"Sacred hours," 56, 132-35
  See also Children's hours; Visits
Sameness
  of life style, 160
  of provider, 66 ff.
Sample, kibbutz, 8 ff., 13
Sanctions
  group, 232-33, 235-36
  supernatural, 210
Schizophrenia, 196
Scholastic achievement, 289-90
School
  and child's radius, 315
  exclusion from, 236
School age, lowering of, 59
School children, interviews with, 325
Schools, kibbutz, 289-90
  See also Education; Kibbutz education